√ 17

'E F(' ' 'JR

S all Claim Procedure
in the County Court

A Practical Guide to
Mediation and Litigation

SIXTH EDITION

Small Claims Procedure in the County Court

A Practical Guide to Mediation and Litigation

SIXTH EDITION

Her Honour Judge
Patricia Pearl
and
District Judge
Christopher Dodd

WS
&H

Wildy, Simmonds & Hill Publishing

© Patricia Pearl and Christopher Dodd, 2014

Contains public sector information licensed under the Open Government Licence v1.0

ISBN: 9780854900527

British Library Cataloguing in Publication Data

A catalogue record for this book is available from the British Library

The right of Patricia Pearl and Christopher Dodd to be identified as the authors of this Work has been asserted by them in accordance with the Copyright, Designs and Patents Act 1988.

Fifth edition 2010

This edition published in 2014 by

Wildy, Simmonds & Hill Publishing
58 Carey Street
London WC2A 2JF
England
www.wildy.com

Typeset by Cornubia Press Ltd, Bristol.
Printed in Great Britain by CPI Antony Rowe, Chippenham, Wiltshire.

Table of Contents

Preface   xvii
Small Claims in the County Court – A Simplified Flowchart   xix
Glossary   xxi
Procedural Table – Overview of Small Claims Procedure   xxvii
Table of Cases   xxix
Table of Statutes and Conventions   xxxi
Table of Statutory Instruments   xxxiii

PART 1
CLAIMS   **1**

1 Preliminary Topics   **3**
    1.1   How to use this book   3
    1.2   Preliminary topics   4
       1.2.1   The overriding objective   4
       1.2.2   Speedy – effective – proportionate   5
       1.2.3   The small claims track – history and overview   5
       1.2.4   Electing to use the small claims track   6
       1.2.5   Terminology   6
       1.2.6   District judges   7
       1.2.7   Reference materials   8
    1.3   Evaluating the case and avoiding court proceedings if possible   9
       1.3.1   The four basic questions   9
       1.3.2   How to decide if the proceedings are worthwhile   9
       1.3.3   Avoid court proceedings if possible   11
    1.4.   Letters before action and pre-action conduct   12
       1.4.1   Introduction   12
       1.4.2   Terms of the practice direction   13
       1.4.3   Detailed guidance on exchange of information
             (Annex A)   14
       1.4.4   Special pre-action steps where the claimant is a
             business and the defendant is an individual
             (Annex B)   14

		1.4.5	Consequences of non-compliance	15
	1.5		European Convention on Human Rights	15
	1.6		Help with legal fees, court fees and getting free advice	15
		1.6.1	Help with court fees	16

2 | **Step-by-Step Guide to Starting a Small Claims Case** | | | **17**
	2.1		Overview	17
	2.2		Issuing claims	20
		2.2.1	By post	20
		2.2.2	Online	21
		2.2.3	Over the counter	21
		2.2.4	Ways of issuing a claim – summary	22
	2.3		Checklist for starting a small claims case, including information to help with completing the claim form online	22
		2.3.1	Decide if the claim is to be specified or unspecified (step 1)	23
		2.3.2	Name the claimant (step 2)	24
		2.3.3	State the claimant's address (step 3)	25
		2.3.4	Give the claimant's address for sending documents and payments (step 4)	26
		2.3.5	Identify the defendant (step 5)	26
		2.3.6	Name the defendant (step 6)	29
		2.3.7	State where the defendant is to be served (step 7)	29
		2.3.8	Brief details of the claim (step 8)	31
		2.3.9	Particulars of the claim (step 9)	32
		2.3.10	Complete the tick box about any human rights element (step 10)	32
		2.3.11	Calculate the interest (step 11)	33
		2.3.12	Statement of truth (step 12)	34
		2.3.13	Value – check that the case is within the small claims limit (step 13)	36
		2.3.14	Amount claimed (step 14)	36
		2.3.15	Calculate the court fee (step 15)	37
		2.3.16	Calculate the legal representative's costs on the claim form (step 16)	37
		2.3.17	Choose a preferred court (step 17)	37
		2.3.18	Ask the court to issue the claim form or submit the claim online (step 18)	38
		2.3.19	Make a diary note (step 19)	39
	2.4		The next steps	40
	2.5		Overview of procedure between response and allocation	40

3 **Responding to the Claim (Including Obtaining Judgment in Default or on an Admission)** **41**
3.1 Introduction 41
3.2 Time for response 42
3.3 Admitting the claim 43
    3.3.1 Judgment on admission 43
    3.3.2 Discretionary judgment 45
    3.3.3 Judgment of the court's own initiative 45
    3.3.4 Request for time to pay 45
    3.3.5 Admitting the claim – summary table 46
3.4 Acknowledging the claim 48
3.5 Dispute of jurisdiction 48
3.6 Defending the claim 49
    3.6.1 Type 1: the bland denial 49
    3.6.2 Type 2: the states paid defence 49
    3.6.3 Type 3: the full defence 50
    3.6.4 Type 4: the defence by way of set off or counterclaim 50
3.7 Defence to counterclaim 51
3.8 When the defendant wants to pass the claim onto someone else 51
3.9 Judgment in default – the consequence of not responding to the claim in time 51
3.10 Judgments for unspecified sums – getting the court to determine the amount payable 52
    3.10.1 Deciding the value without a hearing 52
    3.10.2 Disposal hearings 53
    3.10.3 Amount to be decided by the court – upon allocation to the small claims track 53
3.11 Reply to defence 54

4 **Directions Questionnaires and Allocation** **55**
4.1 Introduction 55
4.2 What does 'allocation' mean? 55
4.3 What is a 'track'? 56
4.4 How does a case qualify for the small claims track? 56
4.5 Principles of allocation – the court is in charge 57
4.6 A value in dispute not exceeding £10,000 58
    4.6.1 Housing claims 58
    4.6.2 Personal injury claims 59
    4.6.3 Claims involving disputed allegations of dishonesty 59
    4.6.4 Injunctions 60
    4.6.5 Claims of no financial value 60

4.6.6	Views of the parties	60
4.6.7	Claims which do not qualify on financial grounds	60
4.6.8	Small claims in the Intellectual Property Enterprise Court	61
4.7	The directions questionnaire	61
4.7.1	Court fee	62
4.7.2	Time limit for returning the directions questionnaire	62
4.7.3	Co-operate	62
4.7.4	Which court?	62
4.8	Step-by-step guide to completing the directions questionnaire	62
4.8.1	A – Settlement/Mediation	63
4.8.2	B – Your contact details	63
4.8.3	C – Track	64
4.8.4	D – About the hearing (hearing venue; expert evidence; witnesses; hearing)	64
4.8.5	Signature	65
4.9	Consequences of failure to return or complete the directions questionnaire	65
4.10	What happens when the court receives the directions questionnaires?	65
4.11	Final disposal of the case can be without a hearing	66
4.12	Orders of the court's own initiative	66
4.13	Allocation hearing	67
4.14	Can the court dispense with directions questionnaires?	67
4.15	Can the allocated track be changed or challenged?	68
4.16	Can the parties elect for the case to be allocated to the small claims track even if the case does not qualify on financial grounds?	68
4.17	Hearings in Welsh	69
4.18	Allocation – what next?	69
5	**Other Parts of the Civil Procedure Rules**	**71**
5.1	Introduction	71
5.2	Overriding objective	71
5.3	The court's case management powers	72
5.3.1	When can the district judge exercise these case management powers?	73
5.3.2	Striking out	73
5.3.3	Civil restraint orders	74
5.3.4	Other sanctions	74
5.3.5	Relief from sanctions	74

	5.3.6	Case management orders made on the court's own initiative	77
5.4		Applications generally	77
	5.4.1	Overview	78
	5.4.2	Consent applications	79
	5.4.3	Costs on applications in small claims cases	79
	5.4.4	Hearing an application by telephone	79
	5.4.5	Applications without notice	80
	5.4.6	Orders without a hearing	80
	5.4.7	Applications to adjourn	81
5.5		Statement of truth	81
	5.5.1	Wording of the statement of truth	81
5.6		Rules about service of the claim form and other documents	82
	5.6.1	Address for service of the claim form	82
	5.6.2	Deemed day of service and rules about dispatch	83
	5.6.3	Service by an alternative method	85
	5.6.4	Delay in service of the claim form (the 4-month rule)	86
5.7		Transfers of cases between courts	86
	5.7.1	Overview	87
	5.7.2	Definitions	87
	5.7.3	Transfer after allocation	87
5.8		Summary judgment	88
	5.8.1	Overview	88
	5.8.2	Summary judgment in detail	88
	5.8.3	Orders that the court can make on an application for summary judgment	90
	5.8.4	Costs on an application for summary judgment	90
5.9		The slip rule and correcting procedural errors	90
5.10		Time for complying with a judgment or order	91
5.11		Calculating time limits	91
5.12		Rules which are excluded on the small claims track	92
5.13		European small claims procedure	96
5.14		Small claims in intellectual property proceedings	97
5.15		Low value personal injury claims	98
6		**Drafting Rules and Precedents in Small Claims Cases**	**99**
6.1		Introduction	99
6.2		Letters before action	100
6.3		Statements of case including defences and counterclaims	100
	6.3.1	Guidelines for preparation of a statement of case and defence	100
	6.3.2	Detailing the claim	101
	6.3.3	Detailing the defence	101

	6.3.4	Reply to defence	102
	6.3.5	Defence to counterclaim	102
	6.3.6	Admission	103
	6.3.7	Amendments	103
6.4		The court's management powers – a reminder	103
6.5		Styles for setting out a small claims case	104
6.6		Witness statements	104
6.7		Precedents	104
	6.7.1	Letters before action	104
		Precedent A: Simple debt claim	105
		Precedent B: Complaint to a holiday company	105
		Precedent C: Cases where the claimant is a business and the defendant is an individual	107
		Precedent D: Defendant's response (simple debt claim)	108
	6.7.2	Starting the case	109
		Precedent E: Letter to the court manager at the start of the case (suitable for any case)	109
	6.7.3	Brief description of type of claim	110
	6.7.4	Statement of case including defences and counterclaims	110
		Precedent F: Claim by landlord for unpaid rent and service charges (includes a claim for statutory interest)	110
		Precedent G: Defence to claim by landlord for unpaid rent and service charges	111
		Precedent H: Claim against garage for negligent repairs	111
		Precedent I: Defence to claim against garage for negligent repairs	111
		Precedent J: Claim by a business for an unpaid invoice including a claim for interest under the Late Payment Act	112
		Precedent K: Holiday claim	112
		Precedent L: Admission to holiday claim	113
		Precedent M: Claim for unpaid professional fees (includes a claim for statutory interest)	113
		Precedent N: Defence and counterclaim to claim for unpaid professional fees	114
		Precedent O: Defence to counterclaim in unpaid professional fees case	114
		Precedent P: Road traffic case	115

		Precedent Q: Defence and counterclaim to road	
		traffic case	117
		Precedent R: Defence to counterclaim in road	
		traffic case	117
		Precedent S: Personal injury claim	118
		Precedent T: Defective goods	119
		Precedent U: Unpaid school fees	120
	6.7.5	Other precedents	121
		Precedent V: Witness statement road traffic case	121
		Precedent W: Witness statement contract	
		dispute	122
		Precedent X: Grounds for appeal to be included	
		in section 5 of Form N164	123
		Precedent Y: Application to set aside	123
		Precedent Z: List of complaints	124
	6.8	How to calculate statutory interest	125

PART 2

MEDIATION **127**

7 **Mediation of Small Claims through the County Court** **129**
7.1	Overview of features	129
7.2	Definition of mediation	130
7.3	Selecting cases for mediation	131
	7.3.1 Selection by category of case	131
	7.3.2 Selection by willingness to negotiate through	
	mediation	131
	7.3.3 Selection by the district judge	132
7.4	Procedure between selection for mediation and mediation	132
	7.4.1 What the court does	132
	7.4.2 What the parties do next	133
	7.4.3 What the mediator does next	133
7.5	Mediation appointment	134
	7.5.1 Role of the mediator	134
	7.5.2 Preparation for mediation	135
	7.5.3 Telephone mediations	135
	7.5.4 Face-to-face mediations	135
7.6	Outcome of the mediation	136
	7.6.1 If the outcome of the mediation is a settlement	136
	7.6.2 If no settlement is reached on mediation	136
	7.6.3 Other matters	137
7.7	Mediation – frequently asked questions	137
7.8	Finding a civil mediation provider outside the court system	138
7.9	The past and future of small claims mediation	138

PART 3
HEARINGS   **141**

8   Steps between Allocation and the Hearing, and Checklist for
Preparation for the Hearing   **143**
   8.1   Introduction   143
   8.2   Standard directions   144
   8.3   Final decision about the hearing venue   145
       8.3.1   Transfer by court order   145
       8.3.2   Last-minute change of venue by the court   149
   8.4   What documents are needed for the case?   149
   8.5   Documents for a small claims hearing – frequently asked
       questions   151
   8.6   Witness statements (non-experts)   151
   8.7   Witness summons   152
   8.8   Expert witness evidence   153
       8.8.1   Single joint experts   154
       8.8.2   What does an expert need to know about preparing
               a report for a small claims hearing?   154
   8.9   Lists of disputed items (or list of complaints)   156
  8.10 Photographs and sketch plans   156
  8.11 Inform the court if the case is settled before the hearing   157
  8.12 Time estimate   157
  8.13 Special directions   158
  8.14 Preliminary hearing   158
  8.15 Applications for directions by the parties   159
  8.16 Checklist for preparing for a small claims hearing   160
      8.16.1 Note the date and time (step 1)   160
      8.16.2 Evaluate and consider settlement (step 2)   160
      8.16.3 Prepare and serve documents (at least 14 days
            before the hearing) (step 3)   161
      8.16.4 Prepare and serve witness statements (at least 14
            days before the hearing) (step 4)   161
      8.16.5 Prepare a list of items in dispute (if needed or
            ordered) (step 5)   162
      8.16.6 Obtain expert evidence (but only if permission has
            been given) (step 6)   162
      8.16.7 Decide whether to attend the hearing (CPR
            rule 27.9(1)) (at least one week before the hearing)
            (step 7)   162
      8.16.8 Pay the hearing fee (step 8)   163
  8.17 Visiting the court before the hearing date   163

9   The No Costs Rule   **165**
  9.1   The no costs rule – basics   165
      9.1.1   Definition of costs   165
      9.1.2   The rule   166
      9.1.3   Electing to use the small claims track by
            agreement   167
      9.1.4   Quantifying the costs   167
      9.1.5   Overall discretion   167
      9.1.6   Offers of settlement and compliance with the
            practice direction on pre-action conduct   167
  9.2   Routine awards for costs   167
      9.2.1   Court fees   167
      9.2.2   Fixed commencement costs   168
      9.2.3   Expert fees   168
      9.2.4   Witness expenses   169
      9.2.5   Lay representatives   170
      9.2.6   Injunction cases   170
      9.2.7   Costs of enforcement   170
      9.2.8   Costs of appeal   170
      9.2.9   Photographs and sketch plans   170
      9.2.10 Low value personal injury claims   171
  9.3   Unreasonable behaviour   171
      9.3.1   The rule   171
      9.3.2   Stage 1: What amounts to unreasonable
            behaviour?   171
      9.3.3   Stage 2: Assessing the costs for unreasonable
            behaviour   173
  9.4   The court's discretion on costs   174
  9.5   Standard basis and indemnity basis   175
  9.6   Procedure for summary assessment   175
  9.7   Costs terminology   176
  9.8   Costs on the small claims track – frequently asked questions   176
  9.9   Costs following allocation, re-allocation and non-
      allocation: the rules   178
  9.10 Costs schedule   179

10   The Hearing   **181**
  10.1 Overview   181
  10.2 Dealing with cases justly   181
  10.3 Rights of audience (advocacy)   182
      10.3.1 Lawyers   182
      10.3.2 Lay representatives   183
      10.3.3 Companies   183

10.4   Hearings are in public   184
        10.4.1   It is never too late to settle   185
10.5   Recording the hearing – tapes and notes   185
10.6   Layout of the court and courtroom etiquette   186
        10.6.1   Addressing the court and the district judge   187
        10.6.2   Documents   187
        10.6.3   Introduction of new documents at the final hearing   187
        10.6.4   Interpreters in various languages and hearings in
                 Welsh   188
        10.6.5   Witnesses   189
        10.6.6   Friends and observers, including McKenzie
                 friends   189
        10.6.7   Parties with special needs or concerns about their
                 personal safety   191
10.7   Procedure at small claims hearings   191
        10.7.1   A fair hearing method   191
        10.7.2   At the start of the hearing (preliminaries)   192
10.8   Organisation of the hearing   192
        10.8.1   Usual sequence in civil trials   193
        10.8.2   Order of hearing for small claims cases   193
        10.8.3   Informality   195
        10.8.4   Contempt of court   195
        10.8.5   Where a party has given notice that they are not
                 coming to court   196
        10.8.6   Consequences of not attending where no notice
                 has been given   196
10.9   Evidence and the small claims hearing (including the burden
        and standard of proof)   196
        10.9.1   Proof – a burden and a standard   196
        10.9.2   Rules of evidence   197
        10.9.3   The usual rules of evidence   197
        10.9.4   Documents   198
        10.9.5   Witness evidence   198
        10.9.6   Do not tell the judge about settlement discussions
                 outside court   199
        10.9.7   Expert evidence   199
        10.9.8   Categories of prohibited evidence   200
        10.9.9   Taking evidence on oath   200
        10.9.10 Limiting cross examination   200
10.10   Advocacy skills and the small claims hearing – making the
        most of your time in court   200
        10.10.1 Opening speech   200

10.10.2 Asking questions of your own witnesses
(examination in chief) 201
10.10.3 Asking questions of the other party and his or her
witnesses (cross examination) 202
10.10.4 Re-examination 203
10.10.5 Closing speech 203
10.10.6 Legal points 203
10.10.7 Practical tips 204
10.10.8 Taking a note 204
10.11 The judgment 204
10.11.1 A reasoned decision 205
10.11.2 Costs and witness expenses 205
10.11.3 Time to pay 206
10.11.4 Permission to appeal 206
10.11.5 Court order 207
10.12 Small claims hearing – frequently asked questions 207

11 Appeals and Applications to Set Aside Judgment **209**
11.1 Introduction 209
11.1.1 Terminology 211
11.2 Appeals 211
11.2.1 The appeal rules 211
11.2.2 Grounds for appeal 212
11.2.3 Permission to appeal 213
11.2.4 Review and not re-hearing 214
11.2.5 Appeals against case management decisions 215
11.2.6 Paperwork for the appeal 215
11.2.7 Respondent's cross appeal 216
11.2.8 Hearing of the appeal 217
11.2.9 Second appeals 217
11.2.10 Small claims appeal flowchart 218
11.3 Setting judgment aside and re-hearing 218
11.3.1 Procedure 219
11.4 Setting aside a judgment in default 220
11.4.1 Mandatory grounds 220
11.4.2 Discretionary grounds 221
11.4.3 Procedure 221
11.5 Credit repair applications 222

12 Enforcement of Small Claims Judgments in the County Court **223**
12.1 Preliminary 223
12.2 Finding out about a debtor's assets 224
12.3 Order to obtain information 225
12.4 Register of judgments, orders and fines 226

12.5 Bankruptcy and company insolvency 226
12.6 Warrant of control 227
12.7 Third party debt order 228
12.8 Attachment of earnings 228
12.9 Charging order on land 229
    12.9.1 Charging order on securities 229
    12.9.2 Order for sale 229
12.10 Timescale for enforcement and interest 230
12.11 Steps after a small claims judgment – overview 230

Appendices **233**
1 Court Fees Payable in Small Claims Cases – Commencement and Hearing Fees 235
2 Court Fees Payable in Small Claims Cases – Applications and Appeals 237
3 Fixed Commencement Costs (CPR Rule 45.2) 239
4 Fixed Costs on Entry of Judgment 241
5 Practice Direction (Pre-Action Conduct), Extracts 243
6 Civil Procedure Rules, Part 1 255
7 Civil Procedure Rules, Part 27 257
8 Civil Procedure Rules, Practice Direction 27 265
9 Directions Questionnaire (Small Claims Track), Form N180 273
10 Costs Schedule 277
11 Mediation Settlement Agreement, Form N182 279

Index 283

Preface

This book includes everything which a professional adviser or one-off court user needs to be confident and successful in pursuing or defending a claim allocated to the small claims track in the county court. The name 'small claims' is something of a misnomer, given that the qualifying limit for money claims is now £10,000 and high fees payable to the court makes pursuing claims through the system a significant expense for most people.

Cases allocated to the small claims track enjoy unique privileges. The court service provides a mediation service exclusively to cases allocated to the small claims track which is described as being 'free', but in reality is provided at no charge in addition to the court fees which the claimant has already paid to start and pursue the claim. Small claims cases have the benefit of a 'no costs' rule which generally prevents the loser from having to pay any legal costs incurred by the other side. The no costs rule does not include the court fees which are usually paid by the loser and it is certainly not a hard and fast rule because the judge can order the loser to pay the other side's costs if they have behaved 'unreasonably'. All aspects of costs relative to the small claims track are discussed in the book. If a case goes to a hearing before a judge, the parties in a small claims case can be represented by an unqualified 'lay representative' who can address the court. Small claims cases also enjoy a simplified procedure before a hearing and, when the case is heard by a judge, procedures will be less formal than is usual for cases allocated to the fast or the multi-track. The small claims track also has a unique and little-used procedure for the judge to decide the case on the papers alone without the attendance of the parties.

Lawyers advising in small claims cases are faced with the challenge of providing a cost-effective service, and this can only be achieved with a good understanding of the rules of the court and the pitfalls of the process; this book provides that knowledge.

This sixth edition takes into account a large number of changes in procedures and rules over the last two years, and is as up to date as we could make it as at 7 April 2014. This includes the introduction of the single county court and new rules and terminology concerning enforcement. The previous editions assumed that most claims would be issued by filling in a paper form, but it is now obligatory for all money claims to be issued online, and the parties will not usually need to visit a court building unless the case goes to a final hearing; even the mediation process is conducted by telephone. Litigants, even those acting for themselves, must ensure that they always comply with court orders and ensure that deadlines are not missed; failure to comply will result in claims and defences being permanently struck out. It is also essential for every case (whether a claim or defence) to be fully and properly explained because failure to do so may result in it being disallowed; this book includes a chapter giving guidelines on how to set out a case in writing.

We have tried to demystify a process which can be overwhelming to new court users. We have laid out the book as in previous editions to include summaries of key rules and procedures, with more detailed text following on. We have used checklists to guide users through key stages of a court case and answered frequently asked questions. The glossary is a useful tool for any court user who is unfamiliar with legal jargon. We have added all necessary case and rule citations and there is a full index. Key court rules plus up-to-date court fees are reproduced at the back of the book.

The authors bring to this book not only their experiences as practitioners but also over 20 years of combined experience as judges; we are proud that the book has built up a loyal following in its 15 years in print, being used not only by legal professionals but also lay advisers, in-house lawyers and litigants in person, and is often recommended as reading material for lawyers who aspire to become district judges. We are also delighted that the book has found its way into many public libraries and is borrowed regularly and, we hope, returned so that it can be used by others who might otherwise be daunted by having to deal with a small claims case.

Patricia Pearl
Christopher Dodd
London and Cumbria
June 2014

Small Claims in the County Court –
A Simplified Flowchart

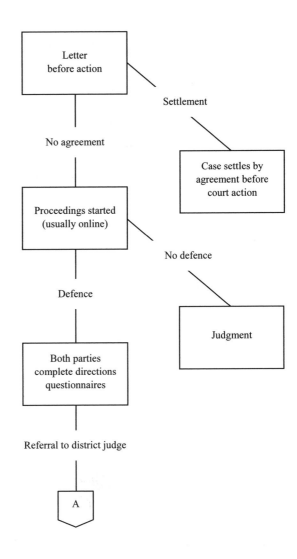

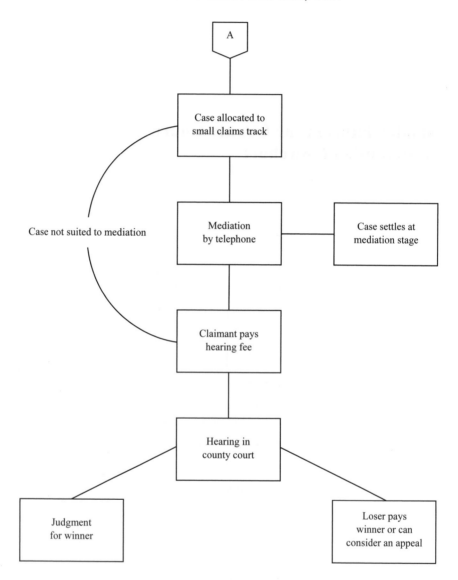

Glossary

Some specialist legal terms explained.

Advocate	Anyone who represents someone in court (see also 'Barrister', 'Solicitor', Lay representative' and 'McKenzie friend')
Allocation	The procedure by which a district judge decides if a case qualifies for the small claims track or some other track
Alternative Dispute Resolution	Collective description of methods of resolving disputes other than by the normal trial process (see also 'Mediation')
Arbitration	A method of settling disputes by which the parties agree to a determination by an umpire or arbitrator; commonly used in the settlement of commercial disputes (the term previously denoted the small claims procedure in the county court)
Assessment	See 'Detailed assessment (of costs)' and 'Summary assessment (of costs)'
Barrister	A specialist professional advocate lawyer who has been called to the Bar by one of the Inns of Court and undertaken the required practical training
Boxwork	The work done by a district or circuit judge on a court file where there is no hearing and the parties are not present
Caseman	The computer records on civil cases held by the courts (a printout of the information held electronically is termed a 'caseman printout')
Case management	The process by which the district judge controls the progress of a case by making orders and imposing sanctions
CCMCC (County Court Money Claims Centre)	The place where claims forms are sent when a claim form is not issued online: PO Box 527, Salford M5 0BY
Circuit judge	A county court judge senior in rank to a district judge (circuit judges hear appeals in small claims cases)
Claimant	The party who starts the legal proceedings by making a claim

Costs terminology	See Chapter 9, para 9.7 for definitions of 'no order for costs', 'costs reserved' and 'costs in the case'
Counterclaim	A claim by a defendant against a claimant (see also 'Part 20 claim/ counterclaim')
Courts Service	HM Courts & Tribunal Service – the government service responsible for running all courts in England and Wales[1]
CPR (the rules)	The Civil Procedure Rules 1998[2]
Damages	A sum of money awarded by the court as compensation for wrongdoing
Default judgment	A judgment entered because a defendant has not filed an acknowledgment or defence to a claim within the time specified by the rules
Defence	Defendant's statement of case
Defendant	The party against whom a claim is made
Deputy district judge	Part-time district judge
Detailed assessment (of costs)	When the costs of a case are decided after the case has been completed: the process involves costs being detailed in a bill and a hearing if they are not agreed (the procedure is not used in small claims cases)
Directions	Orders made to govern the procedure in a case
Directions questionnaire	The form which both sides complete and send to the court to assist the district judge when giving initial case management orders and when allocating the case to a track
Disclosure	The process whereby each party notifies the others of any documents he or she intends to use at a hearing
Disposal	A hearing after judgment when the amount due to the claimant is determined by the court
District judge	A member of the judiciary appointed to conduct business in the county court including small claims cases
Evidence	Information given to the court to support a case. Evidence takes a number of forms including information on the claim form supported by a statement of truth, witness statements, oral evidence given in court and documents

---

[1]   www.justice.gov.uk/about/hmcts.

[2]   www.justice.gov.uk/courts/procedure-rules.

Fast track	Case management regime for cases of up to £25,000 in value which can be heard in one day or less and which do not qualify for the small claims track
Filing	Sending or taking a court document to the court office – the court staff then put the document on the court file relevant to the case
Home court	The county court hearing centre for the district in which the defendant resides or carries on business (CPR rule 2.3)
Intellectual Property Enterprise Court (IPEC), formerly the Patents County Court	The court dealing with disputes about copyright, designs and inventions. As to small claims in this court, see Chapter 5, para 5.14
Jurisdiction (as in the area of jurisdiction)	The geographical area to which the CPR apply – this is England, Wales and adjacent territorial waters. Note that Scotland and Ireland (including Northern Ireland) are not within the jurisdiction (CPR rule 2.3)
Lay representative	Someone other than a lawyer exercising limited rights of audience at a small claims hearing (see also 'McKenzie friend'). Lay representatives are not legal representatives (CPR rule 2.3(1)) (see Chapter 10, para 10.3.2)
Legal Aid Agency	The organisation which organises public funding for court cases; such funding is not available in small claims cases[3]
Legal executive	A professional qualified under the Rules of the Institute of Legal Executives (ILEX). Specially qualified legal executives – ILEX advocates – can appear as advocates in open court county court hearings, including small claims hearings
Legal representative	A barrister or solicitor, solicitor's employee or other authorised litigator (as defined in the Courts and Legal Services Act 1990) who has been instructed to act for a party in relation to a case (CPR rule 2.3(1))
Litigant in person	Someone who acts for himself or herself without using a lawyer or lay representative
Litigation friend	Someone authorised by the court to conduct a case on behalf of a person under 18 or a person under a mental disability. Full details are set out in CPR rule 21
McKenzie friend	Someone who assists a litigant in person in court but does not present the case to the judge (see also 'Lay representative') (see also Chapter 10, para 10.6.6)

---

[3] www.justice.gov.uk/legal-aid.

Mediation	A voluntary, private dispute resolution process in which a neutral person helps the parties try to reach a negotiated settlement, the contents of which remain confidential and 'without prejudice' unless or until a settlement is achieved (see Chapter 7)
Multi-track	Case management regime applicable to cases of over £25,000 in value which do not qualify for the fast track
Overriding objective	The underlying principle of the CPR which is to deal with cases justly taking in certain criteria as to even and open-handedness and proportionality (CPR rule 1.1)
Part	The CPR are divided into over 80 parts, each containing rules and often one or more practice directions (e.g. Part 27 contains rules 27.1 to 27.15 and PD 27)
Part 20 claim/ counterclaim	Claims made in an action other than by a claimant – third party proceedings and counterclaims are types of Part 20 claims being governed by CPR Part 20
Part 36 offers and payments	CPR Part 36 describes the rules which apply if a party wishes to make a formal offer to settle including the costs consequences. These procedures are of limited application in small claims proceedings
Particulars of claim	Claimant's statement of case
Practice direction	The CPR are supported by formal guidance notes – in the case of small claims the practice direction includes the routine directions orders
Pre-action protocol	A series of procedural steps intended to promote settlement before litigation
Preferred court	The court hearing centre which the claimant has specified in the claim form as the place to which the case should be sent if necessary
Procedural judge	Any judge who takes decisions about the procedure in a case; in the county court this can be the district judge or circuit judge
Reply	The claimant's answer to a defence (generally unnecessary in small claims cases)
Right of audience	Being allowed to present a case in court on behalf of someone else or on one's own behalf (see Chapter 10, para 10.3)
Rule	One of the Civil Procedure Rules
Small claims court	A term often used colloquially to mean the small claims procedure in the county court – a misnomer because there is no separate small claims court as such

Small claims track	The special case management regime applicable to cases of limited financial value (see Chapter 4 for more detail of which cases qualify for the small claims track)
Solicitor	Someone who has passed the Law Society examinations and is on the Law Society's roll of solicitors (Solicitors Act 1974, section 1)
Specified claim	Cases where the amount of the claim is stated by the claimant as a fixed sum of money (see Chapter 2, para 2.3.1)
Statement of truth	Formal confirmation that the contents of a court document are true, for example a statement of case or a witness statement (see Chapter 2, para 2.3.12)
Statements of case	Formal documents setting out a party's case in outline
States paid defence	A defence when the defendant claims that the sum claimed has already been paid (see Chapter 3, para 3.6.2)
Stay	A court imposed halt on proceedings; a case can only continue if the stay is removed (see also '*Tomlin* order')
Strike out	Striking out means either the court ordering an end to the case as a whole or that certain written material within a case be deleted so that it may no longer be relied upon
Summary assessment (of costs)	If the district judge decides that any costs are payable in a small claims case, the amount will be decided there and then at the hearing and this process is called summary assessment
Summary judgment	Procedure under CPR Part 24 for obtaining a judgment without a full hearing (see Chapter 5, para 5.8)
Third party claim	A claim where the defendant wants to shift blame on to a party who was not brought into the action by the claimant (see also 'Part 20 claim/counterclaim')
Track	One of the special case management regimes under the CPR (see also 'Small claims track', 'Fast track' and 'Multi-track')
Tomlin order	An order of the court made with the agreement of the parties where proceedings are to be stayed on agreed terms which are attached to the order as a schedule (see Chapter 7, para 7.6.1)
Unspecified claim	Cases where the claimant leaves the amount of the claim to be determined by the court (see Chapter 2, para 2.3.1)
Without notice application (and order)	An application made (and resulting order) without giving notice to the other side (NB under the CPR this term replaced the obsolete 'ex parte application')

Without prejudice	Negotiations with a view to a settlement are usually conducted 'without prejudice', which means that the circumstances in which the content of those negotiations may be revealed to the court are very restricted (and usually not until after the judge has delivered judgment)
Witness statement	A written statement of the evidence which a witness will or would give at a hearing, which should be divided into numbered paragraphs for ease of reference

Procedural Table – Overview of Small Claims Procedure

Stage of action	Step to be taken	Notes
Before the start of the action	Claimant writes a letter before action and parties exchange information before starting the court action	
	Both parties try to negotiate a settlement	
At the start of the court action	Claimant completes Form N1 and sends it by post or online to the CCMCC with the court fee	See checklist in Chapter 2
When the court receives the claimant's papers	Court staff give the case an action number (proceedings are issued)	The papers may be referred to the district judge by the court staff for directions at any stage of the case
	Court serves the proceedings by sending to the defendant by first class post	
14 days after service	Last date for responding to the case by defence acknowledgment or admission	The table in Chapter 2, para 2.5 gives more detail of the steps to be taken at the allocation stage
28 days after service	Last date for defence (if acknowledgment has been filed)	
After filing of defence	Court sends out directions questionnaires	The case is transferred to the defendant's home court if the amount is specified and the defendant is an individual

Stage of action	Step to be taken	Notes
14 days after receiving directions questionnaires	Both parties return questionnaire (claimant pays fee if amount claimed is above a certain sum)	
	District judge considers directions questionnaires – case is allocated to small claims track and in some cases referred to mediation; directions are given	In a few cases the district judge may direct that there be a preliminary hearing
Either on the direction of the district judge or with the consent of the parties	Case referred to the small claims mediation service	If mediation is not successful the case returns to the system for a final hearing
Before the hearing	Parties send each other the documents that they will use at the hearing	This is usually 14 days before the hearing but may be at a different time if the district judge so directs
The hearing		It is usual for both sides to attend the hearing but the rules do allow the parties to make arrangements for the case to be heard in their absence
Within 21 days of the date of the decision	Loser can lodge an appeal; the decision must be wrong or there must be a serious procedural irregularity	Permission is required which can be requested at the hearing itself or later by application to a circuit judge

Table of Cases

References are to page numbers

Afzal and Others v Ford Motor Co Ltd [1994] 4 All ER 720, CA	58, 172
Ashktar v Boland [2014] EWCA Civ 943, CA	170
Bank of Credit and Commerce International (in liq) v Zafar [2001] All ER D 21 (Nov)	221
Bank of Scotland v Pereira & Pain & Pain [2011] EWCA Civ 241	219
Bashir v Hanson CC [1999] 12 CL 143	172
Berridge (Paul) (t/a EAB builders) v RM Bayliss, Lawtel, 23 November 1999	58
Clohessy v Homes [2004] CL 418, Bristol CC	172
Credit Agricole Indosuez v Unicof Ltd [2002] EWHC 77 (Comm), Lawtel, 4 February 2003	220
Denton & Ors v TH White Ltd & Ors [2014] EWCA Civ 906	76, 77
Dulce Maltez v Damien Lewis and Anr (1999) *The Times*, 4 May, ChD, [1999] All ER (D) 425	183
English v Emery Reimbold & Strick Ltd [2002] EWCA Civ 605, [2002] 3 All ER 385	213
Geoffrey Arnold Wheen v Smithmann and another, Lawtel, 25 September 2000	59
Guidance for McKenzie Friends (Civil and Family Courts) [2010] 4 All ER 272	189
Joyce v Liverpool City Council [1996] QB 252	58, 60
Kenny v Abubaker [2012] EWCA Civ 1962	219
Lacey v Melford CC [1999] 12 CL 37	172
Ladd v Marshall [1954] 3 All ER 745, CA	214

Lunnan v Hart Singh and others, *Times Law Reports*, 1 July 1999,
    unreported   53

Madden v Pattni CC [1999] CLY 540   72
Maes Finance and Mac No 1 Ltd v Al Phillips & Co (A Firm), *Times Law
    Reports*, 25 March 1997, unreported   53
Mitchell v News Group Newspapers Limited [2013] EWCA Civ 1537   76
Mount v Oldham Corporation [1973] 1 All ER 26, CA   120
Moyse v Regal Partnerships Ltd [2004] EWCA Civ 1269   214

R v Leicester City Justices ex parte Barrow and another [1991] 3 All ER
    935, CA   189
Reed Executive plc v Reed Business Information Ltd [2004] EWCA Civ
    887, [2004] 4 All ER 942   206
Regency Rolls Ltd and Another v Carnall [2000] EWCA Civ 379, (2000)
    LTL, 16 October   221

Samara v MBI & Partners UK Ltd and Another [2014] EWHC 563 (QB)   221

Tanfern Ltd v Cameron-Macdonald [2000] 2 All ER 801   213

Voice and Script International Ltd v Alghafar [2003] EWCA Civ 736,
    [2003] All ER (D) 86   53

Table of Statutes and Conventions

References are to page numbers

Statutes

Business Names Act 1985

    s 4   27

Consumer Credit Act 1974

    s 189(1)   230

Contempt of Court Act 1981

    s 9   207

County Courts Act 1984

    s 69   113, 116

    s 118   196

Courts and Legal Services Act 1980

    s 11   170

Data Protection Act 1998   60

Highways Act 1980

    s 58   123

Human Rights Act 1998   15, 33

Judgments Act 1838

    s 17   125

Late Payment of Commercial Debts (Interest) Act 1998   34, 112

Welsh Language Act 1993

    s 22(1)   69

Convention

European Convention for the Protection of Human Rights and

    Fundamental Freedoms 1950   5, 15, 185

    Art 6   15, 184

Table of Statutory Instruments

References are to page numbers

Charging Orders (Orders for Sale: Financial Thresholds) Regulations 2012 (SI 2012/491)	230
Civil Procedure Rules 1998 (SI 1998/3132)	3, 4
Pt 1	71
r 1.1	71, 183
r 1.1(1)(c)	57
r 1.1(2)	145, 155, 181
r 1.1(2)(a)	10, 182
r 1.1(2)(b)	182
r 1.1(2)(c)	153
r 1.1(2)(d)	72
r 1.2	175
r 1.3	72
r 1.4	72, 182
r 1.4(1)	145
r 1.4(2)(e)	130
Pt 2	91
r 2.3(1)	26, 35
r 2.8	91
r 2.8(4)	91
r 2.9	91
Pt 3	45, 72
r 3.1	52
r 3.1(2)	73
r 3.1(2)(a)	219
r 3.1(2)(f)	220
r 3.1(3)	220
r 3.2	73
r 3.3	77
r 3.4	73
r 3.4.6	74
r 3.7(4)	65

Civil Procedure Rules 1998 (SI 1998/3132) *(continued)*

r 3.8(2)	75
r 3.8(4)	77
r 3.9	75, 77
r 3.9(1)	76
r 3.10	91
r 3.11	74
PD 3A	73
PD 3C	74
PD 3C, para 2.2	74, 80
Pt 6	82
r 6.4	82
r 6.5	84
r 6.9	30
r 6.9(3)	30
r 6.14	84
r 6.15	86
r 6.17	82
r 6.26	84
r 7.4(1)	42
r 7.4(1)(b)	32
r 7.5	20, 83, 86
r 7.5.1	83
r 7.6	86
r 7.6(3)	86
r 7.6(4)	86
PD 7A, para 5A.3	28
PD 7A, para 5C	27
PD 7E	38
PD 7E, para 10	35
Pt 10	48
Pt 11	48
r 12.3(2)	51
r 12.4	52
r 12.4(1)	51
r 12.5(2)	91
r 12.5A	52, 65
Pt 13	210, 220
r 13.2	210, 220
r 13.2(c)	47
r 13.3	210
r 13.4(3)	221
PD 13, para 16.3(3)	101
r 14.1(3)	45
r 14.1(4)	43

r 14.2(3)	47
r 14.3	45
r 14.4	43, 46
r 14.5	43, 46
r 14.5(9)	91
r 14.6	43, 47
r 14.7	44, 47
r 14.7(9)	47
r 14.7(10)	44, 47
rr 14.9–14.13	45
r 15.8	54
r 15.11	52
PD 15, para 3.2	54
r 16.2(2)	32
r 16.4(1)	32
r 16.4(1)(a)	101
r 16.4(1)(b)	101
r 16.4(2)	33, 101
r 16.5	49, 50
r 16.5(1)(a)	102
r 16.5(1)(b)	102
r 16.5(1)(c)	102
r 16.5(2)(a)	102
r 16.5(2)(b)	102
r 16.5(5)	101
r 16.7	102
r 16.7(1)	54
PD 16, para 2.2	26
PD 16, para 2.4	26
PD 16, para 3.4	32
PD 16, para 4	32, 101
PD 16, para 4.3	154
PD 16, para 7.3(1)	101
PD 16, para 7.3(2)	101
PD 16, para 8.2(1)	101
PD 16, para 8.2(2)	101
PD 16, para 8.2(3)	101
PD 16, para 8.2(8)	101
PD 16, para 10.2	101
PD 16, para 12	102
PD 16, para 13.3(1)	101, 102
PD 16, para 13.3(2)	101, 102
PD 16, para 13.3(3)	102
PD 16, para 15.1	33
r 17.1	103

Civil Procedure Rules 1998 (SI 1998/3132) *(continued)*
Pt 18   66, 92, 93
Pt 20   50, 51
r 20.2(1)   50
r 20.4(2)   50
r 20.5(1)   51
r 20.6   51
PD 20, para 6.1   50
Pt 21   25
r 21.1(2)   25
PD 21   25
r 22.1   81
r 22.1(3)   81
r 22.2   81
r 22.2(1)   36
r 22.2(2)   36
r 22.3   81
PD 22   81
PD 22, para 3   35
PD 22, para 3.1   82
PD 22, para 3.8   35
Pt 23   78, 79
r 23.1   78
r 23.3(2)   79
r 23.7   78
r 23.7(1)(b)   78
r 23.8(c)   80
r 23.10   80
PD 23A   78, 79
PD 23A, para 2.1   78
PD 23A, para 2.7   78
PD 23A, para 3   80
PD 23A, para 10   79
PD 23A, para 11.1   53
PD 23A, para 11.2   53
Pt 24   45, 88, 89
r 24.2   89
r 24.4   89
r 24.4(1)(a)   48
r 24.4(2)   88
PD 24   89
Pt 25   92
Pt 26   57
r 26   73
r 26.2A   66

r 26.3(6)	62
r 26.3(7A)	65
r 26.3(10)	65
r 26.4(2)	63
r 26.4(3)	63
r 26.4(5)	63
r 26.6(1)(a)(ii)	59
r 26.6(2)	59
r 26.7(4)	56, 58
r 26.8(1)	57, 60
r 26.8(1)(e)	50
r 26.8(2)	57, 59
PD 26	67
PD 26, para 6.2	67
PD 26, para 7.5	68
PD 26, para 8.1(1)(d)	59
PD 26, para 8.1(2)	68
PD 26, para 11.1(1)	68
PD 26, para 11.2	68
PD 26, para 12.4	53
PD 26, para 12.8	53
Pt 27	7, 56, 71, 97, 182, 197, 219
r 27.1(2)	56, 58
r 27.2	92
r 27.2(1)(b)	149
r 27.2(3)	93, 158
r 27.3	95
r 27.4(1)(c)	158
r 27.4(2)(a)	143
r 27.5	153
r 27.6	73, 159
r 27.6(2)	159
r 27.8	191, 192
r 27.8(1)	212
r 27.8(3)	81, 197
r 27.8(4)	198, 200, 202
r 27.8(5)	200
r 27.8(6)	205
r 27.9	162, 210
r 27.9(1)	160, 162, 196, 198, 205, 219
r 27.9(2)	162, 196
r 27.9(3)	162, 196
r 27.9(4)	162, 196
r 27.10	66, 205
r 27.11	210, 218

Civil Procedure Rules 1998 (SI 1998/3132) *(continued)*
r 27.11(2)									219
r 27.14								166, 217
r 27.14(2)					165, 168, 170, 177
r 27.14(2)(b)								170
r 27.14(2)(e)								169
r 27.14(2)(f)								168
r 27.14(2)(g)					15, 103, 167, 171
r 27.14(2)(h)								166
r 27.14(3)						96, 167, 172
r 27.14(4)								170
PD 27						7, 144, 146–8, 192
PD 27, para 3.2(1)							182
PD 27, para 3.2(2)						183, 217
PD 27, para 3.2(4)							183
PD 27, para 4.1(1)							184
PD 27, para 4.1(2)							185
PD 27, para 4.1(3)							185
PD 27, para 4.3								191
PD 27, para 5.1								216
PD 27, para 5.3(1)							204
PD 27, para 5.3(2)							204
PD 27, para 5.4						162, 205
PD 27, para 7								170
PD 27, para 7.2								170
PD 27, para 7.3								166
PD 27, para 7.3(1)							169
PD 27, para 7.3(2)							168
PD 27, Appendix A							144
PD 27, Appendix C							158
Pt 28									56
Pt 29									56
r 30.3									145
PD 30, para 6.1								149
Pt 31									92
r 31.1(2)								149
Pt 32								92, 94
r 32.1								92, 94
r 32.2									151
r 32.14								34, 84
PD 32									94
Pt 33								92, 95
Pt 34									152
Pt 35								92, 95
r 35.1							92, 95, 153

r 35.3	154, 155
r 35.4	155
r 35.5	92, 95
r 35.7	92, 95, 154
r 35.8	92, 95, 154
r 35.8(4)	154
r 35.8(5)	154, 155
Pt 36	92, 96, 172–3
r 36.2(5)	96, 173
Pt 39	92
r 39.2	184
r 39.3	219
r 39.9(2)	185
PD 39A	184
PD 39A, para 1.10	185
PD 39A, para 1.12	184
PD 39A, para 6.2	186
r 40.11	91, 206
r 40.12	90
PD 40B	90
r 44.2	167, 174
r 44.3(5)	90, 174
r 44.4	174
r 44.4(3)	174
r 44.7	177
r 44.9	65
r 44.10	176
Pt 45	168
r 45.1(1)	168
r 46.13	178
r 46.13(2)	177
PD 46, para 7.1	178
PD 46, para 7.1(1)	177
PD 46, para 7.1(2)	177
PD 46, para 8.1	178
PD 46, para 8.2	179
r 48.6(6)	176
Pt 52	209
r 52.3(4)	214
r 52.3(6)	213
r 52.3(7)	214
r 52.4(2)(b)	213
r 52.5	216
r 52.11(2)	214
r 52.11(3)	212

Civil Procedure Rules 1998 (SI 1998/3132) *(continued)*
   r 52.11(5)   215
   r 52.13   217
   PD 52A, para 4.6   215
   PD 52B, para 4.2   215
   PD 52B, para 6.2   215
   Pt 71   225
   Pt 72   228
   Pt 73   230
   Pt 78   96, 97
   PD 78, Annex 1   97
   Pt 83   228
   Pt 84   228
   Pt 85   227, 228
   Sch 2   229
County Court Fees Order 1999 (SI 1999/689)   37
County Court Rules
   Ord 19   58
   Ord 27   229

Package Travel, Package Holidays and Package Tours Regulations 1992
   (SI 1992/3288)
   reg 2(i)   25

Taking Control of Goods Regulations 2013 (SI 2013/1894)
   reg 4   228

Part 1

Claims

Chapter 1

Preliminary Topics

1.1 HOW TO USE THIS BOOK

It is natural to skip chapters in a reference book and to seek out the parts that are needed. Even so, it is highly recommended that this chapter and in particular para 1.3 'Evaluating the case and avoiding court proceedings if possible' are read in full before advancing to other sections. The book contains numerous cross references and for those in a rush the boxes in the text contain basic information about the detail which follows.

Court cases have their own vocabulary and readers confronted with a new word or term in this book should consult the glossary which appears at the front of this book.

References to 'rules' in this book are to the Civil Procedure Rules 1998,[1] referred to in shorthand as 'the rules' and 'CPR'.

This book has three parts:

- *Part 1* (Chapters 1 to 6) is relevant to all claims and includes guidance on how to start the claim, preparing the case and any defence. There is a procedural table and drafting rules and precedents which are useful for small claims cases. This part is a 'must read' for anyone new to small claims cases or to court procedure in general.

---

[1]   Civil Procedure Rules 1998 (SI 1998/3132) (as amended).

- *Part 2* (Chapter 7) deals with mediation. The court will encourage the parties to seek a settlement without a court hearing and where cases are allocated to the small claims track a mediation service is provided at no additional charge. The service is confidential and very effective. This chapter contains a procedural table and guidance on how to get the most out of mediation; it explains which cases are suitable for mediation and those which are not.

- *Part 3* (Chapters 8 to 12) deals with judges' hearings. It gives guidance where the case is not suitable for mediation or where mediation has failed, including everything to do with appeals.

In addition, the book contains appendices of court fees and extracts of the rules. Navigation through the chapters is designed to be as easy as possible with numerous separate sections with descriptive headings.

1.2   PRELIMINARY TOPICS

1.2.1   The overriding objective

This book is about the procedural rules which apply to running a small claims case in the county court and the practical and effective ways in which these rules are applied to cases of limited financial value.

The CPR govern the procedure applicable to small claims. The overriding objective of the rules is to enable the court to deal with cases justly and at proportionate cost. Part 1 describes the way in which the court seeks to achieve this objective, for example by active case management and encouraging the parties to settle. Throughout this book, references are made to the considerable case management powers which enable judges to control the preparation of the case for the final hearing. Parties cannot expect poorly prepared or hopeless cases to run to a hearing; such cases are likely to be identified by the district judge at an early stage and may be struck out or at least subjected to rigorous case management. The court will also scrutinise steps taken by the parties before the commencement of court action, including letters before action and compliance with the practice direction relating to 'pre-action conduct' (see para 1.4).

> The overriding objective is discussed in detail in Chapter 5, para 5.2

1.2.2   Speedy – effective – proportionate

The overall procedure for dealing with small claims cases is set out in CPR Part 27. It provides a speedy, effective and proportionate method of dealing with disputes of limited financial value.

The procedure is ideally suited to litigants in person. Practitioners advising in small claims cases are faced with the challenge of providing a cost-effective service. The efficiency of the small claims procedure depends on all court users understanding the rules applicable to small claims cases and applying them in a practical way.

1.2.3   The small claims track – history and overview

The procedure has evolved over the years, initially limited to claims involving sums in dispute for not more than £100; the current financial limit is £10,000 for money claims. Such a sum is not a 'small' sum for most people, neither are small claims insignificant in any way for the county court. Every year, between 80,000 and 100,000 cases are started which qualify for the small claims track. Going by the sheer number of hearings, most disputes that are decided by civil judges in England and Wales are dealt with by the small claims procedure.

The small claims procedure was an integral part of the reforms recommended by Lord Woolf.[2] It was inspired by the so-called arbitration procedure which existed under the old rules. The old arbitration proceedings were conducted by the district judge in private, the appeal procedure was very limited, there was a no costs rule and the procedure between issue and hearing was considerably simplified.

When the rules were introduced, the name of the small claims system was changed and the description 'arbitration' abandoned; the old procedure was never, in any true sense, an arbitration. The right of appeal under the new rules was, at first, limited but later a full appeal process was introduced to bring the system in line with other cases. The rules were also changed to open the hearings to the public. These changes were made with the European Convention for the Protection of Human Rights and Fundamental Freedoms 1950 (ECHR) in mind (see para 1.5). Over the last decade there have been changes to the rules which increased the procedural steps between issue and hearing, including introducing allocation questionnaires for small claims cases. The no costs rule has survived the decade, but now there is a specific warning in the rules that certain forms of unreasonable conduct, including failure to follow the pre-action protocol (see

---

[2]   The Right Honourable Lord Woolf, Master of the Rolls, *Access to Justice, Final Report*, July 1996.

para 1.5) and failing to engage in settlement discussions, may attract an adverse award for costs. The small claims track is now subject to more sophisticated and complex procedures than ever applied to the arbitration procedure.

A recent innovation for small claims cases is that the courts service now offers a mediation scheme for cases allocated to the small claims track. This scheme has been running since 2008 nationwide. Chapter 7 discusses the scheme in detail and offers practical advice on how to make the most of small claims mediation. There is no equivalent court-run scheme for cases allocated to other tracks, although parties in cases on other tracks may be advised to seek the assistance of the National Mediation Helpline service. It is possible to see the new mediation scheme as an attempt to return to simplicity as far as claims of limited financial value are concerned. A small claims procedure now exists in the Intellectual Property Enterprise Court (IPEC), aimed at small businesses which claim that their intellectual property rights have been enfringed. For an overview of this procedure, which was initiated in October 2012, see Chapter 5, para 5.14.

Counter service and use of email

At the time of writing, all public services are being subjected to cuts and economies. Although courts remain open for hearings, public counters now often have restricted opening hours, and telephone calls are routed to call centres. The public are strongly encouraged to deal with courts by email.

1.2.4   Electing to use the small claims track

Parties may consent to a claim being allocated to the small claims track where the financial value of the claim exceeds the usual qualifying amount. The parties then have the benefit of the reduced procedures of the small claims track and an informal hearing plus the protection of the no costs rule.

> Chapter 4, para 4.16 covers the topic of electing to use the small claims track in more detail

1.2.5   Terminology

> A list of definitions of legal terms and frequently used jargon is set out in the glossary which appears at the front of the book

The unfortunate word 'arbitration' which was formerly used to describe cases before the introduction of the new rules has now been abandoned. The term 'claimant' was substituted for 'plaintiff' in 1999 for all civil cases. The rules contain technical words but the glossary will help the reader of the book with those terms.

Virtually all small claims cases are dealt with by district judges save for the very few that are dealt with by circuit judges at first instance and on appeal. Although the rules often refer to 'the court' taking steps, in this book it is made clear where decisions are taken by a judge and where steps are taken by members of the court staff.

All county courts deal with small claims cases and there is no separate building or court called a 'small claims court'. Nearly all hearings are conducted in the normal county court buildings.

Small claims are mainly governed by CPR Part 27, but other parts of the rules are also relevant to small claims and these are referenced in this book where necessary.

The rules are supported by practice directions. Specific practice directions are referred to in this book by the letters PD. The practice direction which supports Part 27, PD 27, is reproduced at Appendix 8.

1.2.6　District judges

Suitably experienced and qualified lawyers may become district judges. They apply for the job following public advertisements for the selection process which is via competitions. The judges who are appointed in this way come from a wide variety of professional backgrounds including high street firms, larger commercially based practices, local authority and government employment plus legal academics. In their work as judges they deal with all the work of the county court, not just small claims. Their daily work includes:

- case management of cases on all tracks;
- matrimonial matters;
- cases involving children;
- bankruptcy;
- landlord and tenant cases, including mortgage possession;
- fast track trials;
- assessment of costs;
- disposal hearings.

When dealing with small claims cases district judges apply their accumulated knowledge and experience; they have a good working knowledge, sometimes considerable expertise, in the law relevant to cases which often appear on the small claims track. This will include:

- consumer matters;
- contract law;
- agency law;
- the law of negligence.

Deputy district judges usually work full time as solicitors or barristers and in addition sit for several days a year in county courts covering the lists of the full-time judges when they are absent. Those attending a small claims hearing may sometimes notice an additional district judge watching the work of the court – that judge will be appraising the work of the deputy district judge and takes no part in the hearing as a judge.

Small claims in the IPEC are heard by the specialist district judges in that court (see Chapter 5, para 5.14).

1.2.7   Reference materials

The rules without commentary and downloadable leaflets explaining basic procedures and setting out current court fees can be found at the Ministry of Justice website.[3]

This book is a comprehensive handbook with sufficient extracts from the rules to cover most procedural situations encountered in small claims cases.

The major legal publishers produce annual volumes of the rules with expert commentary and other material useful for conducting litigation at all levels; these civil practice books can be found in legal offices and the different publishers' books are called 'the green book',[4] 'the white book'[5] and 'the brown book'[6] after the colour of their covers.

---

3   www.justice.gov.uk.

4   *The Civil Court Practice 2013* (Butterworths, 2013).

5   *Civil Procedure 2013* (Sweet & Maxwell, 2013).

6   *Civil Court Service 2013* (Jordan Publishing Ltd, 2013).

1.3 EVALUATING THE CASE AND AVOIDING COURT PROCEEDINGS IF POSSIBLE

1.3.1 The four basic questions

Each side must step back from the case and ask four basic questions:

Question 1: Do I have a good chance of winning?
Question 2: If I win, will I be able to recover the money from the other side?
Question 3: Is the amount at stake worth the cost to me of the court case (time and money)?
Question 4: Have I done everything I can to avoid issuing court proceedings by trying to negotiate a settlement?

This evaluation must take place not only at the start of the case, but when the defence and any counterclaim is received, and in the light of all changing circumstances before the hearing or the mediation – for example when the other side's documents are received before the hearing.

1.3.2 How to decide if the proceedings are worthwhile

Each side should:

- consider the strength of their evidence
- find out if the law is in their favour
- weigh the personal and financial cost of proceeding
- consider if the other side can afford to pay their claim and court fees if they win

Evidence

When considering disputed issues of fact, the judge has to consider the written and oral evidence and make a finding. The ordinary civil standard of proof applies which is the 'balance of probability', namely whether a particular fact or matter is likely to be true. The strict rules of evidence do not apply to small claims cases and this means that the judge can look at all the evidence without being limited by over formality. The judge will weigh all evidence depending on its relevance and credibility. In other words, the judge will take a common-sense approach to the evidence to decide if what is claimed is likely to be true. Basic original documents, for example invoices and records, must be available for the hearing; and the parties must be able to bring to court with them any witnesses who will support their case. See Chapter 10, para 10.9 for a discussion of the use of evidence at a small claims hearing.

The court may give permission for an expert to assist at the hearing. The parties should consider at the outset whether a person may be approached to act as an independent expert and how the fees of that expert will be met. The cost of the expert could well be more than the £750 allowance which may be awarded for expert's fees in favour of the winner (Chapter 8, para 8.8 deals with expert evidence in small claims cases).

Applying the law

District judges are keenly aware of the need to apply the law accurately in small claims cases. If a mistake in the law is made, the loser will have grounds for appeal (see Chapter 11).

The district judge will not act as legal adviser to the parties. The overriding objective provides that the court will, so far as practicable, ensure that the parties are on an equal footing (CPR rule 1.1(2)(a)).[7] If an important point of law is raised at the hearing which takes either party by surprise then an adjournment may be necessary for each party to seek legal advice.

The parties and their legal advisers must therefore ensure that they check and research any legal points before a hearing to avoid the delay and expense of an adjournment or the risk of a case going to appeal if the district judge makes a mistake on the law.

The cost of proceeding (time and money)

The claimant must pay the initial court fee. A defendant must pay a fee to start a counterclaim. There is no extra charge for mediation but if there is no mediation or if a mediation fails and the case goes to a judges hearing then a hearing fee will be payable in addition to the issue fee and allocation fee.

Litigation involves not only money, but also time. Litigants must be prepared to set aside adequate time to prepare the case for the hearing and to attend court on the day of the hearing itself. The hearing may be quite short, but the parties may have to wait some hours at court before the case is called for hearing.

---

[7] See Appendix 6.

The parties must consider that if they lose they will be ordered to pay the other side's court fees and witness expenses. If the court decides that either party has behaved unreasonably an award for costs may be made (the issue of costs in small claims cases is dealt with in Chapter 9).

Does the other side have funds?

Chapter 12 considers methods of enforcement and some practical hints on how to find out about the likely ability of the other side having funds to pay and should be consulted before starting a court case.

A litigant must make an informed decision about whether the other side has funds to pay before starting any court action. Even if a judgment is obtained, the loser may refuse to pay and the winner then has to embark on enforcement action which can be slow and expensive. Litigants are strongly advised to take a realistic view about whether the other side is likely to pay a judgment before they start the court action.

1.3.3 Avoid court proceedings if possible

> The overriding objective encourages settlement out of court proceedings which can be achieved by:
>
> * small claims and pre-action protocols
> * trade arbitration and ombudsman schemes
> * mediation after the start of a court action

The court rules are designed to deal with cases fairly but it is all too easy to get bogged down with the technicalities and forget that avoiding court action may be a cheaper and more effective way of resolving a dispute. It is also incorrect to assume that actions taken or not taken before the start of a court action are immune from the scrutiny of the court process. There is a no costs culture in small claims; even so, the district judge may penalise a party who has continued unreasonably to litigation and not tried to settle out of court. This point is pressed home as far as pre-action protocols are concerned; parties who do not comply with the practice direction relating to pre-action conduct[8] may be liable to pay costs even where the case is later allocated to the small claims track (see para 1.4).

---

[8] Practice Direction – Pre-Action Conduct, updated September 2013.

In every case the potential claimant should send a letter of claim and give a reasonable time to respond before starting the action. Failure to do this may result in the district judge finding that the claimant has acted unreasonably and costs sanctions may follow. It is clear that this principle applies to small claims cases (for more detail, see para 1.4).

Many large organisations and trade groups run free, independent mediation or arbitration services or complaints may be referred to an ombudsman scheme. The potential small claims litigant who ignores these routes to satisfaction does so at the real risk of forfeiting a routine award of costs at a hearing before the judge (this is discussed in more detail at Chapter 9, para 9.3).

It used to be the case that out of court settlement meant putting together a deal in the court waiting room just before a hearing before a judge. These settlements are still possible but HM Courts & Tribunals Service (the Courts Service) now offers a professional mediation service to small claims litigants which is available to the parties after the allocation of the case to the small claims track. Chapter 7 deals with this procedure in full.

The court fees structure also encourages out of court settlement. The fees charged to potential litigants have rocketed in recent years and the cost of court-based justice cannot be said to be cheap. Paying the fee on commencement is only the start. Then there is a further fee for the hearing.

1.4.   LETTERS BEFORE ACTION AND PRE-ACTION CONDUCT

1.4.1   Introduction

The rules enable the court to take into account the conduct of the parties at all stages of litigation including before the start of the court case. In every case where the matter is likely to be disputed, the court will expect the parties to have exchanged information before starting a court case and to have given the other party a chance to settle the claim. If this is not done the offending party may be asked to provide an explanation and ordered to pay costs.

It has always been good advice to write a letter before action. The general practice direction on pre-action conduct was introduced in April 2009 and applies to all cases, including and not related exclusively to those cases destined for the small claims track. Previously, in relation to small claims, it could be said that compliance with the spirit of specific pre-action protocols, for example those drafted to deal with personal injury claims, was voluntary. Compliance with the pre-action conduct practice direction is now compulsory.

This section is a guide to the protocol tailored to cases destined for the small claims track.

For the purpose of this book on small claims, those key sections of the pre-action conduct practice direction most relevant to these cases are reproduced at Appendix 5. These are:

- exchanging information before starting proceedings;
- Alternative Dispute Resolution;
- Annex A: guidance on pre-action procedure where no pre-action protocol applies;
- Annex B: information to be provided in a debt claim where the claimant is a business and the defendant is an individual;
- compliance.

> Reference to the relevant paragraphs of the pre-action conduct practice direction concerning experts is included in Chapter 8, para 8.8

1.4.2 Terms of the practice direction

> The two key elements of the pre-action conduct practice direction are:
>
> - exchange of information before starting proceedings
> - trying to settle the case out of court including engaging in an appropriate form of Alternative Dispute Resolution

The claimants must write a letter before action and provide a reasonable time to respond. If the case is straightforward then 14 days is a reasonable time to respond. If the other side is expected to refer the matter to an insurance company, for example to house insurers or to car insurers, then it is suggested that about 30 days is allowed for a response. Longer periods of up to 90 days are suggested for more complex cases but this is unlikely to apply to small claims cases; it is really a matter of common sense but a period of 14 days should be treated as an absolute minimum.

Annexes A and B to the pre-action conduct practice direction set out detailed guidance on the information to be provided in the letter before action and the terms of the response (see paras 1.4.3 and 1.4.4).

The pre-action conduct practice direction provides that court action should only be started when all attempts at settlement have failed and no court action should be started when settlement discussions are underway. Privately funded professional mediation is often too expensive for a small claims case. However, the increase in the qualifying limit to £10,000 may now make it a viable option for more cases than when the limit was lower. It is always worth investigating, for a particular dispute, if there is a relevant trade-run arbitration or ombudsman scheme. Where they exist, ombudsman schemes are free to the consumer; for example the Banking Ombudsman Scheme. The most well-known scheme related to a trade organisation is the independent scheme used by ABTA (Association of British Travel Agents). A search on the internet will quickly reveal if a suitable scheme operates for a particular problem.

1.4.3   Detailed guidance on exchange of information (Annex A)

Annex A to the pre-action conduct practice direction gives detailed guidance on pre-action conduct (see Appendix 5).

A letter before action must contain basic information which includes not only the assertion of the claim but also details of documents relied on and must say what documents the claimant asks the other side to provide.

The defendant must give a 'full response'. If the defendant cannot respond within the time specified it is reasonable to say why a response is delayed and the date upon which a full response is forthcoming. The defendant must set out full reasons why the claim is disputed with full reference to any document relied upon. If documents have been requested they should be supplied and if not a reason should be given.

Overall, the contents of Annex A are really no more than common sense allied with courtesy, and the pre-action conduct practice direction formalises steps that sensible litigants have long since been taking. The real innovation is the attention that judges now pay to the actions of parties who do not comply with these steps (see para 1.4.5).

1.4.4   Special pre-action steps where the claimant is a business and the defendant is an individual (Annex B)

This is an innovation. The claimant must now provide the defendant with details of organisations which can offer free advice, and this information is set out in Annex B to the pre-action conduct practice direction. The information must accompany or precede the letter before action. The defendant may need more than 14 days to take debt advice and, if so, must say so in the response, giving detail of the timescale involved. The claimant should allow 14 days to obtain debt advice.

1.4.5 Consequences of non-compliance

The guidance is flexible, therefore the district judge will have to look at the matter in the round. Matters to be taken into account will include whether the steps taken before proceedings were in proportion to the size and importance of the matter. Urgency of the matter will be taken into account.

Failure to comply may result in an adverse order for costs and, for the avoidance of doubt, the guidance specifically mentions CPR rule 27.14(2)(g); this is the rule that a party to a small claims action may be liable to pay costs insofar as the judge considers he or she has acted unreasonably. Chapter 9 deals with the issue of costs in small claims cases in detail (see, in particular, para 9.3).

The guidance also suggests that any party who has failed to take reasonable pre-action steps can be ordered to make an explanation of his or her conduct and may be penalised when interest is awarded. The court may also suspend a court case until steps which ought to have been taken are taken.

1.5 EUROPEAN CONVENTION ON HUMAN RIGHTS

The Human Rights Act 1998 gives effect in England and Wales to the ECHR. It is a legally enforceable charter of human rights and fundamental freedoms. The Act became part of UK law on 2 October 2000 and it has been influential in modelling the current procedures on small claims cases. For example, the fact that small claims hearings are no longer held in private is a reflection of ECHR, Article 6 (right to a fair and public hearing). All courts and tribunals, including county courts hearing cases allocated to the small claims track, are able to consider arguments raised under the ECHR. Further discussion of the interaction of UK and European law is beyond the scope of this book.

1.6 HELP WITH LEGAL FEES, COURT FEES AND GETTING FREE ADVICE

Although litigants in person are welcome on the small claims track, cases can be conducted using a solicitor or barrister. Their fees will have to be paid for privately and, due to the no costs rule, it is unlikely that the fees will be recovered from the loser.

For those on low incomes and with limited savings, the Community Legal Services Fund ('legal aid') strictly offers no opportunity for public funding of litigants whose case is, or is likely to be, referred to the small claims track.[9] Some firms of solicitors which hold a legal aid contract may be prepared to offer up to 2 hours of legal advice or help at court to a person of limited financial means. It is worth enquiring if a local firm is able to assist under such a scheme.

There are free legal advice units attached to some colleges and universities and it is worth contacting local higher education establishments and asking if their pro bono unit can help with a particular case.

Some house insurance policies offer free legal advice on some cases. Members of motoring organisations can enquire about assistance for relevant cases. Various websites, including those of Trading Standards and the Which? Organisation, offer sound advice on practical legal issues.

Citizens Advice Bureaux will assist litigants with procedures and offer advice on legal matters.

1.6.1   Help with court fees

People in receipt of benefits or on low incomes should go to the local county court and ask about fee remission. They will be asked to complete a means testing form (EX160[10]) and if they qualify will then be entitled to pay reduced court fees or may even get the court fees waived completely. The explanatory booklet EX160A is available on the Courts Service website.[11]

---

[9]   *The Funding Code, Part 1 – Criteria*, Section 5 – The General Funding Code, para 5.4.6.

[10]   Available on the Courts Service website.

[11]   www.justice.gov.uk/courts/fees.

Chapter 2

Step-by-Step Guide to Starting a Small Claims Case

2.1 OVERVIEW

Basics

- The court case is started by the claimant:
    - filling out a court form (a claim form)
    - setting out the claim in writing and
    - paying a court fee

    All either online or by post

- The defendant defends by sending a written defence to the court within 14 days of service or within 28 days if an acknowledgment is filed

- A counterclaim is started by the defendant:
    - setting out the counterclaim in writing and
    - paying a court fee

- Any claim, counterclaim or defence must be verified by a statement of truth

---

The filling out of the claim form, Form N1, comes after sending a letter before action and waiting a reasonable time for a response. Consideration to out of court settlement must be given before launching a court action.

Chapter 1, paras 1.3 and 1.4 deal with how to evaluate a case and avoid court proceedings, and letters before action and pre-action conduct

---

Click here to reset form | **Click here to print form**

Claim Form

In the
Step 18

for court use only

Claim No.

Issue date

Claimant(s) name(s) and address(es) including postcode

Step 2 (name the claimant)
Step 3 (claimant's address)

SEAL

Defendant(s) name and address(es) including postcode

Step 5 (identify the defendant)
Step 6 (name the defendant)

Brief details of claim

Step 8

Value

Step 13

You must indicate your preferred court for hearings here *(see notes for guidance)*

Step 17 (choose a preferred court)

Defendant's name and address for service including postcode			£
Step 7	Amount claimed	Step 14	
	Court fee	Step 15	
	Solicitor's costs	Step 16	
	Total amount		

When corresponding with the court, please address forms or letters to the Court Manager and quote the claim number.

N1 Claim form (CPR Part 7) (12.12)   © Crown Copyright 2012

Claim No.	

Does, or will, your claim include any issues under the Human Rights Act 1998? ☐ Yes ☐ No

Step 10
Particulars of Claim (attached)(to follow)

Step 1 (specified or unspecified)
Step 9 (particulars of claim)
Step 11 (interest)

Statement of Truth
*(I believe)(The Claimant believes) that the facts stated in these particulars of claim are true.
* I am duly authorised by the claimant to sign this statement

Full name _Step 12_____

Name of claimant's solicitor's firm _____

signed _____ position or office held _____
*(Claimant)(Litigation friend)(Claimant's solicitor)   (if signing on behalf of firm or company)
*delete as appropriate

Step 4

Claimant's or claimant's solicitor's address to which documents or payments should be sent if different from overleaf including (if appropriate) details of DX, fax or e-mail.

Thoughtful preparation of the claim may be the difference between success and disaster – if a claim is poorly drafted or the parties are wrongly described, the matter may become unnecessarily complicated. The essence of a small claims case is its simplicity, and this benefit will be lost if mistakes are made at the outset.

This chapter covers the main topics to be thought through by the claimant at the outset of the case. It is a checklist of how to commence a small claims case, the steps of which are explained in the order they are listed below.

The claim form must be served within 4 months of issue otherwise it expires (CPR rule 7.5). An application can be made to extend the life of the claim form (see Chapter 5, para 5.6.4).

Note: although mediation can occur after the issue of proceedings, it makes sense to consider mediation as an option before you issue proceedings (see para 1.3.3 for more about avoiding court proceedings).

2.2   ISSUING CLAIMS

The formal beginning of a claim at court is known as its 'issue'. Litigants are expected to issue proceedings by post or online; issuing by attending a local county court hearing centre in person (over the counter) is now reserved to limited types of cases.

2.2.1   By post

A claim for money is issued when a form which is filled out by hand is sent to the County Court Money Claims Centre (CCMCC) in Salford.[1] This office is not open to the public and does not take personal callers. Queries are dealt with by a telephone helpline[2] or by email.[3]

The process of filling out the claim form (Form N1) and sending to the CCMCC is explained in detail in this chapter.

For small claims in the IPEC, see Chapter 5, para 5.14.

---

[1]   County Court Money Claims Centre, PO Box 527, Salford M5 0BY.

[2]   Helpline telephone number: 0300 123 1372.

[3]   Email address: ccmcccustomerenquiries@hmcts.gsi.gov.uk.

The process is started by completing and sending a Form N1, which can be obtained either from a local county court or downloaded from the Courts Service website.[4]

2.2.2　Online

The online service can only be used for claims for a 'specified' sum of money which are claims for a fixed sum of money. Claims for general compensation (damages) must be issued by post or over the counter.

The online service is called Money Claim Online, sometimes just referred to as MCOL.[5]

The online form is the same as the paper form which is filled out by hand. The process of filling out the form and submitting online is explained in detail in this chapter.

2.2.3　Over the counter

A local county court hearing centre will only issue a claim over the counter if the case relates to something other than money – for example a claim for an injunction or a declaration. These cases cannot be issued online or by posting to the CCMCC.

Local county court hearing centres have limited opening hours and sometimes only see personal callers by appointment.

There is no need to be concerned about the difficulties of travelling to Salford. Any hearings will almost always take place at a court convenient to at least one of the parties.

---

4   www.justice.gov.uk/courts/procedure-rules/civil/forms.

5   www.moneyclaim.gov.uk.

2.2.4   Ways of issuing a claim – summary

	Specified claim for money (debts and fixed sums)	Unspecified claim (compensation and damages)	Injunctions and declarations including claims for declarations
Online service, at www.moneyclaim.gov.uk	Yes	No	No
By post by sending to the CCMCC (no personal callers)	Yes	Yes	No
Over the counter or by post to a local county court	No	No	Yes

2.3   CHECKLIST FOR STARTING A SMALL CLAIMS CASE, INCLUDING INFORMATION TO HELP WITH COMPLETING THE CLAIM FORM ONLINE

Step 1   Decide if the case is to be specified or unspecified
Step 2   Name the claimant
Step 3   State the claimant's address
Step 4   Give the claimant's address for sending documents and payments
Step 5   Identify the defendant
Step 6   Name the defendant
Step 7   State where the defendant is to be served
Step 8   Brief details of the claim
Step 9   Particulars of the claim
Step 10   Complete the tick box about any human rights element
Step 11   Calculate the interest
Step 12   Statement of truth
Step 13   Value – check that the case is within the small claims limit
Step 14   Amount claimed
Step 15   Calculate the court fee
Step 16   Calculate the legal representative's costs on the claim form
Step 17   Choose a preferred court
Step 18   Ask the court to issue the claim form or submit the claim online
Step 19   Make a diary note

Reminder

The matters discussed in this chapter cover the mechanics of the case

The claimant's case must be carefully evaluated at all stages – not only at the outset but also when the defence has been received

This topic is discussed in more detail in Chapter 1

The starting point is the claim form, Form N1.[6] Rather than filling in the form from top to bottom, follow the steps in the order of the checklist and this should result in a perfect claim form every time (see para 2.1 for an annotated version of the claim form). The form is available on the Courts Service website.[7]

When filling in the form by hand, use capital letters and black ink.

2.3.1 Decide if the claim is to be specified or unspecified (step 1)

A claim which is specified, for example a debt claim, is for a fixed amount of money. A claim is 'unspecified' if the amount involved is not precisely known at the outset (e.g. 'damages for distress').

This is relevant to a number of practical matters, namely:

- the choice of issue court and transfer between courts if the defendant is an individual (see para 2.3.17 (step 17));
- checking that the value is within the small claims limit (see para 2.3.13 (step 13));
- calculating the court fee (see para 2.3.15 (step 15));
- entering judgment in default (see Chapter 3).

---

[6] There is an alternative method of commencing proceedings, namely the Part 8 procedure. This alternative method is used in cases where there is unlikely to be substantial dispute of fact. The form that is used to start such cases is N208, which is also used for certain specialist claims as defined by Part 8. A case started by the alternative method may be allocated to the small claims track at the allocation stage, but this is rarely found in practice.

[7] www.justice.gov.uk/courts/procedure-rules/civil/forms.

Specified claims

All claims which are simply for money of a specified amount (e.g. a £50 debt or £100 for general inconvenience) are 'specified'.

The key features of a claim which is specified are that:

- if the defendant does not file a defence in time then the claimant enters judgment in default for the amount claimed and the judgment can be enforced straight away;
- if the defendant is an individual and defends a specified claim then, upon receipt of the defence, the case will be automatically transferred to the defendant's court (see para 2.3.17 (step 17));
- the court fee is calculated on the basis of the sum specified.

Unspecified claims

Any claim where the amount is left to the court to decide is 'unspecified' (e.g. 'damages' claims).

The key features of a claim which is unspecified are:

- if the defendant does not file a defence in time the damages have to be decided by the court (see Chapter 3, para 3.10) so the judgment cannot be enforced straight away;
- there is no automatic transfer to the defendant's home court on filing of a defence;
- to qualify for the small claims track, the claim should be limited to 'a sum not exceeding £10,000' (or any amount under £10,000) (but note that if the amount can be limited to a lower amount this may reduce the court fee payable).

2.3.2   Name the claimant (step 2)

The basic rules to be followed when naming the claimant are set out in Table 2.1.

Table 2.1   Rules for naming the claimant and defendant

Where the claimant or defendant is	Notes
An individual	Give full name
A sole trader carrying on business in a name other than his or her own	Must use personal name but should add trading name for clarity, for example John Smith trading as Smiths the Grocers
Partners (i.e. more than one individual carrying on business together)	Name of partnership or individual names of partners (see note (a))
Co-claimants	Where more than one person has a claim then each must be named as a claimant (see note (b))
A child or mentally disabled person	The claimant's name must be followed by the name of an adult 'litigation friend' (see note (c))
A limited company	Give name of company and state whether it is 'limited' or 'plc'
More than one defendant	List the parties separately as 'first', 'second', etc defendant

Notes

(a)   Partnerships, for example firms of solicitors or accountants, can sue or be sued either in their trading name or in the name of some or all of the individual partners.

(b)   In cases involving a group in a holiday case, sometimes only the leader of the party need be named as claimant (Package Travel, Package Holidays and Package Tours Regulations 1992,[8] regulation 2(i)).

(c)   A child is anyone under the age of 18 at the date of the issue of the proceedings (CPR rule 21.1(2)). There are special procedures which must be followed before embarking on a case by a litigation friend, which are set out in CPR Part 21 and PD 21 (not discussed in detail in this book).

2.3.3   State the claimant's address (step 3)

If the claimant is an individual, the claim form requires the residential address to be given – in the case of an individual suing in a business capacity, the business address can be used.

---

[8]   Package Travel, Package Holidays and Package Tours Regulations 1992 (SI 1992/3288).

If the claimant is a limited company, the registered office must be shown; alternatively, the place of business which is most closely connected with the claim.

The claim form must provide a residential or business address for the claimant in addition to any solicitor's address (PD 16, para 2.2).

Any address provided must include the postcode (PD 16, para 2.4).

2.3.4   Give the claimant's address for sending documents and payments (step 4)

This is the claimant's 'address for service', namely the address used by the court and by the other side for any correspondence about the case and the place where the defendant will send any money. This information is added on the back of the claim form in the box at the foot of the form.

The claimant must give an address for service in the United Kingdom.

The address of a solicitor can be used as the claimant's address for service.

If the claimant is a limited company, a business address will have already been inserted under step 2 (see section 2.3.2). However, a company's trading address is often different from the registered office. If the company is not using a solicitor, the business address of the actual person in the company who is running the case should be added here so that any papers from the court or the other side go to that person direct and not to the registered office.

There is no restriction on a litigant in person or a company conducting a case without a solicitor, but if the litigant has a non-solicitor to advise and assist, the adviser cannot 'conduct' the proceedings (e.g. sign legal documents on his or her behalf).

The address for service can be the party's own address or that of a solicitor. A legal representative includes solicitors and their employees but not general lay agents (CPR rule 2.3(1)).

2.3.5   Identify the defendant (step 5)

Wrongly identifying the defendant is one of the most common errors in small claims cases. If the incorrect defendant is sued, the proceedings will be delayed and may become muddled.

Claims against shops

Every business is obliged to display a prominent notice at its premises which gives the names and addresses of the owners of the business (Business Names Act 1985, section 4).

If the name of the owner of the business is not known, proceedings can be issued in the trading name of the business (PD 7A, para 5C).

Claims against firms

The use of the word 'firm' in this chapter means a business which does not reveal on its notepaper, or otherwise, whether it is a limited company, partnership or sole trader.

If details of the owners of the business or firm cannot be found, proceedings can be issued in the trading name of the business (PD 7A, para 5C). The position is the same as for claims against shops.

A firm which does not reveal details of its ownership on its business paper or at its place of business is, of course, in breach of Business Names Act 1985, section 4.

Claims against limited companies

If the firm's notepaper, website or the notice displayed at the shop reveals that the defendant is a limited company, that is the name which should be used on the claim form. Any individual director or employee should not be named as the defendant, as it is unlikely that they will be personally liable to meet the claim (see below).

Claims against directors of limited companies

The general rule is that where the claim is against a limited company then it is the company and not the directors or managers who are sued.

There are situations where a director can be held liable for a debt incurred by a company. For example, when a company director signs cheques knowing that the company does not have funds to honour them. However, remedies against directors in these circumstances are not available to litigants commencing county court proceedings. The claim or complaint should be referred immediately to the liquidator of the company, who will invite the claimant to 'prove' in the liquidation. If there are circumstances that justify a claim against the directors personally, such proceedings are brought by the liquidator, who will probably require a financial contribution towards legal costs from the claimant before starting proceedings.

Details of the liquidator will be found by making a search at Companies House (see Chapter 12, para 12.2 for contact details for Companies House).

Claims against partnerships

Partners should be sued in the trading name of the partnership, unless it is inappropriate to do so, in which case the claim can be brought against the individual partners themselves (PD 7A, para 5A.3).

Claims against principals and agents

This is a difficult area and will require careful thought before issuing proceedings. However, the following basic legal principles should be borne in mind:

- an agent does not deal on his or her own behalf but only on behalf of the principal;
- any court action must be against the principal and not the agent.

It is sometimes difficult to tell who is the principal and who is the agent. The situation is confused by the fact that some professionals call themselves 'agents' when, in strict legal terms, they are not:

- *travel agents*: may be giving advice in a professional capacity to clients as 'travel consultants' or may be acting as an agent for a travel company. As a rule of thumb, a travel agent will be acting as a true agent (and as such should not be sued) if a booking has been made; the claim should then be against the tour operator who is the principal;
- *estate agents*: usually act as agents for sellers, not buyers;
- *letting agents*: act as agents for landlords;
- *managing agents*: usually act for landlords, but may act on behalf of a residents' association or management company.

If there is any doubt or confusion about whether an individual or company is acting on its own behalf or on behalf of someone else, this should be researched at the outset and before proceedings are issued. A litigant in person should certainly consider taking legal advice if there is any doubt at all about who should be sued.

If the confusion cannot be resolved, an option is to sue both potential defendants. In the small claims procedure this is not particularly risky, as an order for costs cannot be made against the claimant unless it is shown that he acted 'unreasonably' in joining a particular defendant as a party to the action. However, if the situation is clarified by the defence, for example if one of the defendants admits to being the 'principal', it may well then be unreasonable to pursue the case against both to the full hearing.

Claims against companies in liquidation

Proceedings should not be issued against companies in liquidation and any claim must be referred to the liquidator – details of the liquidator will be found at Companies House (see Chapter 12, para 12.2).

Claims against bankrupts

Proceedings cannot be issued against a bankrupt for any debt or claim which arose before the date of bankruptcy except with the permission of the court. Most claims against bankrupts should be referred to the Trustee in Bankruptcy. If the claim or debt arose after the date of bankruptcy then the bankrupt can be sued. However, if the claim involves the bankrupt obtaining credit after the date of bankruptcy then an offence may have been committed and the Trustee in Bankruptcy should be notified immediately. (See Chapter 12 for how to find out if someone is bankrupt.)

2.3.6   Name the defendant (step 6)

Once the defendant has been identified, follow the guidance on naming as set out in Table 2.1.

2.3.7   State where the defendant is to be served (step 7)

This will usually be straightforward and will be the address where the defendant is known to live or carry on business. Where there has been correspondence before the start of the proceedings the defendant may have named a solicitor to accept service, in which case that address should be used. The defendant can give an address for service anywhere in the United Kingdom; however, if the address is in Scotland or Northern Ireland, extra time is allowed for the defendants to respond to the claim form.

In all cases, the address must include a postcode.

In cases where a solicitor has not been named to accept service, the rules about the place of service are set out in CPR rule 6.9 (see the following table). This should be considered as the address for service only to be used where the proposed defendant has not already said to where the court papers should be sent:

Nature of defendant to be served	Place of service
1. Individual	Usual or last known residence
2. Individual being sued in the name of a business	Usual or last known residence of the individual; or principal or last known place of business
3. Individual being sued in the business name of a partnership	Usual or last known residence of the individual; or principal or last known place of business of the partnership
4. Limited liability partnership	Principal office of the partnership; or any place of business of the partnership within the jurisdiction which has a real connection with the claim
5. Corporation (other than a company) incorporated in England and Wales	Principal office of the corporation; or any place within the jurisdiction where the corporation carries on its activities and which has a real connection with the claim
6. Company registered in England and Wales	Principal office of the company; or any place of business of the company within the jurisdiction which has a real connection with the claim
7. Any other company or corporation	Any place within the jurisdiction where the corporation carries on its activities; or any place of business of the company within the jurisdiction

Note that in the case of an individual being sued in his or her personal capacity, the address is the 'residential' address and not the work address. If only the work address is known and not the residential address then the rules about alternative addresses for service apply (see Chapter 5, para 5.6.3).

Individuals who move around, including those who are evasive about where they live or work, can create problems, and the concern is that a claim form sent to the last known address will be returned in the post or that the defendant may claim that he or she did not receive it. Here, the rules assist the claimant who acts reasonably.

If the claimant has reason to believe that the defendant is no longer at the last known address, he or she must take *reasonable steps* to ascertain the address of the defendant's current residence or place of business (CPR rule 6.9(3)). This wording was introduced by an amendment to the rules in 2008 and the previous, somewhat convoluted, case law on this topic is now of only limited relevance, but may continue to influence the courts in deciding if the steps taken to locate the defendant were reasonable.

Reasonable steps include:

- searching for an individual's new address in his or her professional or trade directory;
- checking the Yellow Pages;
- physically checking the premises of a business that has moved to see if the new address is displayed for the public;
- checking online;
- contacting any relevant trade organisation;
- visiting the business address to see if there is a notice in the window or if the new occupants have been given a forwarding address.

None of these steps should, however, be necessary if the case is started promptly. It has to be said that the case law on this topic mainly concerns cases where parties have delayed 2 or 3 years, or even longer, after the event before starting a court action.

If the outcome of that search is the finding of a new address then that address must be used for service.

If the outcome of that search is that a new address cannot be found, an alternative address should be considered or even an alternative method of service. If these steps still draw a blank then the last known address can be used; however, this is very much a last resort. The topic of alternative methods of service is covered in Chapter 5, para 5.6.3.

Once the proceedings have been properly served on the last known address, that counts as good service. If the envelope is returned to the court office marked 'not known', this does not raise a presumption that the proceedings have not been served – but it could raise a question about whether the claimant has taken reasonable steps to find the defendant.

2.3.8 Brief details of the claim (step 8)

There is space on the front of the claim form to give a brief description of the case. This will provide anyone looking at the claim with an at-a-glance view of what it is about. Some suggested wordings appear in Chapter 6, para 6.7.3.

2.3.9   Particulars of the claim (step 9)

> See Chapter 6 for guidance on how to draft the claim, including
> precedents

The particulars must include a concise statement of the facts on which the claimant relies (CPR rule 16.4(1)). In many small claims cases the space on the back of the claim form will be sufficient to set out the claim fully. The claim may be set out on a separate sheet, in which case write 'see attached' on the back of the form.

Note: when issuing a claim online, the space for the claim form is limited to 1,080 characters and up to 24 lines. However, it is now possible to issue a claim online and serve the statement of case (otherwise known as full particulars) separately.

In small claims cases it is best to set out the claim in full at the time of issue as service of particulars later will only complicate matters. However, if the particulars of claim are to be served at a later date, the words 'to follow' should be written on the back of the form (CPR rule 16.2(2)).

If the statement of case is served separately, the following rules apply:

- the statement must be served within 14 days of the claim form (CPR rule 7.4(1)(b));
- the statement of case must be verified by a statement of truth (PD 16, para 3.4);
- a copy of the statement and a certificate of service must be filed at the court within 7 days of service.

If the claim involves a claim for personal injury, it is unlikely that the case will qualify for the small claims track because the maximum value of a personal injury claim in small claims case is £1,000. If there is a personal injury claim and the claimant relies on medical evidence, a medical report must be attached to the statement of case. In cases involving minor injuries where the claimant can give direct evidence of the injuries, a medical report may be unnecessary (PD 16, para 4).

2.3.10   Complete the tick box about any human rights element (step 10)

The tick box has been introduced to help the Courts Service to keep tabs on the issue of such claims. If the claim does rely on any provision or right under the

Human Rights Act 1998, the statement of case must set out all the information required by PD 16, para 15.1 (not covered in this book).

2.3.11   Calculate the interest (step 11)

See Chapter 6, para 6.8 for a method of calculating statutory interest

The Money Claim Online website[9] also provides a prompt for claiming interest and explains how to calculate it

---

If the claimant is seeking interest then the claim must be fully set out on the claim form (CPR rule 16.4(2)). Failure to set out a claim for interest on the claim form is likely to prevent the claimant from being awarded interest at the hearing.

Contractual interest

This only applies if it was set out in the original agreement between the claimant and defendant. For example:

- interest on a credit card, loan or bank overdraft;
- interest on unpaid professional fees, but only where the professional has made it plain from the outset that interest will be charged at a specific rate on unpaid invoices (accountants and solicitors often have a provision for interest in their terms of business);
- interest specified in the small print of the contract, for example for goods sold and delivered;
- interest on unpaid rent and service charges where interest is set out in a lease or tenancy agreement.

Statutory interest

This applies in debt claims where the rate of interest was not set out in the contract. The award is discretionary but, if claimed, is routinely made in most cases. The award of interest is not a penalty but recognition that the defendant, and not the claimant, has had the use of the money.

The rate of interest awarded is also within the discretion of the district judge: although a rate of 8% per year is often claimed and used to be awarded almost

---

[9]   www.moneyclaim.gov.uk.

as a matter of routine, many district judges now award a much lower rate (2% to 4%) to reflect the fact that in current economic conditions, higher rates risk overcompensating the recipient.

By contrast, the rate of interest payable after judgment is fixed by law at 8%.

Failure to set out a claim for interest on the claim form is likely to prevent the claimant from being awarded interest at the hearing.

Interest in other cases

Other interest, including interest on sums awarded for 'damages', is discretionary and there are special rules covering interest in personal injury cases.

Late payment of commercial debts

Extra interest plus a sum for compensation on a sliding scale is payable on commercial debts under the Late Payment of Commercial Debts (Interest) Act 1998. This gives any business, irrespective of size, a statutory right to claim interest on late payment of commercial debts. Full information about the Act can be found on the Pay on Time website.[10] The interest that can be claimed is 8% above the official dealing rate of the Bank of England. The wording of the claim for commercial interest is set out in Chapter 6. A commercial debt is a debt that results from contracts made between businesses and does not apply to consumer claims.

2.3.12   Statement of truth (step 12)

- Various documents filed at court must be supported by a statement of truth
- The statement is signed by the person filing the document or his or her solicitor
- If the person signing the statement does not believe the statement is true, then this can amount to contempt of court (CPR rule 32.14)
- Failure to sign the statement will restrict the use of the document in evidence

A statement of truth should be signed to support the claim form, plus any defence, witness statement and expert's report.

---

[10]   www.payontime.co.uk.

Wording of the statement of truth

> ### STATEMENT OF TRUTH
>
> *(I believe) *(the Claimant believes) that the facts stated in these particulars of claim are true. *(I am duly authorised by the claimant to sign this statement).
>
> * delete as appropriate

When issuing online, the claimant is invited to confirm the statement of truth by adding his or her name; this fulfils the requirement to sign the statement of truth (PD 7E, para 10).

Who can sign the statement of truth? (PD 22, para 3)

Where statement is made by	*The statement can be signed by*
An individual	The individual A legal representative*
A limited company	Director Treasurer Company secretary Chief executive Manager Other officer A legal representative*
A partnership	Any of the partners A person 'having control or management of the partnership business' A legal representative*

Note: the person who signs a statement of truth must print his or her name clearly beneath the signature. Where the statement of truth is signed by a legal representative they must use their own name plus state the capacity in which they sign; the firm's name should also be stated. A lay representative cannot sign a statement of truth – the definition of a legal representative in CPR rule 2.3(1) does not include a lay representative.

---

*   If the person making the statement is represented by a legal representative, he or she will be taken by the court as having:

- been authorised to sign the statement on behalf of the client;
- explained to the client that, by signing it, he or she is confirming the client's belief the statement is true; and
- explained to the client the possible consequences if the client does not have an honest belief in the truth of those facts.

PD 22, para 3.8

Consequences of failure to sign the statement of truth

The proceedings are effective, even without a statement of truth, unless subsequently struck out. However, if it is not signed, the claimant will not be able to rely on the statement of case in evidence (CPR rule 22.2(1)).

A defendant who receives a claim which has not been verified by a statement of truth can apply to the court for an order that the case be struck out (CPR rule 22(2)(2)).

See also Chapter 5, para 5.5 for more about statements of truth

---

2.3.13   Value – check that the case is within the small claims limit (step 13)

The value of the claim must be written on the front of the claim form beside the word 'value'.

In summary, the claim will only qualify for the small claims track if:

- it is for £10,000 or less;
- it does not include a claim for possession of land or a claim for harassment or unlawful eviction; and
- it includes a claim for personal injury or compensation against a landlord for repairs but the sum claimed in that respect is £1,000 or less.

How does a case qualify for the small claims track? See Chapter 4, para 4.4 for more details

---

If a case is outside the qualifying limit then consider:

- electing to use the small claims track by agreement (see Chapter 4, para 4.16);
- reducing the amount claimed to £10,000 or less.

2.3.14   Amount claimed (step 14)

Insert the amount claimed in the box on the form. If the claim is for an unspecified amount then write 'to be assessed' in the box (see para 2.3.1 (step 1)).

2.3.15 Calculate the court fee (step 15)

Court fees payable on issue are set out at Appendix 1 and Appendix 2.

The court fee payable to commence a small claims case is calculated on a sliding scale depending on the amount of the claim.

If the claim is limited to £10,000 and damages in general are claimed, the court will require the maximum scale fee.

If damages are likely to be limited, for example to the expected cost of repairs – say £550 – it is best to limit the damages to the sum expected. Then the fee will be charged at the rate relative to the maximum damages claimed.

Those on low incomes may obtain a part reduction of the court fee (or even a total exemption) at the discretion of the court manager. Application for a fee exemption or remission of fees should be made to the court manager. The applicant will be asked to fill out a form so that the reduction can be assessed.[11]

The fee can be paid in cash or by cheque in favour of 'HM Courts & Tribunals Service'.

Interest is not taken into account when deciding if the case qualifies for the small track but interest is taken into account when calculating the court fee.

2.3.16 Calculate the legal representative's costs on the claim form (step 16)

The scale of charges is set out at Appendix 3.

If a solicitor has issued the proceedings, fixed charges should be calculated and can be included on the claim form.

2.3.17 Choose a preferred court (step 17)

> See also Chapter 5, para 5.7 (transfers of cases between courts) and Chapter 8, para 8.3 (final decision about the hearing venue)

---

[11] County Court Fees Order 1999 (SI 1999/689).

- The claimant nominates a preferred court on the claim form.
- The district judge will make the final decision on the venue for a case if the parties cannot agree.

Note: claims issued online start their life in Northampton. If defended, the final hearing will be in the claimant's home court or, if the defendant is an individual, the defendant's home court. (The rules about this are set out in PD 7E which deals with money claims online.)

The claimant must specify a preferred local court on the claim form, to which the case should be transferred at the appropriate time.

Defended claims are transferred to a local county court hearing centre after the parties have returned their directions questionnaires (see Chapter 4, para 4.7):

(a) where the defendant is an individual, in a claim for a specific amount of money, there will be transfer to the defendant's home court;

(b) if the claimant or defendant specifies a different court on the directions questionnaire to the claimant's preferred court, the claim will be transferred to that court (the district judge will decide if the parties specify two different local courts);

(c) in all other circumstances, the claim will be transferred to the claimant's preferred court.

2.3.18 Ask the court to issue the claim form or submit the claim online (step 18)

If using the CCMCC, write 'County Court Money Claims Centre' in the box at the top right of the first page.

If using Money Claim Online, that box will already contain a reference to the County Court at Northampton.

The claim form should now be fully completed.

If you have proceeded logically through all the previous steps, the exercise of issuing the claim form should be trouble free.

If using the CCMCC, you will need to send to the court at the address above at para 2.2.1:

- the completed Form N1 plus at least two copies (one for the court and one for the defendant);
- a further copy of Form N1 for each additional defendant;
- the court fee, in cash, postal order or a cheque in favour of 'HM Courts & Tribunals Service'.

Note: the court does not return a copy of Form N1 to the claimant after the proceedings have been issued, so make a copy to keep before posting the original to the court.

The court will then formally issue the claim.

Normally, the proceedings will be served (i.e. sent to the defendant(s)) by the court by first class post but if you want to serve the proceedings yourself, then ask the court to return the papers to you for service (see para 2.3.7 (step 7) for more about service of proceedings).

Delay in serving the claim form

A word of warning. If the claim form is issued and not served immediately this can create problems. The claim form expires after 4 months, see Chapter 5, para 5.6.4.

2.3.19 Make a diary note (step 19)

The process of issuing involves giving the case a number and sending the papers to the defendant. The case number, including the letters at the start, remain with the case throughout, and should be used to identify the case whenever letters are sent to the court about the case. The case number should appear on any statements of case or witness statements.

The cheque will be paid in immediately upon receipt, but it could be a few days before the issuing process is complete. The Courts Charter promises that proceedings will be issued within 10 working days of the papers being received, but in practice proceedings are usually issued more quickly than that.

When the court notifies you of the case number you will also be told the date of service. Make a note in your diary of the date when the defence is due so that you can apply for judgment in default if none is received. The defence or an acknowledgment will be due 14 days after service (see Chapter 3 for more detail).

2.4   THE NEXT STEPS

The following chapters explain all the steps to be taken by both parties and the court up to and including the allocation of the case to the small claims track. The steps must all be taken within a strict timetable. Practitioners and litigants must carefully note all relevant time limits in their diaries and make sure that deadlines are met.

2.5   OVERVIEW OF PROCEDURE BETWEEN RESPONSE AND ALLOCATION

14 days after service	Last date for responding to the case by defence acknowledgment or admission	See Chapter 3, para 3.2
28 days after service if an acknowledgment has been filed	Last date for defence or admission	See Chapter 3, paras 3.3 and 3.4
	Last date for contesting the jurisdiction of the court	See Chapter 3, para 3.5

Once a defence has been received, the court provisionally allocates the claim to a track and sends out directions questionnaires

14 days after receipt of directions questionnaires	Both parties must complete and return directions questionnaires to the court and to each other	See Chapter 4
	Claimant should file defence to counterclaim and any reply. *Note*: failure to file a defence to counterclaim may result in judgment in default	See Chapter 3, para 3.7
As soon as possible after receipt of directions questionnaires	If either party wishes to make an application for summary judgment, this should be done now	See Chapter 5, para 5.8

District judge considers the directions questionnaires, allocates to a track and gives directions

Chapter 3

Responding to the Claim (Including Obtaining Judgment in Default or on an Admission)

3.1 INTRODUCTION

This chapter covers the steps to be taken by the defendant by way of acknowledgment, defence, counterclaim and admission. It also deals with matters relating to default judgments and disposal hearings.

Basics

- The defendant must respond to the claim by acknowledgment admission or defence within 14 days
- The defendant must give reasons for defending the claim
- Any counterclaim should be set out at the same time as the defence
- The claimant can enter judgment on certain types of admissions
- In some cases where liability has been admitted, the amount payable can be decided at a 'disposal hearing' and a full small claims hearing will not be necessary

---

The court sends the defendant a 'response pack', which includes notes and guidance to the defendant on how to proceed.

The response pack contains:

- the claim form and the particulars of claim plus 'notes for the defendant on replying to the claim form';
- an acknowledgment of service form;
- an admission form;
- a form for a defence and counterclaim.

The court sends out different types of response pack, depending on whether the claim is specified or not specified.

Where a claim has been issued online the response can be done online – the response pack issued by the claims issue centre provides the defendant with instructions on how to proceed including a unique access code for each claim.

Reminder

The matters discussed in this chapter cover the mechanics of the case. The defendant's case must be carefully evaluated before a defence is prepared, see Chapter 1, para 1.3.1. At the outset, the defendant should be concerned about the viability, including the cost effectiveness, of fighting the case, and should give careful thought to using mediation, see Chapter 1, para 1.4

3.2   TIME FOR RESPONSE

The response can be an acknowledgment, admission, defence or counterclaim. In default of a response the claimant is entitled to a judgment in default (see para 3.9).

The time for responding does not start to run until the particulars of claim have been served.[1] If the claim form states that the particulars of claim are to follow then they should follow within 14 days of the claim form (CPR rule 7.4(1)).

The first thing that the defendant or legal adviser should do on the receipt of the papers is to make a careful note of the date that the papers were received and make a diary note of the last date for responding. If the response to the court is to be made by post, make sure that plenty of time is allowed for postal delays. The diary note should be at least 3 working days before the court's deadline.

The time for response depends on whether the defendant is an individual or a limited company, and on the method of service.

---

[1]   Confusingly, this may be a date after the documents were received – this is explained at Chapter 5, para 5.6.2.

> See the table at Chapter 5, para 5.6.2 for the deemed date of service relative to the method of service used

The basic rule is that the court must receive the defence or acknowledgment 14 days after the defendant receives the particulars of claim.

See also:

- rules about service of the claim form and other documents including a description of the various methods of service are set out in Chapter 5, para 5.6;
- calculating time limits (Chapter 5, para 5.11);
- judgment in default (para 3.9).

3.3 ADMITTING THE CLAIM

When admitting a claim, the steps to be taken depend on whether the claim is specified or unspecified, and whether the defendant admits all or part of the claim.

If the defendant admits all or part of the claim, the claimant may:

(1) accept the sums offered or paid and take the matter no further; or
(2) apply for a judgment on admission (see para 3.3.1); or
(3) apply for a discretionary judgment (see para 3.3.2).

3.3.1 Judgment on admission

This is a judgment which the claimant is entitled to as of right under CPR rule 14.1(4).

Judgment on admission is only available where:

- the claim is for payment of money; and
- there is an admission of a whole claim for a specified sum (CPR rule 14.4); or
- there is an admission of a part of a claim for a specified sum (CPR rule 14.5) – if the claimant accepts the amount admitted; or
- there is an admission of the whole of the claim for an unspecified sum (CPR rule 14.6) – the court will then determine the amount payable; or

- the defendant offers a sum in payment of an unspecified claim (CPR rule 14.7) – if the claimant does not accept the sum offered, a judgment on admission can be obtained with the amount to be decided by the court (rule 14.7(10)).

The documents which accompany the particulars of claim when sent to the defendant include a form for making an admission.

If the defendant wishes to admit the whole of a claim for a specified sum of money, the admission form or some other written record of the admission should be sent to the claimant within 14 days. The claimant can then obtain judgment for the admitted sum simply by requesting it – by returning to the court a completed Form N225, which is available on the Courts Service website.[2]

If, on the other hand, the defendant wishes to admit part of a claim for a specified sum or in respect of a claim for an unspecified sum, the admission form or some other written record of the admission should be sent to the court within 14 days.

Upon receiving an admission of part of a specified amount, or an admission of an unspecified amount, the court staff will send the claimant a standard form which prompts the claimant to apply for judgment.

Where the claimant files a request for judgment on an admission of a specified amount, the court will enter judgment for that sum.

Where the claimant files a request for judgment on an admission for an amount to be decided by the court, the claim will be transferred from the CCMCC to the preferred court.

No court fee is payable to enter judgment on admission

---

[2]   www.justice.gov.uk/forms/hmcts.

3.3.2 Discretionary judgment

The claimant can ask the court for judgment in cases which do not fall neatly into the categories set out in CPR rule 14.1(3) by making an application under rule 14.3. The application can be an application on notice (see Chapter 5, para 5.4 for applications generally) or an application for summary judgment under CPR Part 24 (see Chapter 5, para 5.8).

3.3.3 Judgment of the court's own initiative

The court's management powers under CPR Part 3 give the district judge the discretion to enter judgment in appropriate cases (see Chapter 5, para 5.3). For example, if the terms of the defence amount to an admission, the district judge may order judgment on his or her own initiative. In suitable cases, a claimant could write to the court to prompt the district judge to review the defence and enter judgment. The defendant will be entitled to apply for such a judgment to be set aside within a specified number of days (usually 7 days).

> The overriding objective and the courts case management powers are considered in Chapter 5

3.3.4 Request for time to pay

When admitting the whole or part of the claim, the defendant can ask for time to pay. The usual procedure is for a senior member of court staff to look at the admission form and financial information and to determine the rate of payment as a paper exercise; the figures are based on set criteria balancing income against various standard allowances. Once the determination has been made, the parties are notified and can choose to accept or reject the determination. Either side can apply for a hearing before a district judge to change the determination. The application for a re-determination hearing must be made within 14 days. If the claim is for a specified sum, it will be automatically transferred to the preferred court unless the defendant is an individual, in which case it is transferred to the defendant's home court for the re-determination hearing (CPR rules 14.9 to 14.13).

3.3.5   Admitting the claim – summary table

	Defendant wishes to	Steps to be taken within 14 days after receipt of the statement of case [1]	Consequence
	Admit and pay the whole claim (CPR rule 14.4)	Pay full amount (including court fee and costs on summons) to the claimant direct. It is not strictly necessary to return the response form to the court [2]	Provided the claim has been paid in full and the payment safely received, the action will be over [3]
	Admit the whole claim but request time to pay [4] (CPR rule 14.4)	Fill out the admission form including the income details	Court will send a copy of the admission form to the claimant who is entitled to enter a judgment on admission [5] – the rate of payment can then be agreed between the parties or will be set by the court
Specified Claims	Admit and pay part of the claim (a part admission) [6]	Pay the amount admitted to the claimant direct and file a defence as to the balance	Court will send the defence to the claimant together with allocation questionnaires to both parties Claimant can either accept the sum paid and take the matter no further or rerun the completed allocation questionnaire to the court and request a hearing date to determine the balance due
	Admit some of the claim (a part admission) but request time to pay or defend the balance [4] (CPR rule 14.5)	Fill out the admission form including the income details and file a defence as to the balance	Apply to the court for judgment on admission on Form N225A [7] Alternatively, apply for a judgment on admission [5] of the amount admitted and do not pursue the balance
	Have more time to consider a response	Return the acknowledgment	This gives a further 14 days (28 days in total) to respond

Unspecified claims	Admit the whole claim (CPR rule 14.6)	State on the defence form that the claim is admitted, subject to the court determining the amount due [8] [9]	Claimant will be sent a copy of the admission form and is entitled to a judgment on admission [5] for damages to be decided by the court [8] Claimant applies for judgment on Form N226 [7]
	Make an offer to settle (CPR rule 14.7)	The defendant should say how much the he or she offers to pay [9] Also, if time is required to pay, [4] complete the financial information on the admission form	If the claimant accepts the offer then he or she can enter a judgment on admission [5] for the amount admitted If the claimant does not accept the offer then the claimant can apply for a judgment on Form N226 with the amount to be decided by the court (CPR rule 14.7(9) and (10))
	Have more time to consider a response	Return the acknowledgment	This gives a further 14 days (28 days in total) to respond

Notes

1   The defendant can take any of the steps mentioned after 14 days provided the claimant has not in the meantime entered judgment in default (CPR rule 14.2(3)).

2   The payment must be made to the claimant direct and not to the court. It makes sense to insist on a receipt if paying by cash.

3   If the defendant pays the whole amount of the claim before judgment is entered then he is entitled to have the judgment set aside (CPR rule 13.2(c)).

4   Request for time to pay (see para 3.3.4).

5   Judgment on admission (see para 3.3.1).

6   A defendant will often want to admit the 'claim' (or part of the claim) but may wish to dispute the court fee, interest, and solicitor's costs on the summons. As a general rule the claimant who has been forced to issue proceedings to recover money due will be entitled to recover these sums. In some cases, however, the proceedings may not have been justified. In such cases the 'part admission procedure' should be followed.

7   Available on the Courts Service website at www.justice.gov.uk/forms/hmcts.

8   The defendant will be given a chance to be heard when the court decides how much the defendant has to pay (see para 3.10.2).

9   Make an offer to settle – there is no facility to pay the money into court.

3.4   ACKNOWLEDGING THE CLAIM

There are two possible reasons for returning the acknowledgment form, rather than just sending in a defence straight away, namely:

(1) returning the acknowledgment form automatically gives the defendant a further 14 days to file and serve a defence; or
(2) to give the defendant time to make an application to the court to dispute the jurisdiction of the court.

Although the 14 days extra time sounds useful, bear in mind that the case cannot be allocated to the small claims track until after the defence has been filed. The defendant will not be automatically protected by the no costs rule until allocation has taken place (see Chapter 9, para 9.8).

The claimant can apply for summary judgment once an acknowledgment has been filed (CPR rule 24.4(1)(a)) (see Chapter 5, para 5.8).

Rules about acknowledging the claim are in CPR Part 10.

3.5   DISPUTE OF JURISDICTION

A dispute of jurisdiction means challenging whether the court has the right to determine the dispute: the objection might relate to geography, or to an agreement made in advance by the parties not to go to court but to settle any dispute by private arbitration. For example, it is usual for parties to a formal signed building contract to agree that any disputes should be referred to arbitration.

To dispute jurisdiction, the defendant must make an application either before acknowledgment or before the time for filing a defence has expired. The application should be supported by evidence (e.g. documents, or reasons on the application form supported by a statement of truth). A defendant can dispute jurisdiction even though an acknowledgment has been filed, but not usually after a defence has been filed. It is therefore important to apply to dispute jurisdiction before filing a defence.

Rules about disputing jurisdiction are in CPR Part 11; the detail is outside the scope of this book.

3.6 DEFENDING THE CLAIM

- See Chapter 6, para 6.3 for guidance on how to draft the defence (plus a few precedents) and the matters which a defence must include
- Each separate defendant must file and serve their own defence (but they may be combined in one document)

Four types of defence will be considered:

- *Type 1*: the bland denial (or holding defence).
- *Type 2*: the states paid defence.
- *Type 3*: the full defence.
- *Type 4*: the defence by way of set off or counterclaim.

3.6.1 Type 1: the bland denial

Sending a few lines (or just one) to the court to state that the claim will be contested and without giving reasons is not enough. The defendant must give the reasons for the defence (CPR rule 16.5) (see Chapter 6, section 6.3.3 for guidance on how to prepare a defence).

A district judge can strike out a defence if it is flimsy and insubstantial (see Chapter 5, para 5.3.2).

3.6.2 Type 2: the states paid defence

The response form to a specified claim invites the defendant to state if the debt has already been paid, and if so when. If it has been paid, and the defendant says so, this is called a states paid defence.

A states paid defence is sent to the claimant when the court receives it, and the claimant is asked to comment before the matter proceeds further. If the claimant accepts that the debt has been paid, the case will be at an end.

Costs will ultimately be in the discretion of the district judge but the defendant should not expect to pay the court fee and the other costs on the claim form if the claim was paid in full before the proceedings were issued. However, if the proceedings were issued before payment, even if they were served later, the defendant should expect to pay the costs on the summons, especially if the claimant sent a 'letter before action'.

3.6.3   Type 3: the full defence

> There are rules about what a defence must include and these are
> set out in Chapter 6, para 6.3.3

The defence must say:

- what parts of the claim are disputed (and why);
- which parts of the claim the defendant does not know enough about to admit or dispute, but which the defendant wants the claimant to prove;
- what parts of the defence are admitted (CPR rule 16.5).

The defence can be written or typed on the response form or set out in a separate document.

3.6.4   Type 4: the defence by way of set off or counterclaim

A counterclaim can be made without obtaining permission from the court at the time of the defence. If a defendant wants to put in a counterclaim at a later date the court will have to give permission (CPR rule 20.4(2)) and this permission must be obtained by making an application (see Chapter 5, para 5.4 for details on how to make an application).

The court will require a fee from the defendant based on the amount of the counterclaim. The fee is calculated on the scale of fees shown at Appendix 1 and is paid on the full amount of the counterclaim.

If the amount of the counterclaim exceeds £10,000, this may prevent the claim from being allocated to the small claims track (CPR rule 26.8(1)(e)).

A counterclaim is a statement of case (CPR rule 20.2(1)). When preparing the counterclaim, the guidance for drafting a statement of case should be followed (see Chapter 6), and it should be noted that the counterclaim should be supported by a statement of truth.

The counterclaim and defence should be one document – the counterclaim usually runs on at the end of the defence (PD 20, para 6.1).

A defendant who makes a claim against a claimant by way of counterclaim is technically a Part 20 claimant. If the claimant withdraws a claim the counterclaim will remain unless that is also withdrawn.

3.7 DEFENCE TO COUNTERCLAIM

A claimant must respond to the counterclaim within 14 days by serving and filing a defence or admission. There is no acknowledgment procedure.

The defendant can enter judgment in default of defence to counterclaim if none is filed (CPR rule 12.3(2)).

Often, a simple defence to counterclaim will suffice – a possible wording is set out in Chapter 6, para 6.7.4, precedent O.

3.8 WHEN THE DEFENDANT WANTS TO PASS THE CLAIM ONTO SOMEONE ELSE

If the defendant wishes to defend by saying 'I am not liable or to blame, someone else is' – the 'someone else' is called the third party. To pass the buck in this way, the defendant makes a claim in what are called 'third party proceedings'. An example of this type of claim would be if the claimant's car was hit in the rear by the defendant and the defendant's defence is that he or she was shunted into the claimant by a driver at the back driving into their car. The defendant would then start third party proceedings against the driver at the back of the shunt.

The court must give permission for the defendant to add another party to the proceedings (CPR rule 20.5(1)) (see Chapter 5, para 5.4 for details of how to make an application).

A formal application is not needed if the defendant wishes to make a claim against another existing defendant and the claim is made at the time of the defence (CPR rule 20.6).

Rules about claims against third parties are in CPR Part 20.

3.9 JUDGMENT IN DEFAULT – THE CONSEQUENCE OF NOT RESPONDING TO THE CLAIM IN TIME

If the defendant does not respond to the claim in time (see para 3.2), the claimant can apply for judgment in default by using the correct form (CPR rule 12.4(1)). The form is supplied to the claimant when the court notifies the claimant that proceedings have been issued and served. If the claimant is represented by a solicitor, fixed costs will be allowed in addition to those set out on the claim form – these are set out at Appendix 4. No court fee is payable on applying for a default judgment.

If the claim is for a specified amount (e.g. debt claims) the judgment is for the full claim plus interest to the date of judgment. If the claim is for an unspecified amount then the judgment is for 'an amount to be decided by the court' (CPR rule 12.4).

Judgment in default of defence cannot be obtained if the claimant has already made an application for summary judgment (see Chapter 5, para 5.8) or if the proceedings have been commenced by the alternative Part 8 procedure (see Chapter 2, para 2.3, n 6).

An application for judgment in default cannot be made until after the date for service of the defence or acknowledgment has expired but must be made within six months after the date for filing the defence – if not, the claim is stayed and the claimant has to apply to the court to progress the action (CPR rule 15.11).

When a judgment in default for an amount to be decided by the court is obtained, the case will automatically be transferred to the claimant's preferred court (see para 2.3.17) (CPR rule 12.5A).

3.10 JUDGMENTS FOR UNSPECIFIED SUMS – GETTING THE COURT TO DETERMINE THE AMOUNT PAYABLE

If the amount of the judgment is to be decided by the court then, immediately after transfer, the papers will be put before a district judge who will decide how the amount is to be determined or calculated. The district judge can:

- decide the value without a hearing;
- list for a 'disposal' hearing;
- allocate the case to the small claims track;
- have directions questionnaires be sent out before allocating the case.

3.10.1 Deciding the value without a hearing

This will only be done in the simplest of cases, the decision being made under the district judge's case management powers (CPR rule 3.1). In these circumstances the order will state that, because the decision has been made without a hearing, any party affected by the order can apply for the order to be set aside. The order will also state the time period within which the affected party may apply for the order to be set aside, often 7 days (see Chapter 5, para 5.3 (PD 23A, paras 11.1 and 11.2)).

3.10.2 Disposal hearings

A disposal hearing offers a simplified method of determining a case where it is only being defended as to value (quantum), and is suitable in simple cases where a judgment has been obtained by default or through an admission. The case goes straight from the judgment stage to a final hearing without having to go through the process of allocation directions (PD 26, para 12.8). The district judge who orders a disposal hearing will give simple directions, usually limited to the claimant serving a witness statement and documents to support the claim.

The disposal hearing will not normally last for more than 30 minutes, during which the court will not usually hear oral evidence (PD 26, para 12.4). The defendant will be notified of a disposal hearing and can argue with the amount being claimed by the claimant. The defendant can comment on any issue affecting the amount of the claim, including commenting on the claimant's evidence, raising issues of contributory negligence, mitigation and causation, so far as these are not inconsistent with any matter determined by the judgment.[3]

Both the district judge who lists the case for a disposal hearing and the district judge on that hearing can, if they wish, allocate the case to the small claims track and have the case proceed, in which case the rules about small claims costs will apply. Even if the case is disposed of without allocation, if it is a case which would have been allocated to the small claims track, the general rule is that the small claims costs regime will apply.[4]

3.10.3 Amount to be decided by the court – upon allocation to the small claims track

If the district judge decides to allocate a case to the small claims track, the action will then take on the structure of small claims case. Examples of cases which might be allocated after judgment include 'holiday cases', or others where the amount of the judgment can only be determined after considering detailed evidence. Chapter 8 deals with preparation for a small claims hearing.

---

[3] See *Lunnan v Hari Singh and others*, Times Law Reports, 1 July 1999, unreported, and *Maes Finance and Mac No 1 Ltd v Al Phillips & Co (A Firm)*, Times Law Reports, 25 March 1997, unreported.

[4] See *Voice and Script International Ltd v Alghafar* [2003] EWCA Civ 736, [2003] All ER (D) 86.

3.11   REPLY TO DEFENCE

A claimant does not usually need to file a reply to defence because, by not doing so, he or she will not be taken as having admitted any part of the defence (CPR rule 16.7(1)). If the claimant wants to make a reply to the defence then the reply must be filed and served with the directions questionnaire (rule 15.8). If the claimant is also filing a defence to counterclaim, they should usually form one document, with the reply first (PD 15, para 3.2). Replies are not usual in small claims cases. The general aim on this track is to limit the number of procedural steps to be taken and it will rarely be necessary or proportionate to serve a reply to defence.

Chapter 11 covers applications to set aside default judgments

---

Chapter 4

Directions Questionnaires and Allocation

4.1 INTRODUCTION

There is one last chance at the allocation stage for the proceedings to be stopped in order for settlement discussions to take place. Otherwise, the impetus of the case is maintained and the parties must continue to be vigilant about time limits and following court directions, otherwise the claim, defence or counterclaim may be struck out. The court is in charge.

An overview of the steps to be taken at this stage of the case is set out at Chapter 2, para 2.5.

Basics

- The case will usually be allocated to the small claims track if it meets the financial qualifications of the track
- The parties are all required to return completed directions questionnaires to the court before the district judge can make an allocation decision
- Some cases may require an allocation hearing

4.2 WHAT DOES 'ALLOCATION' MEAN?

The rules recognise that all cases do not need the same treatment in preparation for a hearing and not all cases need a formal or lengthy trial. To cater for this variety, and to ensure that procedures are proportionate to the value of the claim, the rules create three distinct categories of case. Once the district judge knows what the claim and defence involve, he or she can assign, or allocate, the case to the most suitable category. This process is termed 'allocation'.

4.3   WHAT IS A 'TRACK'?

The three case management categories are termed 'tracks'. They are shown in the following table.

Small claims track CPR Part 27	Cases up to £10,000 in value subject to specific exceptions in personal injury and housing claims
Fast track CPR Part 28	Cases above the small claims limit (see above) but of not more than £25,000 in value and where the case can be heard in one day or less
Multi track CPR Part 29	Cases which do not qualify for the small claims or fast track including all cases of over £25,000 in value

Once a case has been allocated to a track, the management of the case and the hearing are in accordance with the rules of that track. The track which the case is suited to by the rules is termed its 'normal track'.

4.4   HOW DOES A CASE QUALIFY FOR THE SMALL CLAIMS TRACK?

The financial ceiling for claims on the small claims track is £10,000 for most cases.

The small claims track is the normal track for:

- a claim which has a financial value of not more than £10,000 (except for personal injury and housing claims);
- any claim which is or includes a claim for personal injuries which has a financial value of not more than £10,000 where the claim for damages for personal injuries is not more than £1,000; and
- any claim which includes a claim by a tenant of residential premises against his landlord for repairs or other work to the premises where the estimated cost of repairs or other work is not more than £1,000 (and the financial value of the claim for damages in respect of those repairs is not more than £1,000) (CPR rule 27.1(2)).

The small claims track cannot be used for:

- a claim by a tenant of residential premises against his or her landlord in respect of harassment or unlawful eviction (CPR rule 26.7(4));

- claims which must be allocated to the multi track (e.g. defamation claims).

There is a special small claims procedure in the IPEC which caters for claims for infringement of copyright, trademark and unregistered design rights (see Chapter 5, para 5.14).

4.5   PRINCIPLES OF ALLOCATION – THE COURT IS IN CHARGE

When deciding the track for a claim, the matters to which the court shall have regard include:

(1)   the financial value of the claim, if any;
(2)   the nature of the remedy sought;
(3)   the likely complexity of the facts, law or evidence;
(4)   the number of parties or likely parties;
(5)   the value of any counterclaim or other Part 20 claim and the complexity of any matters relating to it;
(6)   the amount of oral evidence which may be required;
(7)   the importance of the claim to persons who are not parties to the proceedings;
(8)   the views expressed by the parties; and
(9)   the circumstances of the parties.

It is for the court to assess the financial value of a claim, and in doing so it will disregard:

(1)   any amount not in dispute;
(2)   any claim for interest;
(3)   costs; and
(4)   any contributory negligence.

See rule 26.8(1) and (2).

As well as the list of points in CPR Part 26 as quoted above, the district judge will have the overriding objective firmly in mind (see Appendix 6 and Chapter 5, para 5.2), including the need to achieve justice by dealing with the case in a manner which is proportionate (rule 1.1(1)(c)). The experience of the district judge will be that most types of case can be sensibly managed by small claims directions, even those which the parties may find complex or difficult. It is the essence of the small claims procedure that a case can be kept in proportion by stripping the pre-hearing procedure to its bare essentials.

The district judge will also recall that the Court of Appeal, in the past, when considering whether a case was suitable for the old-style arbitration procedure under CCR Order 19, took a robust view of the matter. It decided that even cases involving accidents at work[1] or disrepair to houses[2] were not to be excluded from the small claims process.

4.6   A VALUE IN DISPUTE NOT EXCEEDING £10,000

The money in dispute is the factor primarily taken into account in deciding whether the case qualifies for the small claims track (CPR rule 26.8(1)).

The district judge looks at the amount which the claimant states as the claim, but he or she may put a different valuation on the claim and this is determinative for allocation purposes. In making the allocation decision, the claim and counterclaim are not added together, and the fact that the counterclaim may be in excess of £10,000 does not automatically disqualify the case from the small claims track.[3]

It is the *disputed* amount which is considered for allocation purposes. So, if a claim starts out at, say £12,000 and the defendant pays £8,000 after the issue of proceedings and before allocation, the case will qualify for the small claims track (PD 26, para 7.4) (see also Chapter 9, para 9.8).

4.6.1   Housing claims

Cases for harassment or unlawful eviction will not be allocated to the small claims track (rules 26.7(4) and 27.1(2)).

Cases of housing disrepair where either the cost of the repair or the damages for non-repair are expected to be £1,000 or less each do not qualify for the small claims track (CPR rule 27.1(2)). The expected cost of repair and damages each have a separate £1,000 limit making the total up to £2,000.

---

[1]   *Afzal and Others v Ford Motor Co Ltd* [1994] 4 All ER 720.

[2]   *Joyce v Liverpool City Council* [1996] QB 252.

[3]   *Berridge (Paul) (t/a EAB builders) v RM Bayliss*, Lawtel, 23 November 1999.

If the tenant claims only for the cost of repairs which have already been carried out, then the case will qualify for the small claims track, if the amount claimed is not more than £10,000.

4.6.2 Personal injury claims

The small claims procedure can be used for personal injury cases, including claims arising from accidents at work. However, if the personal injury aspect of the claim is above £1,000 the case will not qualify for the small claims procedure (CPR rule 26.6(1)(a)(ii)).

Some claims mix personal injury and non-personal injury aspects. If either the personal injury aspect exceeds £1,000 in value, or the combined injury and non-personal injury aspect exceeds £10,000, the case will not qualify for the small claims track. 'Damages for personal injuries' means sums claimed as compensation for pain, suffering and loss of amenity (CPR rule 26.6(2)). Medical expenses, loss of earnings and damage to clothing do not count as personal injury elements of a claim when calculating whether the case qualifies for the small claims track.

In reality, few cases involving a claim for personal injury will qualify for the small claims track – only the most superficial of personal injuries are likely to merit an award of £1,000 or less.

It is the assessment of value put on the case by the district judge which matters, and not assessment made by the claimant (CPR rule 26.8(2)). The district judge will assess the potential value of the claim on the basis of the injuries as described in the claim or supporting medical report and will disregard the claimant's own estimate if necessary.

4.6.3 Claims involving disputed allegations of dishonesty

If there is a disputed allegation of dishonesty this will usually make the case unsuitable for the small claims track (PD 26, para 8.1(1)(d)). For example in the case of *Geoffrey Arnold Wheen v Smithmann and another*,[4] the Court of Appeal confirmed that a case involving allegations of fraud against estate agents was plainly not suitable for a small claims hearing. It should be borne in mind that the district judge will decide if the allegation of dishonesty is sufficiently serious to merit the case not being allocated to the small claims track. If a party uses the words 'fraud' or 'dishonest' this will be assessed by the district judge who will decide if the allegation is substantial or a mere insult.

---

[4]   *Geoffrey Arnold Wheen v Smithmann and another*, Lawtel, 25 September 2000.

4.6.4   Injunctions

The small claims procedure is not restricted to money claims and the district judge may, at a small claims hearing, award an injunction or similar relief,[5] for example ordering:

- a shop to supply replacement goods;
- a neighbour to replace a fence or boundary;
- disclosure of information under the Data Protection Act 1998;
- a bank not to close a customer account.

4.6.5   Claims of no financial value

The court will allocate a claim which has no financial value to the track which is most suitable to the case having regard to the factors mentioned in CPR rule 26.8(1) (see para 4.5). The small claims track might well be the best track for such a case – and if the parties themselves tell the court that they want a small claims hearing, this will certainly be taken into account.

4.6.6   Views of the parties

The court will consider what the parties have to say, but this is only one of the factors. The district judge will, in accordance with the overriding case management responsibilities of the court, ultimately make the decision on allocation.

Even if the normal track is not the small claims track, the parties can, by agreement, elect to use the small claims track (see para 4.16).

4.6.7   Claims which do not qualify on financial grounds

The court can allocate the case to the small claims track where the claim is greater than the small claims limit, with or without the agreement of the parties. Judges might adopt this technique to place parties on more equal footing where one of them cannot afford legal representation and no public funding is available.

Voluntary referral to the small claims track is discussed in para 4.16.

---

5   See *Joyce v Liverpool City Council* [1996] QB 252.

4.6.8 Small claims in the Intellectual Property Enterprise Court

Where a claim is for an infringement of copyright, trademark or passing off, the proceedings must be issued in the IPEC, which will decide if the case qualifies for the small claims procedure in that court. The financial ceiling is £10,000 (see Chapter 5, para 5.14).

4.7 THE DIRECTIONS QUESTIONNAIRE

> **Basics**
>
> - Once a defence has been filed at court, a court officer makes a provisional decision as to allocation to track and sends out a notice to this effect to the parties together with a directions questionnaire
> - Each side must complete the directions questionnaire within 14 days of receipt
> - The claim, or counterclaim, can be struck out if the directions questionnaire is not returned
> - The district judge reads the directions questionnaires submitted by all parties to make case management decisions about a case, including deciding to which track the case is to be allocated

The directions questionnaire is sent out to both sides by the court when the defence is received. The form is sent out with another form (N149A) which includes basic information on the date to return the questionnaire and the court it must be sent to.

Form N180 is sent to the parties in cases where it appears to the court staff that the case qualifies to be allocated to the small claims track. Both forms are available on the Courts Service website.[6]

The case can still be allocated to the small claims track even if the proposed allocation is not to the small claims track and the parties received the directions questionnaire tailored for cases destined for the fast track or multi track – all the parties need to do is to complete and return the form indicating why the case should be allocated to the small claims track.

In exceptional cases the court may deal with allocation without first asking the parties to complete a directions questionnaire.

---

6   www.justice.gov.uk/forms/hmcts.

4.7.1   Court fee

The court does not now require a fee from the parties at the allocation stage.

4.7.2   Time limit for returning the directions questionnaire

The directions questionnaire must be returned to the court by the date specified in the accompanying notice which will allow at least 14 days after receipt if the claim has been provisionally allocated to the small claims track (CPR rule 26.3(6)).

> What happens if the directions questionnaire is not returned? The answer is set out at para 4.9

4.7.3   Co-operate

The rules require the parties to co-operate when filling out the form: in fact, the rules require completed directions questionnaires to be sent to the other side as well as the court. In any event, it is sensible for the parties to agree between themselves the court which should be used for any court hearing.

4.7.4   Which court?

The directions questionnaire is returned to the court specified in the notice.

4.8   STEP-BY-STEP GUIDE TO COMPLETING THE DIRECTIONS QUESTIONNAIRE

The directions questionnaire is set out in full at Appendix 9. There are several sections to complete:

- A – Settlement/Mediation;
- B – Your contact details;
- C – Track;
- D – About the hearing (hearing venue; expert evidence; witnesses; hearing);
- Signature.

4.8.1 A – Settlement/Mediation

The parties are introduced to the small claims mediation service in section A of the directions questionnaire. They are invited to use the service which is described as 'free' but in reality is provided at no charge above the court fees already paid by the claimant up to this point in the case. Most consumer-type claims are suitable for mediation but mediation is generally not used for road traffic cases and cases involving issues of law.

> Chapter 7 discusses the county court small claims mediation service
>
> Paragraph 7.3 considers which cases are suitable for this type of mediation and those which are not
>
> The factors which define if a case is suitable for mediation are:
>
> • category of case (most types of case are suitable for mediation)
> • the willingness of the parties to engage in mediation
> • selection by the district judge

The parties should have tried to settle before starting the case but, if there is still scope for discussion, there is one last chance to put the case on hold, or 'stay' the proceedings, particularly pending an attempt at mediation. If all parties request a stay the district judge will direct that the proceedings are stayed, typically for one month (CPR rule 26.4(2)) if the parties are negotiating a settlement themselves but usually for 6 weeks if the case is being referred to the small claims mediation service.

The district judge can allow the stay to continue for more than one month but there must be a good reason, and the stay will be for a defined period of time only (CPR rule 26.4(3)). If the parties stay the case for mediation to take place the court will probably require a report on the outcome.

The court must be told if the case settles during the period of 'stay'. At the end of the stay the district judge will review the file and give directions (CPR rule 26.4(5)).

4.8.2 B – Your contact details

This is self-explanatory.

4.8.3   C – Track

Paragraphs 4.4, 4.5 and 4.6 explain whether the case qualifies for the small claims track. If the case qualifies, the 'yes' box should be ticked.

4.8.4   D – About the hearing (hearing venue; expert evidence; witnesses; hearing)

Hearing venue

This is the opportunity for the parties to tell the district judge where they want the case to be heard. The parties should set out reasons for their choice. Parties should attempt to get the other side to agree the location of the hearing. Where the parties live at opposite ends of the country, it may be rational to agree to the case being tried at a court at a halfway point.

The claimant must specify a preferred local hearing centre on Form N1, to which the case should be transferred at the appropriate time.

Defended claims are transferred to a local hearing centre after the parties have returned their directions questionnaires (see para 4.7):

(a)   where the defendant is an individual, in a claim for a specific amount of money, there will be transfer to the defendant's home court – unless the defendant has specified a different court in the directions questionnaire;

(b)   in all other circumstances, the claim will be transferred to the claimant's preferred court – again, unless the claimant has specified a different court in the directions questionnaire.

Expert evidence

Completing this section is self-explanatory. The appointment and use of experts in small claim cases is explained at Chapter 8, para 8.8. Please note that expert evidence is not allowed unless the court gives permission in advance.

Witnesses

A witness is anyone (apart from an expert) who knows about the case and will give evidence to the court. To distinguish ordinary witnesses from experts, lawyers call them 'witnesses as to fact'. The main witness as to fact is usually the claimant/defendant himself or herself. Therefore, if the claimant is filling out the form and he or she is the only person who will be giving evidence, the number of witnesses is 'one'.

Hearing

Completing this section is also self-explanatory. It is important that the parties state any dates upon which any essential witness is unable to attend the final hearing. Although the court may list the case on 21 days' notice, it is far more likely that the hearing date will be several weeks in the future. Since the hearing date is likely to be up to 4 months hence, it is suggested that important dates to avoid for several months in advance are mentioned in the listing questionnaire.

4.8.5 Signature

The directions questionnaire is usually signed by the litigant or his or her legal representative but it can be signed by a litigation friend. A lay representative cannot sign this form.

4.9 CONSEQUENCES OF FAILURE TO RETURN OR COMPLETE THE DIRECTIONS QUESTIONNAIRE

If a party fails to file a directions questionnaire the court will send out a warning notice requiring compliance within 7 days. If the defaulting party fails to comply, his or her statement of case is then struck out automatically. That would be the end of the case for a defaulting claimant. If a defence is struck out, the claimant would be able to ask the court to enter judgment, at which point the case will be transferred to the preferred court (see CPR rules 26.3(7A) and 12.5A).

It is important to note that if the case is lost by default before it is allocated to the small claims track, the protection of the no costs rule does not apply and the defaulter is liable to pay the other party's costs (CPR rule 44.9). If costs are awarded and the case is later reinstated the award of costs will not automatically be set aside (rules 26.3(10) and 3.7(4)).

4.10 WHAT HAPPENS WHEN THE COURT RECEIVES THE DIRECTIONS QUESTIONNAIRES?

Assuming both directions questionnaires have been safely received, the case is transferred out to a local hearing centre:

- where the claim is for a specified sum of money against a defendant who is an individual, the transfer will be to the defendant's home court, unless the defendant has nominated another court in his or her directions questionnaire;

- in any other case, to the preferred court, unless the claimant has nominated another court in his or her directions questionnaire.

See CPR rule 26.2A.

Once the case has been transferred, the file will be given to the district judge to review.

At this point, the district judge will have the following information on the file:

- the claim, defence and counterclaim (if any);
- any correspondence from the parties;
- the completed directions questionnaires (and any documents sent in with the directions questionnaires).

The district judge will then allocate the case there and then, or fix an allocation hearing.

Upon allocation, the district judge will either stay the case for mediation or settlement discussions or will give directions to move the case through to the final hearing.

> Chapter 8 considers the directions which may be given to manage the case through to a final hearing before a district judge

4.11   FINAL DISPOSAL OF THE CASE CAN BE WITHOUT A HEARING

The district judge can decide a disputed case as a paperwork exercise without the attendance of the parties *but only if both parties agree* (CPR rule 27.10). This is a method of disposal which has not often been used in the past. Parties wishing to use this procedure can write to the court or indicate their agreement in the directions questionnaire.

4.12   ORDERS OF THE COURT'S OWN INITIATIVE

The district judge may use the powers under the rules to strike out a claim or defence which is plainly hopeless, or an abuse of the process of the court. Where cases are allocated to the small claims track, CPR Part 18 (further information) does not apply (see Chapter 5, para 5.12). However, the district judge may of his or her own initiative require a party to clarify its case and this can be done at the allocation stage. If a party wishes the court to make such an order at the allocation stage then this should be asked for in the directions questionnaire.

> See also Chapter 5, para 5.3

4.13 ALLOCATION HEARING

In practice, in small claims cases allocation hearings are rare. The rules make it plain that every case must be dealt with 'proportionately' and where relatively small sums of money are at stake an allocation hearing will not often be justified. In a small claims case, possible reasons for an allocation hearing could be:

- where there is confusion as to the amount in dispute (especially if it is possible that the case may not qualify for the small claims track on financial grounds); or
- where there is an issue of dishonesty which might make the case unsuitable for the small claims track.

Both sides will be given at least 7 days' notice of the allocation hearing (PD 26, para 6.2).

PD 26 sets out the general principles for allocation hearings and the orders which can be made. The allocation hearing is not a formality and must be attended by the parties themselves or, if represented, by someone who has authority to take decisions about the case.

Note the warning on the foot of the notice in Form N153 (notice of allocation hearing) which states, 'if you fail to attend the hearing, the court may order you to pay the costs of the other party, or parties, that do attend. Failure to pay those costs within the time limit stated may lead to your statement of case being struck out'.

4.14 CAN THE COURT DISPENSE WITH DIRECTIONS QUESTIONNAIRES?

Yes, but this is not done often. The decision to dispense with directions questionnaires is taken on a case-by-case basis and only if the district judge is sure that the case can be safely timetabled to a final hearing without the completion of the questionnaire.

4.15   CAN THE ALLOCATED TRACK BE CHANGED OR CHALLENGED?

If either party is not happy with the allocation decision, they can apply for reallocation (PD 26, para 11.1(1)). However, if the allocation decision was made at a hearing at which the disgruntled party was present, he or she cannot simply apply to the district judge for reallocation (unless there has been a significant change in circumstances) – the decision can only be reviewed on appeal (see Chapter 11).

If there has been a change of circumstances since allocation, the parties should notify the court so that the district judge can reallocate (PD 26, para 11.2). For example, this should happen if the case was allocated to the fast track and the amount in dispute was later reduced below the small claims limit by the defendant admitting or paying part of the sum claimed.

4.16   CAN THE PARTIES ELECT FOR THE CASE TO BE ALLOCATED TO THE SMALL CLAIMS TRACK EVEN IF THE CASE DOES NOT QUALIFY ON FINANCIAL GROUNDS?

The answer to this question is 'yes'. This is sometimes termed 'voluntary referral'.

This option will be particularly attractive to litigants in person who have a fairly straightforward case that they wish to be heard promptly and with the minimum of fuss. If the case is allocated to the small claims track, the parties will pay reduced court fees and will not have to complete a pre-trial checklist.

However, allocation to track remains a decision for the court, which is not bound by any agreement of the parties on this point. The judge will not normally allocate to the small claims track if it seems that the case is likely to take more than one day to be heard (PD 26, paras 7.5 and 8.1(2)).

Benefits of voluntary referral to the small claims track

- simplified steps to the final hearing
- relatively informal procedure at the final hearing
- the no costs rule applies
- no pre-trial checklist
- depending on the court, probably an earlier hearing date

4.17 HEARINGS IN WELSH

The court service in Wales has adopted the principle that the English and Welsh languages must be treated equally; this is in line with Welsh Language Act 1993, section 22(1). Those familiar with conducting court proceedings in Wales will know that many of the court forms, including the directions questionnaire, are bilingual. All court hearings, including small claims hearings, may be conducted in Welsh if this is the choice of the parties and certain district judges are able to conduct the hearings in Welsh. Arrangements for coordinating the Welsh speaking parties with a suitable district judge are made by the county court. Welsh speakers are entitled to an interpreter at any hearing if this is needed for them to follow the proceedings.

4.18 ALLOCATION – WHAT NEXT?

If the case has been referred to mediation, then the steps described in Chapter 7 will follow.

If directions have been given to take the case to a hearing before a judge, then the parties will need to prepare for the final hearing. This is covered in Chapter 8.

Chapter 5

Other Parts of the Civil Procedure Rules

5.1 INTRODUCTION

The small claims procedure is set out in CPR Part 27, but that part does not exist in isolation from the other parts of the rules. Some rules which would clash with the objectives of small claims case management are excluded. Of the other rules, some are of particular significance to small claims cases.

This book contains detailed references to various parts of the rules where appropriate. This chapter explains other rules which are most often encountered in the course of a small claims case. They are discussed here with reference to the way they are applied in small claims cases. This chapter also considers those rules that are specifically excluded in small claims cases.

5.2 OVERRIDING OBJECTIVE

> CPR Part 1 defines the overriding objective and the court's duty to manage cases. Part 1 is reproduced at Appendix 6

The CPR are a procedural code with the overriding objective of enabling the court to deal with cases 'justly and at proportionate cost' (rule 1.1).

CPR Part 1 defines and expands on what this means and how the procedural rules achieve it.

Practicality is a central part of case management. Underpinning every aspect of the rules is the emphasis on keeping things in proportion, and so making sure that the cost of litigation is in proportion to the matters in dispute. This is achieved by effective case management, for example requiring the parties to set out their case in writing and restricting the hearing to relevant issues, including the limiting of cross examination. However, the disproportionate use of the court's resources is not of itself a basis for a claim to be struck out, rather, the court will use its case management powers to control the expenditure of time and money by the parties.

The small claims track itself is a proportionate way of dealing with disputes of limited financial value. The fact that there may be a larger claim in the background does not prevent parties from using the small claims track.[1]

The procedures in the rules must be applied by the court 'expeditiously and fairly' (CPR rule 1.1(2)(d)), and the parties are required to assist the court to further the overriding objective (rule 1.3).

CPR rule 1.4 spells out examples of ways in which the court can achieve the overriding objective by use of its case management powers.

5.3   THE COURT'S CASE MANAGEMENT POWERS

CPR Part 3 gives the district judge the powers to promote the overriding objective and manage cases effectively.

The court may:

(a)   extend or shorten the time for compliance with any rule, practice direction or court order (even if an application for extension is made after the time for compliance has expired);

(b)   adjourn or bring forward a hearing;

(c)   require a party or a party's legal representative to attend the court;

(d)   hold a hearing and receive evidence by telephone or by using any other method of direct oral communication;

(e)   direct that part of any proceedings (such as a counterclaim) be dealt with as separate proceedings;

(f)   stay the whole or part of any proceedings or judgment either generally or until a specified date or event;

(g)   consolidate proceedings;

(h)   try two or more claims on the same occasion;

(i)   direct a separate trial of any issue;

(j)   decide the order in which issues are to be tried;

---

[1]   For example *Madden v Pattni CC* [1999] CLY 540.

(k) exclude an issue from consideration;
(l) dismiss or give judgment on a claim after a decision on a preliminary issue;
(m) take any other step or make any other order for the purpose of managing the case and furthering the overriding objective (CPR rule 3.1(2)).

5.3.1 When can the district judge exercise these case management powers?

The district judge can intervene and make directions about a small claims case at a number of stages including:

- if the papers are referred to the district judge for comment by the court staff soon after issue (CPR rule 3.2);
- when the district judge reviews the claim and defence at the allocation stage (CPR rule 26);
- at a preliminary hearing (CPR rule 27.6);
- if any party writes to the court at any stage to bring any matter of procedure to the attention of the district judge;
- at any application hearing;
- at the trial itself.

5.3.2 Striking out

Claims and defences alike are liable to be struck out if they are plainly hopeless or mischievous. Such cases can be struck out at an early stage (CPR rule 3.4 and PD 3A).

A case may be struck out as a whole or in part.

The district judge will ensure that the management of the case is in proportion to the amount in dispute – if the case is plainly hopeless, then to strike it out will save the parties the inconvenience of the hearing.

PD 3A sets out some suggestions for claims that might fall into this category, namely:

- a case setting out no facts, for example 'money owed £5,000';
- a claim or defence which is incoherent and makes no sense;
- a claim or defence which sets out facts which, even if true, do not amount to a legally recognisable case against the defendant;
- a defence which is a bare denial.

A poorly drafted claim or defence will attract the attention of the district judge and may prompt the case to be struck out. To avoid this, litigants must ensure the claim is properly drafted from the outset; the guidance in this book in Chapter 6 will help.

If a case is struck out, it may be reinstated (see para 5.3.5).

5.3.3   Civil restraint orders

A district judge may make a limited civil restraint order, the effect of which is to prevent a party from making any further applications in the proceedings (PD 3C, para 2.2).

An extended civil restraint order has the effect of severely restricting the right of a party from starting new claims. These orders are relatively rare and can only be made by a designated civil judge or a judge of more seniority.

CPR rules 3.4.6 and 3.11 and PD 3C set out the rules concerning civil restraint orders.

5.3.4   Other sanctions

As well as striking out, the district judge will consider other options for case management and will apply sanctions that are relevant to the case management problem in hand. For example, any directions will be proportionate to the case but may involve:

- making an order for costs (see also para 5.3.5);
- if documents are not sent to the other side before the hearing and take the other side by surprise, then the district judge may prevent them from being used in evidence;
- if either party is unprepared at a hearing and as a result requests an adjournment, then the sanction may be that they pay the costs thrown away by the adjournment;
- delay in bringing or pursuing a case may result in the party being deprived of interest;
- requiring a party to clarify details of their case.

5.3.5   Relief from sanctions

A party who does not comply with a case management order – for example by the late filing of evidence – may discover that their case has been struck out or they have been penalised by being ordered to pay costs. This section considers what can be done to reinstate the case and obtain relief from sanctions. The rules are tough, and litigants who do not comply with court orders because they are busy or overlook deadlines by mistake should not assume that the court will grant relief.

CPR rule 3.9 deals with relief from sanctions, which must be read in conjunction with rule 1.1 (the overriding objective).

The matter is approached in steps, which can be simplified as a sequence of questions, as follows.

Question 1

Was the sanction imposed an order for costs against the defaulting party?

- If 'yes' then the *only* way of challenging that sanction is by an appeal (CPR rule 3.8(2)).

- If 'no', then continue to Question 2 (the rest of this paragraph assumes that the sanction applied was to strike out the party's case).

Question 2

Was the sanction properly imposed?

- If 'yes', proceed to Question 3.

  - *Possibility 1*: that the order was *imposed by mistake* – for example before a deadline expired or maybe the court made a mistake and 'lost' a document sent by post. If this is the position, then the party who has had his or her case struck out 'by mistake' should urgently bring this mistake to the court and request the mistake to be rectified. If this does not work, then an application can be made for the district judge to review the decision to strike out. Chapter 11, para 11.4 contains guidance on applications to set aside.

  - *Possibility 2*: that the order was *wrongly imposed* by the district judge, in which case the route is that of appeal (see Chapter 11, para 11.2.5 (appeals against case management decisions)).

Question 3

Should relief against sanction be granted taking into account the guidance in the rules?

There has been recent consideration of the circumstances where the court should grant relief against sanctions in the Court of Appeal in *Mitchell v News Group Newspapers Limited* [2] and *Denton v TH White Limited*.[3] In *Denton*, the court refined the guidance in *Mitchell* and other cases into a three-stage test:

- *Stage 1*: How serious or significant is the failure to comply with the rule or court order?
  If it is neither serious nor significant, relief is likely to be granted. If it is serious and/or significant, the court will proceed to the next stage.
  In deciding upon the level of seriousness/significance, the court will look particularly at the impact of the failure upon the progress of the case and of the other cases with which the court has to deal.

- *Stage 2*: Why did the failure occur? Is there a good reason?
  What is a 'good reason' will depend on the facts and circumstances of each case. The application must be supported by evidence, which means not only a written explanation but also documentary evidence if that evidence is likely to exist. Some reason or excuse outside the control of the party in default is likely to count as a 'good explanation'.
  Therefore, a sudden illness would be a good explanation, but the court may want to see a doctor's note to confirm this. A problem with a computer may not be a good explanation unless the party can show that for some reason he or she could not get access to another computer (e.g. at a public library or internet café).
  Merely overlooking a deadline is unlikely to be found to be a good reason.
  Where there is a good reason for a serious or significant breach, relief is likely to be granted.

- *Stage 3*: If the failure is serious/significant and there is no good reason for it, the court will consider all the circumstances of the case, with particular emphasis on the factors listed at CPR rule 3.9(1), i.e. the need:

  - for litigation to be conducted efficiently and at proportionate cost; and
  - to enforce compliance with rules, practice directions and orders.

---

[2] *Mitchell v News Group Newspapers Limited* [2013] EWCA Civ 1537. By way of interest, and not relevant to the legal analysis, this was part of the so-called 'Plebgate' case.

[3] *Denton & Ors v TH White Ltd & Ors* [2014] EWCA Civ 906.

At this stage, the court will consider if the party concerned has failed to comply with a deadline or other requirement in the past and will be less sympathetic on a second default. The attitude of the other side will also be taken into account, including if the default has caused them inconvenience, distress or prejudice. It is also relevant at this stage to consider whether the defaulting party has made the application for relief from sanctions promptly.

Professional users of this book who make a mistake and overlook a deadline must review CPR rule 3.9 in detail and consider the case law with care, as they may end up being faced with a claim for professional negligence by their own client.

Equally, legal professionals in particular should consider very carefully[4] whether or not to object to relief from sanctions being granted to the other party. An unreasonable objection to relief being granted could amount to unreasonable conduct and the imposition of costs penalties, even in a small claim.

In any case where it should be obvious that relief from sanctions is appropriate, the parties should agree it without the need for a contested application.[5]

5.3.6 Case management orders made on the court's own initiative

At any stage in the case the district judge can make an order of his or her own initiative without notifying the parties in advance. If such an order is made, it must be accompanied by a statement notifying any party affected by the order that they can have the order varied or set aside. The order will specify when the application to vary or set aside must be made. Generally, the period specified is 7 days, but can be a different period (CPR rule 3.3).

5.4 APPLICATIONS GENERALLY

Basics

Applications should:

- be made in writing, and
- give the opposite party 3 days' notice of the hearing

---

[4] Having read *Denton & Ors v TH White Ltd & Ors* [2014] EWCA Civ 906 [40]–[43].

[5] Parties may agree extensions of time for compliance with the rules or court orders of up to 28 days, provided this does not put at risk any hearing date (CPR rule 3.8(4)).

5.4.1   Overview

There should be little need for applications in a small claims case. The objective is for all the issues to be dealt with at a full hearing (the trial) with the minimum of applications. There are, however, a number of situations where applications need to be made in small claims cases. For example, an application to transfer a case to another court, or an application for an alternative method of service. A formal application is also needed if a defendant wishes to add another party to the proceedings or if the defendant wishes to add a counterclaim after the defence has already been filed.

CPR Part 23 sets out the general provisions for making applications. The party making the application is called the 'applicant' and the party against whom the order is sought is the 'respondent' (rule 23.1). PD 23A emphasises the need to make any application promptly (PD 23A, para 2.7). In a small claims case this is especially important, because if there is delay the application is unlikely to be listed until close to the date of the hearing which may defeat the objective of the application.

The court form for making an application is N244.[6] The use of this form is not obligatory (see PD 23A, para 2.1) but is recommended. If the form is filled out fully, the application will be in good order. The court may accept the written application in any format, including a letter, but note the information which the application notice must include (see below).

The application notice must be sent to the other side at least 3 clear days before the hearing of the application (CPR rule 23.7(1)(b)) (see para 5.11 for rules about calculating time limits).

The application notice must set out what the applicant is seeking, plus brief reasons for making the application. If the application notice includes evidence or reasons, then a statement of truth must be signed (see para 5.5). Any evidence in support of the application and any draft of the order sought must be served at the same time as the application notice (CPR rule 23.7).

A fee will be payable to the court when issuing an application. The amount will depend on whether or not it is by consent. (For the fees payable, see Appendix 2.)

---

[6]   Available on the Courts Service website, at www.justice.gov.uk/forms/hmcts.

The district judge has a wide discretion in dealing with applications. In some circumstances:

- an application can be made orally, without a written application notice (CPR rule 23.3(2));
- applications can be made without giving notice to the other side (see below);
- the district judge may make the order without a hearing (see below);
- applications can be dealt with by consent;
- the district judge can reduce (or abridge) the notice time to less than 3 days.

5.4.2 Consent applications

If the parties agree what order the court should make (a consent order), their draft order will be given to the district judge for approval but as the final decision to grant the order will be made by the district judge, the parties must tell the district judge the reason for applying for the order by consent (PD 23A, para 10). An application made by consent attracts a lower court fee (see Appendix 2).

5.4.3 Costs on applications in small claims cases

The no costs rule does not apply to hearings that take place before allocation, but any award for costs will be proportionate to the case. However, it does apply to hearings that take place after allocation (see Chapter 9, para 9.9).

5.4.4 Hearing an application by telephone

What follows is a practical guide to telephone hearings in small claims cases presupposing there is only one claimant and one defendant. Rules about telephone hearings are set out in CPR Part 23 and PD 23A:

- the court will inform the parties if the hearing is to be by telephone;
- unrepresented parties are not expected to make arrangements for the telephone hearing – these must be made by the party who has legal representation;
- if both parties have legal representation, the applicant must make the arrangements for the hearing;
- the hearing takes place as a three-way conference call involving both parties and the district judge. The telecom provider must be on a list of

approved service providers which are identified on the Courts Service website;[7]

- the hearing is recorded by the telecom company;
- the district judge will have the court file and must be sent any other documents, including draft orders, in good time for the hearing: the deadline is 4.00 p.m. on the last working day before the hearing. Documents can be sent to the court by fax or email. All documents must clearly indicate the time and date of the hearing and be marked 'for urgent attention';
- if a party objects to a hearing being conducted by telephone, they must apply for a personal hearing. Such an application must be made at least 7 days before the telephone hearing and the usual application fee will apply;
- the court will aim for the hearing to take place at exactly the time notified on the hearing notice;
- if both parties are in person and not legally represented, the hearing will not take place by telephone (PD 3C, para 2.2).

5.4.5   Applications without notice

In small claims cases, applications made without notice to the other side are rare, so they will not be discussed in detail here. An application without notice can be made if there is 'exceptional urgency' or where the overriding objective would be furthered by such an application (for more detail, see PD 23A, para 3).

A party who has not been told about an application can apply to have any order made at that application varied or set aside, but the application must be made within 7 days (CPR rule 23.10).

5.4.6   Orders without a hearing

The applicant can ask the district judge to make any order without a hearing (CPR rule 23.8(c)).

It is usual for orders by consent to be made without a hearing including orders which confirm the withdrawal or settlement of a case. Where an order is sought to record the terms of a settlement, the district judge will approve the order only if it makes sense.

---

[7]   www.justice.gov.uk/courts/telephone-hearings.

5.4.7 Applications to adjourn

It would be unusual for the district judge to approve a request for a change of hearing date (adjournment) at the request of one party and without the consent of the other side and these applications should usually be made on notice.

The best approach when one side wants an adjournment is to contact the other side direct to ask them to agree to the hearing date being changed. If they agree then the party asking for the adjournment should write to the court including the written consent of the other side to the adjournment. The district judge will then make the final decision as to whether to re-list the case, as the parties request.

5.5 STATEMENT OF TRUTH

5.5.1 Wording of the statement of truth

The wording is varied to accommodate who is signing the statement and the nature of the document and is expressed, with possible variations, as follows:

> [*I believe*][*the claimant/defendant believes*] that the facts stated in this [*claim*][*defence*][*application*] [*witness statement*] are true.

If using a court form, the alternatives are simply deleted but the statement should be amended if a form is not being used. For example:

> I believe that the facts stated in this witness statement are true.

The claim form must be supported by a statement of truth (see Chapter 2, para 2.3.12).

A claim, a defence and a witness statement must all be verified by a statement of truth (CPR rule 22.1). Any application which is supported by evidence written on the application form must also be supported by a statement of truth (rule 22.1(3)). Failure to verify a witness statement may result in the statement not being admissible in evidence (rule 22.3). However, a district judge in a small claims case has a wide discretion about the conduct of a hearing and the strict rules of evidence do not apply (rule 27.8(3)). If there is no statement of truth, the defaulter can usually expect to be allowed to rectify this on the day of the hearing.

Failure to verify a statement of case means that it remains effective until it is struck out, but a party may not rely on the contents of a statement of case in evidence until it has been verified by a statement of truth (CPR rule 22.2 and PD 22).

The statement must be signed by the party personally, or by the party's legal representative (not a lay representative) (PD 22, para 3.1).

Proceedings for contempt of court may be brought against anyone who makes a false statement without an honest belief in its truth in a document verified by a statement of truth (CPR rule 32.14).

5.6   RULES ABOUT SERVICE OF THE CLAIM FORM AND OTHER DOCUMENTS

Basics

- The court will send the claim form by first class post to the address for the defendant which the claimant sets out on the claim form
- The claimant can elect to serve the proceedings instead of the court
- The claim form expires if it is not served within 4 months of issue

---

CPR Part 6 sets out the provisions relevant to the service of the claim form and other documents relevant to a case. What follows is a practical approach to the subject, designed to equip the reader with enough information to cover situations that commonly arise in small claims cases.

The court will serve the claim form and any other documents by first class post (e.g. applications and notices) unless the party on whose behalf the document is to be served notifies the court that he or she wishes to serve it himself or herself (CPR rule 6.4), or the court orders otherwise.

If the claimant chooses to serve the claim form, they must file a certificate of service within 21 days, unless the defendant has already acknowledged the claim; the court provides forms but CPR rule 6.17 sets out what must be set out in a certificate of service.

5.6.1   Address for service of the claim form

This topic is discussed in detail in Chapter 2. For the address to be used on the claim form for the claimant, see Chapter 2, para 2.3.3. For consideration of the address to be used on the claim form for the defendant, see Chapter 2, para 2.3.7.

5.6.2   Deemed day of service and rules about dispatch

Introductory definitions

- 'Deemed day of service' means the day upon which the court treats a claim or other court document as being received, whether or not it was actually received on that day, or not received at all
- 'Relevant step' means what the claimant does to serve the claim form

Importance of relevant steps and the limitation period

A claimant is barred from bringing a claim where the statute of limitations has expired. In the case of personal injury claims, this is 3 days after the event which caused the injury. In most other cases, it is 6 years after the breach upon which the claim is based. A full discussion of limitation periods is outside the scope of this book. Sometimes, claimants start their claim at the very last moment, which causes cases to be on the borderline of whether they have been started within the important limitation period. These borderline cases have been a source of much anxious litigation in the past. A clear set of rules now exists to deal with these complicated issues. The claim is said to have been started within the limitation period if the claimant has taken the relevant step and that step is defined by the date of dispatch.

The most common method of service is sending by first class post and the step required to take the relevant step is to put it in the post. The document exchange can be used, provided it allows for delivery on the next business day. Personal service takes place when it is left with the individual. CPR rule 7.5.1 deals with all the permissible methods of service of the claim form, including by email and fax. If a limitation period is about to expire, then the claimant should study rule 7.5 very carefully and to make sure that the relevant step is taken in good time.

Deemed day of service – definition

The definition of the 'deemed day of service' is different in the case of the claim form and other documents:

- *claim form*: the deemed day of service is 2 business days after dispatch by whatever means. Thus, if a defendant is handed a claim form on a

Saturday or Sunday when the following Monday is a bank holiday, the deemed day of service is the following Wednesday;
- *all other documents*: the deemed day of service of court documents other than the claim form is best explained by the table set out in CPR rule 6.26 (reproduced under 'Deemed day of service – rules' below).

Method of service	Step required
First class post, document exchange or other service which provides for delivery on the next business day	Posting, leaving with, delivering to or collection by the relevant service provider
Delivery of the document to or leaving it at the relevant place	Delivering to or leaving the document in the relevant place
Personal service under CPR rule 6.5	Completing the relevant step required by CPR rule 6.5
Fax	Completing the transmission of the fax
Other electronic method	Sending the email or other electronic transmission

Deemed day of service – rules

The rules about the deemed day of service for a claim form are slightly different from the rules about the service of other documents.

The deemed day of service of the claim form is 2 business days after dispatch by whatever means (CPR rule 6.14).

The deemed day of service of court documents other than the claim form is best explained by the table which is set out in CPR rule 6.26, and reproduced below:[8]

Method of service	Deemed day of service
1. First class post (or other service which provides for delivery on the next business day)	The second day after it was posted, left with, delivered to or collected by the relevant service provider provided that day is a business day; or, if not, the next business day after that day
2. Document exchange	The second day after it was left with, delivered to or collected by the relevant service provider provided that day is a business day; or if not, the next business day after that day

---

[8] Note that the table only applies to service of documents *other than* the claim form, and service of the claim form is deemed 2 business days after dispatch by whatever means.

Method of service	Deemed day of service
3. Delivering the document to or leaving it at the permitted address	It is delivered to or left at the permitted address on a business day before 4.30p.m., on that day; or in any other case, on the next business day after that day
4. Fax	If the transmission of the fax is completed on a business day before 4.30p.m., on that day; or in any other case, on the next business day after the day on which it was transmitted
5. Other electronic method	If the email or other electronic transmission is sent on a business day before 4.30p.m., on that day; or in any case, on the next business day after the day on which it was sent
6. Personal service	If the document is served personally before 4.30p.m. on a business day, on that day; or in any other case, on the next business day after that day

5.6.3 Service by an alternative method

If the defendant is an individual, then the claim form must be sent to a private address[9] unless the defendant has agreed in advance that it can be sent to his or her solicitor. Chapter 2, para 2.3.7S deals with what the claimant is expected to do to take *reasonable steps* to trace a defendant who has moved. If all this fails, then the court may permit service by an alternative method.

The application for service by an alternative method or to an alternative address will be made 'without notice' and must be supported by evidence – the most practical way is to set out on the application form where the defendant is thought to be and why it is thought that the alternative method of service will bring the claim form to his or her attention. An example could be that the personal address of the defendant is not known but the address of a relative or friend who is in touch with him or her will be known. The statement should give as much detail as possible about the problems with service and state why the claimant is sure that by sending the papers to a particular address the defendant will come to know about them. The district judge can be expected to take a robust and practical approach to such applications and may often direct that court papers sent to a defendant's work address are marked 'private and confidential'.

The district judge can order that service on an alternative address was good service, even in retrospect; but whether in advance or in retrospect, the court

---

[9] A private address does not include a place of work.

must be satisfied that there is 'good reason' to authorise service by an alternative method (CPR rule 6.15).

5.6.4   Delay in service of the claim form (the 4-month rule)

A claim form must be served within 4 months of issue otherwise it expires (CPR rule 7.5). To be precise, this means that the claimant must *dispatch* the claim form to the defendant within that period and this must be done 'before 12.00 midnight on the calendar day four months after the date of issue of the claim form'.

This is not a problem that should trouble those issuing claims destined for the small claims track because the best course is to serve the claim form at once (see Chapter 2, para 2.3.18) but if time is passing and the claim form has not been served there is a possible remedy; the district judge can extend the life of the claim form. Note that the application should be issued at the court office before the claim form expires, but the hearing of the application can be after the claim form has expired (see CPR rule 7.6).

The granting of the application to extend the life of the claim will not be a formality and if the application is made after the expiry of the 4-month period, the district judge will only grant the application if the claimant has taken all 'reasonable steps' to serve the claim form or if, for some reason, the court has failed to serve the claim form. In either case the claimant must act promptly. The application can be made without notice and must set out the evidence, or reasons, relied on (CPR rule 7.6(3) and (4)).

5.7   TRANSFERS OF CASES BETWEEN COURTS[10]

Basics

- When a defence is served, the case is transferred *automatically* to the defendant's 'home court' if the claim is for a specified amount of money *and* the defendant is an individual, or to the preferred court in all other cases *unless* a different court has been specified in the directions questionnaire
- The district judge has the final say as to where a case is heard

---

[10]   Strictly speaking, within the CPR, a case moved administratively or by operation of the Rules is 'sent'; whereas a case moved by a judge is 'transferred'. For the sake of clarity and brevity in this book, either kind of move is referred to as a 'transfer'.

5.7.1 Overview

The operation of the transfer rules are of particular importance in small claims cases. Although in most small claims cases there will be no award for costs, the winner can expect to be awarded reasonable travel expenses plus the cost of overnight accommodation. Such expenses may be significant, especially when measured against what may be a relatively small sum of money in dispute. A litigant may think twice about pursuing or defending a case if attending the hearing will involve a lot of travelling. If proceedings are moved from court to court, this may cause delay in the court process. When a case is moved between courts, there is always the chance that papers will get lost or mislaid.

5.7.2 Definitions

Every county court hearing centre has its own geographical district or area for this purpose. The Courts Service website[11] has a 'court finder' section with the facility to check which court applies to a particular postcode. The court staff of a particular court will also be able to tell you if any particular address is within the area of that court.

The defendant's home court means the 'county court for the district in which the defendant resides or carries on business'.

A claim for a specified sum includes any claim where the claimant puts a fixed value on the claim. This will mean all debt claims and any claim for damages where the claimant specifies the amount which is claimed in advance.

It is important to note that the rules about transfer to the defendant's home court only apply where the defendant is an individual, which excludes limited companies. If an individual is a trader, for example 'Mike Smith trading as Aroofer', the case will be transferred to Mr Smith's home court. However, if the defendant is named simply as 'Aroofer' or 'Aroofer (*a firm*)', that rule will not apply and the transfer will usually be to the claimant's preferred court.

5.7.3 Transfer after allocation

An application to transfer the case to another court after automatic transfer should be made to the receiving court. The district judge will consider whether the case (or a part of it) could more fairly or conveniently be heard in another

---

[11] www.justice.gov.uk/about/hmcts.

court, taking into account any need for security or the special needs of the parties or their witnesses.

The need to consider a specific order for transfer is most likely to arise where the parties live at opposite ends of the country. Neither will wish to travel hundreds of miles and possibly pay for an overnight stay where the sum in dispute is relatively small.

There is no perfect answer to this conundrum: one option is to direct that the trial take place at a court roughly halfway between the two parties. These orders can be unpopular with the judges in the 'halfway' courts because it involves them dealing with cases which have absolutely no local connection.

Another option is an order suggesting a determination of the dispute on paper – the parties send in their evidence and the decision is taken in their absence. For obvious reasons, this procedure is unpopular with many parties who feel that it will not allow them to explain their case to the judge fully or to respond to the other side's case.

5.8   SUMMARY JUDGMENT

5.8.1   Overview

CPR Part 24 contains the rules which govern applications for summary judgment, namely judgment on an application without a final hearing on the basis that the other side's case has no real prospect of success. The issuing of an application for summary judgment in a small claims case may delay the final hearing of a case and may result in unnecessary costs being incurred. Although available in small claims cases, it is a procedure more suited to more complex claims and those of higher financial value.

5.8.2   Summary judgment in detail

An application for summary judgment may offer a chance to get a judgment quicker than waiting for a small claims hearing, but consider the disadvantages before proceeding:

- once the application for summary judgment has been made, the case is delayed because the defendant will not be obliged to serve a defence (CPR rule 24.4(2));
- if the application fails, then the case will have to go to a full hearing, so the final determination will be delayed;

- costs can only be awarded if the case has not already been allocated to the small claims track when the application is heard and then only if the award for costs would be proportionate;
- the court fee for making the application is £155 – in addition to the fee payable on issue;
- whereas the procedural route to a small claims hearing is straightforward and the hearing itself relatively informal, an application for summary judgment under CPR Part 24 involves complying with strict procedural formalities.

When considering whether to make an application for summary judgment in a small claims case, the conclusion will usually be that it is better to get on with the case and have the matter determined at a final hearing.

CPR rule 24.2 states that the court may award summary judgment against a claimant or defendant if:

(a) it considers that—
  (i) the claimant has no real prospect of succeeding on the claim or issue; or
  (ii) the defendant has no real prospect of successfully defending the claim or issue; and
(b) there is no other compelling reason why the case or issue should be disposed of at a trial.

A claimant can make an application for summary judgment under this rule as soon as an acknowledgment has been filed. There is no need to wait for the defence. If the application is made before the defence, the defendant does not need to file a defence until the hearing of the application (CPR rule 24.4).

CPR Part 24 and PD 24 set out the procedural steps, and these must be followed:

- the application must state that it is made under Part 24;
- the application must state why the order is being sought;
- the application must identify concisely any point of law or any provision relied on;
- the application must state that it is made because the applicant believes that the other side has no real prospect of success; and
- the application must draw the recipient's attention to the timetable for the filing of evidence in response (see below).

In addition, the notice itself should draw the attention of the other side to the orders that the court can make on the application (see below).

The rule provides that the court will give the parties at least 14 days' notice of the hearing; that the person opposing the application should file evidence in response 7 days before the hearing; and that the party making the application should file any counter evidence 3 days before the hearing.

5.8.3   Orders that the court can make on an application for summary judgment

The court can:

- award judgment on the claim;
- strike out or dismiss the claim;
- dismiss the application;
- make a conditional order (e.g. the court can order that a defendant is only allowed to defend on condition that he or she pays a sum of money into court to abide the event);
- award costs in the case and in the application.

5.8.4   Costs on an application for summary judgment

The no cost rule applies if the hearing takes place after allocation to the small claims track. If the hearing takes place before allocation, note that the district judge has a general discretion on costs and will consider the conduct of the parties, including whether it was reasonable for a party to contest a particular issue (CPR rule 44.3(5)).

If costs are awarded, the costs will be assessed there and then on the day of the application and will normally be payable within 14 days.

5.9   THE SLIP RULE AND CORRECTING PROCEDURAL ERRORS

The correction of errors in judgments and orders is covered by CPR rule 40.12 and PD 40B. Rule 40.12 states that:

(1)   The court may at any time correct an accidental slip or omission in a judgment or order.

(2)   A party may apply for a correction without notice.

If there is an obvious typing mistake or accidental error in an order, then the court will deal with it informally and the matter should be raised initially by letter. If the mistake is somehow contentious or if the order is ambiguous or requires further explanation, then an application should be made for the matter to be dealt with on notice – ideally before the district judge who dealt with the original hearing.

In addition, the district judge may take any steps necessary to remedy any procedural error (CPR rule 3.10).

5.10 TIME FOR COMPLYING WITH A JUDGMENT OR ORDER

The general rule is that any order, including an order for costs, must be complied with within 14 days (CPR rule 40.11) unless:

- the district judge specifies a different time;
- the proceedings or judgment are stayed;
- it is a default judgment, which must be complied with immediately unless the judgment provides otherwise (rule 12.5(2));
- it is a judgment on an admission, which must be complied with immediately (rule 14.5(9)).

5.11 CALCULATING TIME LIMITS

The rules about calculating time periods are refreshingly clear (CPR Part 2). The court will, where possible, put dates and a time of day into the orders rather than leaving the parties to count the number of days for themselves (rule 2.9).

Where the time limit is stated in a number of days, this means 'clear days' (i.e. not the first day of the period or the day on which the defining event occurs).

Weekends and bank holidays plus Christmas Day and Good Friday are not counted if the time period specified is 5 days or less (rule 2.8(4)).

In the case of a claim form posted on a Thursday or Friday, therefore, the deemed date of service will be no sooner than the following Monday or Tuesday; it will be later if a bank holiday intervenes.

The following examples are taken from CPR rule 2.8:

> *Example 1*
> Notice of an application must be served at least 3 days before the hearing.
>> An application is to be heard on Friday 20 October.
>> The last date for service is Monday 16 October

Example 2
Particulars of claim must be served within 14 days of service of the claim form.
    The claim form is served on 2 October.
    The last day for service of the particulars of claim is 16 October.

See also the table in para 5.6.2 'Deemed day of service and rules about dispatch'.

5.12 RULES WHICH ARE EXCLUDED ON THE SMALL CLAIMS TRACK

Some parts of the CPR are specifically excluded from the small claims procedure (rule 27.2). If they were to apply they could promote unnecessary applications and procedures, and this would defeat the overall objectives of the small claims track.

Please refer to the table below. The notes in the right hand column correspond to the numbered paragraphs in the text that follows the table.

CPR	Details	Notes
Part 18	Further information (subject to the fact that the court may of its own initiative order a party to provide further information if it considers it appropriate to do so)	1
Part 31	Disclosure and inspection	2
Part 32	Evidence, except: – rule 32.1 (power of the court to control evidence)	3
Part 33	Miscellaneous rules about evidence	4
Part 35	Experts and assessors, except: – rule 35.1 (duty to restrict expert evidence) – rule 35.3 (experts – overriding duty to the court) – rule 35.7 (court's power to direct that evidence is to be given by single joint expert) – rule 35.8 (instructions to a single joint expert)	5
Part 25	Interim remedies, except where they relate to interim injunctions	6
Part 36	Offers to settle	7
Part 39	Hearings	8

Notes

1 – Further information

Requests for information following the formal procedures set out in CPR Part 18 have no place in the small claims track. The district judge can order the parties to clarify their case by ordering a party to provide further information if it is appropriate to do so (rule 27.2(3)). The determination of a case could hardly be fair if one party is taken by surprise by the other's case, or it is otherwise unclear. Chapter 6 gives examples of possible statements of case and defences in small claims cases and suggests cost-effective techniques of ensuring that the case is put fully to the other side before the hearing. In many cases, the parties will exchange witness statements before the hearing.

If these processes still leave the parties in the dark about how the other side puts their case, then what can be done? Probably the best course will be to write to the opposite party and ask for an explanation of what their case is about. If the matter is then not clarified, turn up at the hearing and – if the case presented by the opposite party is a true surprise – then apply for an adjournment and an order for costs on the basis of the other party's unreasonable behaviour (see Chapter 9, para 9.3.2).

2 – Disclosure and inspection

The essential matter to bear in mind with documents and the small claims track is 'proportionality'.

In the small claims track, 'documents' can mean any papers relating to a case including witness statements. The whole procedure of disclosing documents before a hearing is simplified to sending the other side copies – usually 14 days before the hearing. All the parties need do in a small claims case is to produce documents which they intend to rely on at the hearing. There are no lists of documents in small claims cases.

Therefore, a small claims case will not be burdened with the expense of the formal disclosure procedure. In the overwhelming majority of cases this works very well. Problems sometimes arise if one side has exclusive access to documents which the other side needs in order to win the case or if one side suppresses documents which damage their own case.

In this case, the party affected by such a problem has two possible remedies:

- anticipate the problem and point out the concern in the directions questionnaire – this should prompt the district judge to order the other side to include the problem documents in the papers to be disclosed before the hearing (Chapter 4, para 4.12 considers orders that the court can make of its own initiative); or

- if the problem does not emerge until 2 weeks before the hearing, write firmly to the other side and point out the omission – tell them that if the documents are not sent to you in good time for the hearing, then an adjournment may be necessary. If the documents are not produced then this may be good grounds to apply for an adjournment and an award of costs on the basis of that party's unreasonable behaviour (see Chapter 9, para 9.3).

The district judge can make an award for costs if the conduct of either side is unreasonable. Bear in mind the court's duty to deal with the case justly, which includes managing the case in a way in proportion to the amount in dispute (see para 5.3). The district judge will not permit or require any exercise in disclosure that would put a disproportionate burden on any party. See also Chapter 10, para 10.6.3 for what to do when documents are introduced for the first time at the final hearing.

3 – Evidence

There are a number of formal provisions set out in CPR Part 32 and PD 32 concerning the format of witness statements and how they are used at a hearing. None of these formalities applies to a case allocated to the small claims track. A witness statement will only be required in a small claims case if ordered by the district judge. The statement can be relatively informal, since paragraph numbers and the width of the paragraphs or the size of the paper are not prescribed in a small claims case, as they are in other cases. A statement of truth should be added (see para 5.5).

Chapter 6, para 6.7.5 gives some practical guidance on how to make the most of the witness statements.

The key with witness evidence, as with disclosure (see above) is proportionality.

Power of the court to control evidence is set out in CPR rule 32.1:

(1)   The court may control the evidence by giving directions as to—
    (a)   the issues on which it requires evidence;
    (b)   the nature of the evidence which it requires to decide those issues; and
    (c)   the way in which the evidence is to be placed before the court.
(2)   The court may use its power under this rule to exclude evidence that would otherwise be admissible.
(3)   The court may limit cross examination.

The court's power to restrict the introduction of unnecessary evidence extends to the hearing itself.

4 – Miscellaneous rules about evidence
Much of CPR Part 33 has to do with the subject of hearsay evidence. Guidance is given in Chapter 10 (especially para 10.9) on the use of evidence at a small claims hearing.

5 – Experts and assessors
Although many of the rules controlling expert evidence are excluded, four key elements in CPR Part 35 are retained:

(1)   experts will not be allowed unless necessary (rule 35.1);
(2)   an expert must assist the court first and must not be partisan (rule 35.3);
(3)   the parties should instruct a joint single expert wherever possible (in accordance with rule 35.8);
(4)   the district judge can order the appointment of a single joint expert (rule 35.7).

> See Chapter 8, para 8.8 for more about experts in small claims cases

6 – Interim remedies
Interim remedies can be granted as an emergency and in urgent cases without notice.

It is important to note the distinction between an interim order which is made early in the case and remains in force until the final hearing (or further order), and the final order which is made at the hearing.

The rules include a variety of interim remedies, including search orders, interim payments, and accounts and enquiries. Each of these remedies can only be obtained if special rules are followed, and it would plainly be disproportionate in a case of limited financial value to get involved in such complex legal procedures.

This limitation does not apply to an ordinary injunction that can be obtained in a small claims case on an interim basis (e.g. an order that someone removes scaffolding which is hanging over a neighbour's garden without permission). If considering applying for an interim injunction without notice, then bear in mind that the injunction will only be granted in cases of real emergency or where there is a true impossibility of giving notice.

Note that in a small claims case a final order of any type can be obtained (CPR rule 27.3).

7 – Offers to settle

CPR Part 36 sets out formal rules about offers to settle which are relevant to cases allocated to the fast track and multi track. These rules usually have no place in cases allocated to the small claims track, because of the no costs rule, but it should be noted that there is a discretion under rule 36.2(5) for the court to order 'otherwise' (i.e. re-introducing the provisions of Part 36); something which is rarely done.

Instead of all the complexities of CPR Part 36, the small claims track has its own simple rules for encouraging parties to settle. In brief, a party who unreasonably rejects an offer puts himself at risk of being ordered to pay costs under rule 27.14(3). See Chapter 9, para 9.3.2 for a full explanation of the relevance of Part 36 and other settlement offers in a small claims case.

8 – Hearings

> Chapter 10 deals with the special rules for hearings in small claims cases

Small claims hearings have a uniquely simplified method for hearings, and the rules that apply to hearings in the fast track and multi-track do not apply.

5.13   EUROPEAN SMALL CLAIMS PROCEDURE

With effect from 1 January 2009, the rules were extended by CPR Part 78, which includes a procedure for obtaining a judgment against an individual or company in a foreign EU Member State which can be enforced abroad without the need for a declaration of enforceability. The target users of this new cross-border procedure are businesses doing trade in the European Union and individuals who use goods and services abroad. Litigation where the defendant is abroad is beyond the scope of this book, but this scheme merits a mention because it is tailored for 'small claims' and also invokes most but not all of the rules relative to a small claims case in the event that the claim is disputed.

The features of a case which qualifies for the European Small Claims Procedure (ESCP) are that the defendant must be resident in another European Member State[12] and the claim excluding costs interest and disbursements must be under €2,000. The case will fall outside the qualifying limit if the counterclaim is €2,000 or more. If defended, the small claims track rules apply with the

---

12   Except Denmark.

exception of the no costs rule, as the court has the unfettered jurisdiction to award costs.

All cases must be started using a Form A which is reproduced in Annex 1 to PD 78. Form A can be completed in any language but must have an English translation. The date for responding to the claim is 30 days and, if defended, the court must determine the case within 30 days and it is suggested the determination will usually take place by video link or telephone. The small claims track rules govern the pre-hearing procedure but the rules remain silent as to how the parties are informed of the procedure in detail, and it is difficult to see how the hearings can be conducted within the time limit prescribed by the rules given the busy schedule of most county courts in England and Wales.

Readers of this book who want to know more can access CPR Part 78 at the Ministry of Justice website.[13]

5.14 SMALL CLAIMS IN INTELLECTUAL PROPERTY PROCEEDINGS

> **Overview**
>
> Certain types of intellectual property claims qualify for the small claims procedure in the IPEC:
>
> * the qualifying limit is under £10,000 in value and the simplified hearing procedure and the no costs rule of CPR Part 27 apply
> * to qualify for this specialist small claims track proceedings must be issued in the IPEC in London

A specialist small claims procedure was set up in October 2012 in the IPEC. The judges in this court are specialists and the court itself deals only with intellectual property claims. The procedure was introduced to improve access to justice for individuals and small businesses involved with smaller value intellectual property claims – for example a photographer who finds an image he has photographed reproduced without consent.

The route to a small claim being allocated to the small claims track in the IPEC is through that court and not via the usual county court procedure. The proceedings must first be issued in that court (see the contact details below) and

---

[13] www.justice.gov.uk/courts/procedure-rules/civil/rules.

must either be issued over the counter or by post. The qualifying limit for the claim is the same as for the usual small claims track (£10,000). The request for allocation to the small claims track must be made in the particulars of claim (there is no directions questionnaire in the IPEC). The categories of cases which qualify for the procedure are limited but include actions for:

- infringement of copyright;
- infringement of trade mark or passing off;
- infringement of unregistered design right.

The IPEC adopts the no costs rule and the simplified procedures at hearings and on appeal which are applicable to usual small claims; thus the material contained in this book in Chapters 1 to 3, 5 and 9 to 12 applies equally to those in the IPEC. The district judges who hear the small claims cases are specialists in intellectual property cases.

A helpful guide to procedures in small claims cases in the IPEC can be found at www.justice.gov.uk.

The IPEC is supervised by Mr Justice Birss, and the contact details for the court are as follows:

> Intellectual Property Enterprise County Court
> The Rolls Building
> 7 Rolls Building
> Fetter Lane
> London EC4A 1NL
> DX160040 Strand 4

5.15 LOW VALUE PERSONAL INJURY CLAIMS

Claims for personal injury arising out of accidents at work and road traffic claims of value between £1,000 and £25,000 are covered by specialist pre-action steps and a special costs regime. Discussion of this procedure is outside the scope of this book because these cases are not allocated to the small claims track. The procedures overlap on the issue of costs (see Chapter 9, para 9.2.10).

Chapter 6

Drafting Rules and Precedents in Small Claims Cases

6.1 INTRODUCTION

Modern litigation demands that documents used in the court process are set out clearly and with the minimum of jargon and legal language. Arcane legal phrases, including those in Latin, should not be used. It is vital that the case is set out clearly from the start. The benefits of the relative simplicity and speed of the small claims procedure will be lost if the case is changed or has to be clarified at the last moment. The case management powers of the court can be used to strike out a claim which is imprecise or not properly explained.

This book is a procedural guide and cannot aspire to explaining the legal matters relevant to claims which are heard on the small claims track. Litigants in person requiring guidance on whether to make a claim for a specific sum or how to defend a claim must seek legal advice. This can be accessed through solicitors, Citizen's Advice Bureaux, specialist books on particular types of claims (e.g. holiday claims), consumer forums and specialist websites.

This chapter sets out the basic rules about preparation of statements of case relevant to small claims cases. The material which appears in this chapter does not, for example, cover in detail the rules relevant to the preparation of personal injury cases, as these are rare in small claims cases.

The examples that follow in the rest of the chapter give the reader an idea of what particular documents may look like. The objective is to give the reader an idea of how a case might be presented.

6.2   LETTERS BEFORE ACTION

A letter before action may:

- prompt settlement before court action
- be used later on as the statement of case

But must:

- comply with the practice direction on pre-action conduct (see Chapter I, para 1.4)

Please refer to para 6.7.1, precedents A to D.

6.3   STATEMENTS OF CASE INCLUDING DEFENCES AND COUNTERCLAIMS

6.3.1   Guidelines for preparation of a statement of case and defence

---

Basics

- Failure to set out a claim or defence clearly can result in it being struck out
- The particulars of claim must be a concise statement of the facts relied on and, if possible, should be set out on the claim form
- A copy of any contractual conditions ('the small print') should be attached to the claim form
- The defence must be specific – stating exactly what parts of the claim are admitted/denied and which matters the defendant has no knowledge of and wants the claimant to prove
- The defence must set out any alternative version of events contended for by the defendant
- The claim, defence and any counterclaim must be verified by a statement of truth
- A claimant must file a defence to counterclaim to avoid a default judgment on the counterclaim

---

6.3.2   Detailing the claim

The requirements of the particulars of the claim are as follows:

- it must be a concise statement of the facts on which the claimant relies (CPR rule 16.4(1)(a));
- it must include details of any interest claimed (CPR rule 16.4(1)(b) and 16.4(2));
- it must include details of any alleged misrepresentation (PD 16, para 8.2(3));
- it must set out any facts relevant to mitigation of loss or damage (PD 16, para 8.2(8));
- it must specify any allegations of fraud or illegality (but see Chapter 4, para 4.6.3) (claims involving disputed claims of dishonesty) (PD 16, para 8.2(1) and (2));
- a copy of a contract must be attached to the claim if the terms are relied on (PD 16, para 7.3(1));
- a copy of any relevant conditions of sale must be attached to the claim (PD 16, para 7.3(2));
- in a personal injury case, the claimant's date of birth must be included, and a medical report must be attached to the claim (PD 16, para 4) (but see note below);
- it must be verified by a statement of truth (see Chapter 5, para 5.5).

In addition, the claimant may use the claim to:

- refer to a point of law (PD 16, para 13.3(1));
- give the names of any witnesses (PD 16, para 13.3(2));
- serve any documents to support the claim (PD 13, para 16.3(3)).

Note: see PD 16, para 4 for more detail of how to set out a claim for personal injury.

6.3.3   Detailing the defence

The defence must be more than a bare denial or it is liable to be struck out (see above). Every part of the claim must be dealt with (PD 16, para 10.2). Beginners might find it useful to follow the same paragraph numbers as the claim so that nothing is missed out. Each defendant must file and serve a defence, but can combine forces to serve a joint defence.

If an allegation is not covered in the defence it will be taken as proved (CPR rule 16.5(5)).

The defence must state precisely which allegations are:

- denied (CPR rule 16.5(1)(a));
- admitted (CPR rule 16.5(1)(c));
- not admitted or denied but the defendant requires the claimant to prove (CPR rule 16.5(1)(b)); but this is permitted only where the defendant is unable to admit or deny an allegation because they do not know whether or not it is true.

Also, the defence must:

- state reasons, if an allegation is denied (CPR rule 16.5(2)(a));
- set out the defendant's own version of events if different from the claimant's (CPR rule 16.5(2)(b));
- if the defendant states that the claim is made outside a limitation period, define this (PD 16, para 13.1);
- be verified by a statement of truth (see Chapter 5, para 5.5).

In addition, the defendant may use the defence to:

- refer to a point of law (PD 16, para 13.3(1));
- give the names of any witnesses (PD 16, para 13.3(2));
- serve any documents to support the defence (PD 16, para 13.3(3)).

Note: refer to PD 16, para 12 for matters which the defendant must deal with when defending a claim for personal injuries.

6.3.4   Reply to defence

A reply to defence is not usually needed because a claimant who does not file a reply to a defence is not taken to admit the matters raised in the defence (CPR rule 16.7).

6.3.5   Defence to counterclaim

Counterclaims fall into two categories, each of which needs different treatment when preparing a defence.

Firstly, there are those counterclaims that simply shift the blame for the matter back onto the claimant. In this type of counterclaim there is one set of disputed facts, which relates to the claim and counterclaim. Typically, this is the type of counterclaim raised in a road traffic case. A simple response to counterclaim is needed, for example as shown in para 6.7.4, precedent Q.

Secondly, there are those counterclaims that raise a whole new set of facts and matters. An example would be where a plumber sues for unpaid charges and is then met by a counterclaim alleging defective workmanship. These counterclaims need a full defence to counterclaim, which should be drafted by the claimant with all the care of a defence to a claim.

6.3.6   Admission

The claim can be admitted in whole or in part. The benefit of a partial admission is that it narrows the amount in dispute and this will reduce the amount of work needed to bring the case to a final conclusion. The terms of the admission should indicate the points that will be raised when the court decides the amount payable to the claimant.

6.3.7   Amendments

Once a statement of case has been served, it can only be amended with the permission of the court or with the consent of the other side (CPR rule 17.1). In a small claims case, the no costs rule means that the amendment will not usually attract a penalty in costs unless the amendment can be classed as unreasonable behaviour (rule 27.14(2)(g)). If a case is amended without warning, or close to the hearing date, and the other side is put at a disadvantage as a result, then this may well force an adjournment and the party making the amendment is likely to have to pay the costs of the adjournment. The version of the case before amendment does not have to be shown, unless the district judge so orders. Once amended, the statement of case should be described as 'Amended Claim/ Defence'.

6.4   THE COURT'S MANAGEMENT POWERS –
A REMINDER

Attention is drawn to Chapter 5, para 5.3 and the power of the court to strike out a case which is vague or poorly explained.

A case might be struck out, or the proceedings stayed, under the court's management powers if it is incoherent or makes no sense, if the case sets out facts but those facts, even if true, do not disclose any legally recognisable claim against the defendant, or claims which are vexatious, scurrilous or clearly ill-founded.

6.5   STYLES FOR SETTING OUT A SMALL CLAIMS CASE

In many small claims cases, the statement of case should be short enough to fit on the claim form. In other cases, a document which is already in existence (e.g. an invoice) can be attached to the claim form to avoid having to repeat all the details on the claim form. If using Money Claim Online,[1] the claim can be summarised in the limited space provided (1,080 characters on up to 24 lines) or the claim form can be served separately.

Three styles of presentation are suggested:

- *Style 1*: keeping the style short and simple to fit on to the forms provided (see para 6.7.4, precedents F to J).
- *Style 2*: using attachments effectively (see para 6.7.4, precedents K and M).
- *Style 3*: using clear, informal, specially drafted particulars (see para 6.7.4, precedents P to U).

6.6   WITNESS STATEMENTS

Guidelines for preparing witness statement are set out in Chapter 8, para 8.6. Sample witness statements are set out in para 6.7.5, precedents V and W.

6.7   PRECEDENTS

6.7.1   Letters before action

The essential elements of a letter before action are discussed in Chapter 1, para 1.4.

---

[1]   www.moneyclaim.gov.uk.

Precedent A: Simple debt claim

Dear Mrs Jones

Re: Our invoice 00764 for £550.00

I note that you have not yet paid our invoice dated 24 August, a copy of which I enclose for your reference. I have already phoned you about this more than once and although you promised to pay last week, the cheque has not arrived.

Unless I receive payment from you immediately, and in any event no later than close of business on Friday 7 October, I shall start a claim against you in the county court without giving you any further warning.

When I have started the court action I shall be entitled to claim from you, in addition to the invoice, the court fee (£[*amount*]) plus interest *calculated at the rate of 8% per annum.*

I do hope I will not be forced to issue proceedings against you and I look forward to receiving your cheque for £550 at once.

Yours sincerely

Precedent B: Complaint to a holiday company

To: The Customer Services Manager

[*name of holiday company*] Limited

Dear Sir or Madam

Re: Our holiday, reference 34567GRK
Holiday dates 13 March 2013 to 1 April 2013

My wife and I have just returned from a 'nightmare' holiday on the Greek island of Claxson with your company.

We were booked to stay in the Dormos holiday apartments (self-catering), which were advertised in your brochure on page 45. The description of the apartments especially attracted us because it says the apartments are well away from the lively nightlife of the village and yet close to the beach. We told the agent when we booked that my wife is a light sleeper and she told us that the apartments would be ideal.

The Greek island is lovely. We have no complaints about that. But here is a list of complaints about the Dormos holiday apartments:

(a) There was a noisy disco by the swimming pool next to our room run by the owner's son. The music was not turned off until 2 o'clock in the morning.

(b) The bedroom was dirty and the tiles in the bathroom were cracked. We found cockroaches in the toilet pan (photos enclosed).

(c) Although the hotel was only about 50 yards from the beach, to get to it we had to cross a building site – in fact it was more of a junk yard because there wasn't much building going on and the half-finished buildings were occupied by local teenagers taking drugs who left their mess and dirty bottles everywhere.

(d) The brochure also stated that there would be free Wi-Fi connection, but the Wi-Fi did not work in our room.

(e) Although we complained to your courier, she said she couldn't help, as it was company policy not to deal with customers' complaints until the end of the holiday.

My wife hardly slept a wink at night for the whole holiday and had to catch up with her sleep in the afternoons, this really spoilt the holiday for both of us as we had wanted to go sight-seeing during the days. We were both upset by the state of the room and I was so disgusted by the 'building site' that I hardly went to the beach at all.

We spent £1,259 in total for this holiday and I want to claim a refund and compensation.

I am prepared to discuss a settlement with you without going to court and if you wish to refer this matter to independent mediation I would participate in such a scheme.

Please let me have your answer within 14 days, otherwise we shall start a claim against you in the county court.

Yours faithfully

Precedent C: Cases where the claimant is a business and the defendant is an individual[2]

Dear [ ]

We are writing to claim payment of our unpaid invoice addressed to you dated 9 March 2011 in the sum of £2360. A copy of the unpaid invoice is attached for your reference. Payment of the invoice was due on 9 April 2011 and is long overdue.

We intend to issue court proceedings 14 days after the date of this letter if you have not paid the debt in full or unless you have contacted us and we have agreed to accept payment by instalments.

Your cheque in full settlement should be sent to our accounts office which is the address which appears at the head of this letter. If you want to discuss payment by instalments you can call or email Mrs Bracket, whose telephone number and email address are at the head of this letter.

If you need free independent advice and assistance about this letter or your financial situation you should immediately contact any of the organisations set out in the note which we are attaching.[3]

We are disappointed that we have had to write to you to threaten court action. However, you should be aware that if we do issue court action we shall claim court costs and interest in addition to the debt already owed. In the case of this debt the commencement fee for starting the court action is £80.[4]

Yours faithfully

---

[2] The essential elements of a pre-action letter where the claimant is a business and the defendant is an individual are discussed in Chapter 1, para 1.4.4; Annex B of the practice direction on pre-action conduct is reproduced at Appendix 5.

[3] This information need not be set out in the letter before action if the information has been provided to the debtor previously.

[4] If the debtor is reminded of the commencement fee at this stage this can be an effective incentive to settle.

Independent advice organisations

Organisation	Telephone number	Email address
National Debtline	Freephone 0808 808 4000	www.nationaldebtline.org
StepChange Debt Charity (formerly Consumer Credit Counselling Service)	Freephone 0800 138 1111	www.stepchange.org
Citizens Advice	Check your local Yellow Pages or Thomson local directory for address and telephone numbers	www.citizensadvice.org.uk
Civil Legal Advice (CLA)	0345 345 4 345	www.gov.uk/civil-legal-advice

Precedent D: Defendant's response (simple debt claim)

Dear Mrs Bracket

Thank you for your letter dated [   ]

I have checked my records and confirm that I overlooked this payment for which I apologise. I enclose a cheque in full settlement of the amount claimed.

Or

I confirm that I have spoken to Mrs Bracket who has kindly agreed to accept payment of the sum due in three instalments. As agreed, I enclose a cheque for £1,000 and confirm the balance will be paid by two further cheques of £680 each payable on 13 June and 13 July. Thank you for your assistance in this matter.

Or

I am very sorry but I cannot deal with your letter within 14 days. I know that I owe you some money but I need to check my records to finalise the amount due. Unfortunately, I have been very ill and would like to take advice before I decide if the amount claimed is really what I owe you. Could you please hold off the court action until 13 June to give me time to sort this out and take advice from one of the organisations that you mention. I enclose a copy of the sick note from my doctor that signs me off work until 9 June.

Or

> As you well know I dispute the amount claimed. The invoice was for cleaning services at my premises for the last 6 months and I have called several times to complain about the standard of work. I enclose copies of my letters to you dated [ ] and [ ] detailing my complaints. I am prepared to discuss a settlement and if you would care to pick up the phone and speak to me I shall tell you what I am prepared to offer.

Or

> I have been very unhappy with the accountancy services provided by your company and I intend to counterclaim against you for the cost of instructing another accountant to sort out my finances. I enclose a copy of the other accountant's invoice in the sum of £3,050.

> Yours sincerely

6.7.2 Starting the case

Precedent E: Letter to the court manager at the start of the case (suitable for any case)

> Dear Sir or Madam

> I enclose:

> 1. Form N1 plus copy.
> 2. A cheque for [ ] in favour of HM Courts & Tribunal Service.

> Please issue the proceedings and [*arrange for service on the defendant by post in the usual way*] [*return the summons when issued to me because I want to serve the documents myself*].[5]

> Yours sincerely

---

5   The court will serve the claim form for you – personal service is an option but is not usually necessary.

6.7.3   Brief description of type of claim

This is the box which has to be completed on form N1, which will be used to give the court staff an at-a-glance idea of what the case is about (see Chapter 2, para 2.3.8). Here are some suggestions:

- Unpaid debt.
- Holiday claim.
- Unpaid consultant's fees.
- Road traffic accident.
- Damaged goods.
- Claim against tenant for unpaid rent.
- Claim against landlord for disrepair.
- Computer of unsatisfactory quality.
- Repayment of personal loan.

6.7.4   Statement of case including defences and counterclaims

Precedent F: Claim by landlord for unpaid rent and service charges (includes a claim for statutory interest)

PARTICULARS OF CLAIM

1.   The Defendant is the Claimant's tenant of Flat 3, 23 Green Gardens, London N6 under a long lease.

2.   The Claimant's claim is for unpaid rent and other charges due under the lease amounting to £843.58 according to the Claimant's invoice dated 7 June 2013.

3.   The Claimant claims in addition interest[6] pursuant to the lease at 4% above the base rate of National Westminster Bank plc which amounts to £14.20 to date and mounts at the daily rate of 25p until judgment or sooner payment.

I believe that the facts stated in this claim are true.

Signed [*landlord's signature*]

---

[6]   This is an example of pleading interest under a contract.

Precedent G: Defence to claim by landlord for unpaid rent and service charges

DEFENCE

I dispute the claim because I paid all the rent and service charges by cheque last week and I have checked with my bank and the cheque cleared 29 July 2013.[7]

I believe that the facts stated in this defence are true.

Signed [*tenant's signature*]

Precedent H: Claim against garage for negligent repairs

PARTICULARS OF CLAIM

The Claimant took his Renault car registration R95 0YI in for a routine service at the Defendant's garage on 6 May 2013. During the service the wheel hubs were damaged. This was the Defendant's fault.

The Claimant has had an estimate for the repairs in the sum of £800 plus VAT to have the wheel hubs replaced and claims this sum from the Defendant as compensation.

The claimant believes that the facts stated in this claim are true.

Signed [*claimant's solicitor*]

Precedent I: Defence to claim against garage for negligent repairs

DEFENCE

We discovered the damage to the wheel hubs but we did not cause it. They were already damaged when the car was brought in. Our mechanic Mr Patel will come to court as a witness to confirm this. We deny the claim.[8]

I believe that the facts stated in this defence are true.

Signed [*proprietor of garage*]

---

7   This is an example of a states paid defence (see Chapter 3, para 3.6.2).

8   The defence, although short, is to the point and quite adequate.

Precedent J: Claim by a business for an unpaid invoice including a claim for interest under the Late Payment Act

The claim is for the sum of £2,350 being the unpaid cost of cleaning and maintenance services rendered in the period from [ ] to [ ] 2013.

The claimant claims interest under the Late Payment of Commercial Debts (Interest) Act 1998 at the rate of [*add percentage – official dealing rate of the Bank of England (the Base Rate) + 8%*] from [*the date when interest started to run*] to [*the date you are issuing the claim*] in the sum of £[ ] and continuing at the same rate up to the date of judgment or earlier payment at the daily rate of [*enter the daily rate of interest*].

Precedent K: Holiday claim

PARTICULARS OF CLAIM

We went to Greece on holiday but it was a disaster because of the Defendant's failure to provide the holiday we paid for.

We have written to the Defendant but they ignored our claim and ignored our request to refer the matter to out of court mediation

Our claim is as set out in the letter[9] to the Defendant dated 4 April, a copy of which is attached.

We claim a refund and damages.

I believe that the facts stated in this claim are true.

Signed [*claimant's signature*]

---

[9] The letter in this example is the letter before action, see para 6.7.1, precedent B.

Precedent L: Admission to holiday claim

ADMISSION

The defendants accept that they are responsible for the various problems outlined in the case and will not contest liability. However, the claim for the refund and damages is excessive; the claimants still had excellent value for money for their holiday (which was sold to them at budget rates) and enjoyed a lot of the holiday. The defendants will contest the amount claimed and will invite the claimant to use the small claims mediation service to avoid a final hearing.

Precedent M: Claim for unpaid professional fees (includes a claim for statutory interest)

PARTICULARS OF THE CLAIM

The Claimant's claim is for £2,301.94 being the unpaid cost of accountancy services rendered by the Claimant to the Defendant in accordance with the attached statement of account[10] which is dated 19 February 2013.

The Claimant claims interest[11] under section 69 of the County Court Act 1984 at the rate of 8% per annum calculated from 19 February 2013 to the date of issue, which is £[ ] and continuing until payment or the date of judgment at a daily rate of 50p.

I believe that the facts stated in this claim are true.

Signed [*claimant's signature*]

---

[10] The attachment here is the claimant's computerised printout, which shows the running state of various unpaid invoices. There is no point having it all typed out again.

[11] This is an example of how to claim statutory interest (see para 6.8 for notes on how to calculate the interest).

Precedent N: Defence and counterclaim to claim for unpaid professional fees

DEFENCE AND COUNTERCLAIM

The accountant is not entitled to this money because he did not do our accounts on time. The accountant was negligent. We attach a copy of a letter from our new accountant which confirms the negligence.[12] We had to pay a penalty of £1,000 to Her Majesty's Revenue and Customs ('HMRC').[13]

Counterclaim
Reimbursement of the money paid to HMRC. We paid £1,000 in June 2013.

We believe that the facts stated in this claim are true.

Signed [*defendant's signature*]

Precedent O: Defence to counterclaim in unpaid professional fees case

DEFENCE TO COUNTERCLAIM

The claimant denies the defendant's counterclaim because he acted professionally and competently throughout. He was not negligent – the letter attached to the defence gives an incomplete and biased account of the matter. The claimant's case was fully set out in the letter to the Defendant dated 28 August 2013, which is attached.

We believe that the facts stated in this claim are true.

Signed [*claimant's signature*]

---

[12] Although fairly brief, these particulars are just enough to alert the claimant's accountant to the nature of the negligence claim against him.

[13] The defendant will need the permission of the district judge to call expert evidence in this case but it is likely that the permission will be granted.

Precedent P: Road traffic case

PARTICULARS OF CLAIM[14]

Introduction

1. The accident happened on 5 June 2013 at about 6pm at the junction of Mill Lane and Silver Street in Highgate. The junction is controlled by traffic lights.

2. The claimant was driving her Ford Escort registration H42 DWQ and the defendant's vehicle was a white Renault van registration R99 RIT. The claimant does not know the name of the man who was driving the defendant's vehicle. It was daylight, and the weather conditions were good.

About the accident

3. The claimant was in the inside lane at the traffic lights in Silver Street and indicated to turn right. There was no vehicle in the other lane. As she was turning right, across the junction, the defendant's van crashed into the driver's side of the claimant's car.

4. A sketch of the scene of the accident follows on the next page.

5. The accident was the defendant driver's fault. He was negligent because he was not looking where he was going and misjudged his turn at the junction.

6. The claimant needs her car for work and had to hire a care whilst her car was being repaired. The car hire quoted is the cheapest that could be found.

Details of damage
Cost of repairs £5,092.63
Car rental when car being repaired £453.60
Total £5,546.23

---

[14] There is hardly anything less useful in a small claims case than a list of possible 'standard' allegations of negligence taken from a precedent book, when only one or two of the paragraphs have any relevance at all to the accident in question. Particulars of the type shown should make it plain to the defendant exactly what case will have to be met at the hearing.

The Claimant also claims interest[15] under section 69 of the County Court Act 1984 at the rate of 8% per annum calculated from [*insert the date(s) that the repair and rental invoices were paid*] to the date of issue, which is £[ ] and continuing until payment or the date of judgment at a daily rate of £1.21.

The claimant believes that the facts stated in this claim are true.

Signed [*claimant's solicitor*]

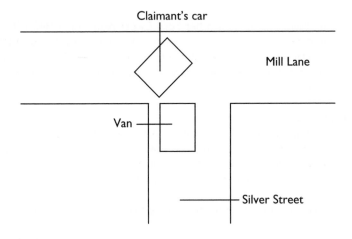

Sketch plan[16]

---

15   This is an example of how to claim statutory interest (see para 6.8 for notes of how to calculate the interest).

16   The sketch plan is less than perfect, and a lot more information could usefully be included by the addition of traffic lights, arrows and other notes. Two sketches, one showing the position of the vehicles before and the other after the accident could also be helpful. However, despite its shortcomings, a simple sketch is better than nothing at all. Photographs will often provide good information about the scene of the accident and make an elaborate sketch plan unnecessary. Google Maps satellite images are often used to illustrate the road layout. Prints of any photographs must be sent to the other side, usually 2 weeks before the hearing in accordance with the directions given by the district judge when the case was allocated to the small claims track.

Precedent Q: Defence and counterclaim to road traffic case

DEFENCE AND COUNTERCLAIM

1. The defendant agrees with paragraphs 1 and 2 of the defence.

2. The claimant's account of the accident is wrong. The claimant pulled out into the defendant's path without warning and she is to blame for the accident.

COUNTERCLAIM

3. The accident was the claimant's fault (see para 2).

4. The defendant has suffered the following losses, which he counterclaims from the Claimant:

   (a) repair to van £576.95
   (b) loss of profit while van is being fixed (3 days at £150 per day) £450.

5. The defendant also counterclaims interest under section 69 of the County Court Act 1984 at the rate of 8% per annum calculated as follows:

   (a) in respect of the cost of repair from [*insert the date that the repair invoice was paid*]
   (b) in respect of the loss of profit from [*insert date profit would have been received*]

   to the date of issue, which is (a) £[ ] and (b) £[ ] respectively and continuing until payment or the date of judgment at a daily rate of [ ]p.

Precedent R: Defence to counterclaim in road traffic case

DEFENCE TO COUNTERCLAIM

The claimant disagrees with all of the defence apart from the admissions. (see Particulars of Claim). The claimant puts the defendant to strict proof of its losses.

Precedent S: Personal injury claim

PARTICULARS OF CLAIM

1.   On 15 December 2013, at about 9 o'clock in the morning, the claimant was riding her bicycle along Silver Street in Highgate in an easterly direction when she was knocked off and fell into the road when the defendant's driver opened his door into her path.

2.   The accident was the defendant's driver's fault because he should have looked to see if it was safe to open the van door and he failed to do so, or at least failed to take sensible precautions to prevent the accident.

3.   The claimant has as a result suffered the following loss and damage.

Particulars of personal injury

The claimant's date of birth is 9 March 1971.
She grazed her right knee and had painful bruising on her right arm.
The graze healed after about 2 weeks and the arm was sore for about 10 days. Full details are set out in the letter from the claimant's GP which is attached.[17]

Particulars of other losses

Ruined jeans and jacket (cost of replacement: £195).
Broken watch (cost of replacement: £89.50).
One day off work (loss of wages: £90).
Repairs to bicycle (£120).

And the claimant claims

Damages for personal injury limited to £1,000 including compensation for the other losses detailed above, plus interest to be assessed.

I believe that the facts stated in this claim are true.

Signed [*claimant's signature*]

---

[17]   The maximum that can be recovered for an expert's report is £750 in a small claims case, so the letter from the GP is a suitable and proportionate way of providing medical evidence in this small claim.

Precedent T: Defective goods

PARTICULARS OF CLAIM

1. The defendant's company sells computers; it advertises its goods in newspapers and magazines, and customers buy the computers over the telephone.

2. On 21 February 2013, the claimant called the defendant after seeing an advert in the *Highgate Daily News*. The claimant spoke to a salesman called 'Mike' and told him that he wanted a computer which would:

    *   enable him to do banking at home on the internet;
    *   enable him to manipulate photos taken on his digital camera;
    *   be good for running computer games;
    *   be supplied ready to use.

3. The salesman told the claimant that their 'Top Dog' computer would be suitable for all these things. On this basis the claimant paid the defendant £975 (including VAT and delivery) for a computer and it was delivered to him on 12 March 2013.

4. When the computer arrived it was in eight different boxes and it took the claimant and his son 5 hours to get it working. The instructions supplied were useless.

5. The computer is not of satisfactory quality and does not match the description given by the salesman, and the salesman misrepresented what the computer would be like because:

    *   the modem is too slow to make home banking possible;
    *   there is insufficient RAM memory to run the 'Photomanipulate' program;
    *   the resolution of the monitor spoils the computer games;
    *   the computer was not supplied ready to use.

6. The claimant therefore claims a refund for the price paid and damages plus interest to be calculated by the court.

I believe that the facts stated in this claim are true.

Signed *John Snapper*
Dated

Precedent U: Unpaid school fees

PARTICULARS OF CASE

1. The claimant claims the sum of £5,542 being one term's school fees. The defendant's son, Darren, was registered at the school in Autumn 2013 and paid one term's school fees in advance. The defendant told the claimant in December 2013 that Darren would be leaving the school and not returning in January 2014.

2. The claimant's terms and conditions (a copy of which are attached)[18] make it clear that one full term's notice must be given otherwise fees must be paid in lieu.

3. The claimant's rely on the decided case of *Mount v Oldham Corporation* [1973] 1 All ER 26, CA.[19]

I believe that the facts stated in this claim are true.

Signed *Dawn Jones (School Administrator)*
Dated

---

[18] See para 6.3.2 for the requirement to attach terms and conditions to a particulars of case.

[19] Case references and law can be set out in a statement of case.

6.7.5 Other precedents

Precedent V: Witness[20] statement road traffic case

1. My name is George Green. I work for Verdant Ices and I drive an ice cream van.

2. On 5 June 2013 at about 6pm I was in Highgate village. It was a warm evening and I had been selling ices to people near Kenwood House.

3. The weather was clear and dry.

4. As I came up to the junction with Mill Lane I indicated to turn right. There was a lady in a red car on my right (offside), she was obviously going to turn left

5. Suddenly and without warning the lady cut in front of me, turning right into the path of my van

6. I tried to avoid the crash but could do nothing. She hit the front of my van and damaged it.

7. I took some photos of the damage the day after the crash and they will be produced in court.[21]

8. After the accident the lady was very upset as she would be because it was her fault. She gave me her name and address and I gave her mine.

9. The van has been repaired through my boss' insurance company.

I believe that the facts stated in this witness statement are true.

Signed *George Green*
Date

---

[20] In the context of a court action, the term 'witness' means anyone who gives a statement at a hearing. This includes the parties themselves plus any bystanders or others who can give evidence about the case.

[21] Spot the deliberate mistake – of course the photographs count as documents and copies must be sent to the other side in advance of the hearing (see Chapter 8, para 8.4).

Precedent W: Witness statement contract dispute

1. My name is Peter Hall. I am a butcher, I specialise in chickens.

2. Between 2010 and 2013 I did a lot of business with the defendant. He would sell me chickens and I would sell them in my shop. He is a butcher as well. Sometimes I would let him have meat for sale if I had too much to sell. We helped each other out. We were friends.

3. I kept a note in a book of the chickens I gave to the defendant to sell. I will bring the book to court with me but copies of the pages with the defendant's account on it are at pages F, G and H of my bundle of documents.[22]

4. The defendant paid for the chickens he had from me when he had money. I got odd payments. Sometimes weekly, sometimes more often. I kept a note of the money he paid in the book and these notes are attached D and E.

5. In 2013 the defendant went out of business. He carried on clearing his debt but he still has not paid it all.

6. In November 2013 I got tired of waiting for payment and sent him an invoice (A). He has not paid the invoice.

7. On 5 December 2013 the defendant wrote me a letter (pages B and C). What he says in the letter is rubbish, if he had kept proper records as I have he would know that he still owes me £2,543.00.

8. I had to issue the court case because the defendant would not pay.

I believe that the facts stated in this witness statement are true.

Signed *Peter Hall*
Date

---

[22] This witness has adopted the excellent approach of attaching his documents to his witness statement and referencing them to the statement itself.

Precedent X: Grounds for appeal to be included in section 5 of Form N164

The district judge's decision was wrong because the evidence was that the defendants had inspected the section of road in question every 3 months; the district judge accepted the defendants' evidence on this point and it was therefore irrational of him to conclude that the defendants had failed to discharge their duty to inspect under section 58 of the Highways Act 1980.

Please refer to Chapter 11 for more about appeals. The appellant must complete all sections of form N164, which includes notes for guidance

---

Precedent Y: Application to set aside

APPLICATION TO SET ASIDE

The defendant applies for the judgment made by District Judge Faulty on 14 June to be set aside. The defendant went away for a 2-week holiday on 13 May with her son. Unfortunately, her son broke his leg and as a result they did not return until 15 June. The defendant then discovered that the case had been heard on 14 June and she had not received the notice of hearing that was posted to her on 14 May. A copy of the tickets and a letter from the tour company confirming the actual dates of travel are attached.

The defendant has a reasonable prospect of defending the claim because ...

I believe that the facts stated in this application are true.

Signed *Brenda Lythe*
Dated

Please refer to Chapter 11, para 11.3 for detail about applications to set aside judgments

---

Precedent Z: List of complaints[23]

IN THE HIGHGATE COUNTY COURT   CASE NUMBER HE [ ]

DISPUTE BETWEEN STEVEN MISHINI AND TONY FRANCIS
(TONI'S CAR REPAIRS)

List of complaints

Claimant's complaint	Defendant's comments
Oil leaking from under the car – inconvenience claimed	A nut was loose. We apologised for this and the matter was rectified the next day
Brakes squeaky – for new brake pads including fitting cost will be £60	Not a fault
The clutch is slipping – I have had an estimate of £150 for repair from another garage	This had nothing to do with the service – Mr Mishini needs a new clutch and we would be happy to fit one at his expense
There is a rattle under the bonnet which was not there before the service – I do not know what the fault is so cannot give an estimate	We know nothing about this
The windscreen wiper was damaged by the defendant and I claim £19.96 as the cost of replacement	We accept this and will pay the Mr Mishini £19.96 to cover this
The car was returned dirty with oil on the driver's seat belt which marked my new jacket. I paid £25 to have the car cleaned by a clean-a-car and £5 dry cleaning	We are a garage not a valet service and we deny that the inside of the car was dirty

Signed   Signed
Claimant   Defendant

Date   Date

---

[23]   In this example both sides have made their comments on the list before the hearing – a useful way of clarifying points in dispute in variety of cases.

6.8 HOW TO CALCULATE STATUTORY INTEREST

Once a claimant has succeeded in obtaining judgment for a sum of money, interest begins to accrue on it at a fixed rate of 8% per year (Judgments Act 1838, section 17).

This must be distinguished from interest awarded by the court when giving judgment, i.e. for the period between the date when the money became due and the date of judgment (usually trial or earlier if by default). The rate of interest awarded at this point is not specified by law but is at the discretion of the judge.

Often 8% per year is claimed and can still be awarded, but with interest rates generally at a historically low level, many judges will decide that a rate of, for example, 4% or 6% best reflects the justice of the case.

This section offers a simple method of calculating interest – this applies to statutory interest only (a precedent for the wording of the interest claim can be found at para 6.7.4, precedent M):

- *Step 1*: count the number of days (N) between the date when the debt was payable and the date of the preparation of the claim.[24]

- *Step 2*: work out the annual interest (A) by multiplying the total debt (D) by 8 (or whatever percentage rate is being applied) and dividing by 100:

  $$A = D \times 8 \div 100$$

- *Step 3*: work out the daily interest rate (R) by dividing A by 365 (write this figure down as it is needed to put in the claim on the summons):[25]

  $$R = A \div 365$$

- *Step 4*: multiply the daily rate (R) by the number of days (N); the answer is the total interest to the date of drafting the summons.

- Total interest = R x N.

---

[24] *Hint*: some diaries conveniently give a number to each day of the year and this number appears discreetly at the bottom of the page – finding this number will save a lot of counting.

[25] *Hint*: if the daily rate is more than £2.19 then something has gone wrong, because the daily rate of interest on a claim of £10,000 at 8% is £2.18.

Part 2

Mediation

Chapter 7

Mediation of Small Claims through the County Court

7.1 OVERVIEW OF FEATURES

Cases which qualify for the small claims track also qualify for out of court mediation at no additional charge. The mediation is conducted by a trained mediator, not a lawyer or a judge, almost always by telephone. If mediation is successful, the parties do not need to come to court for a hearing before a judge. The mediation scheme is an important and integral part of the service offered to parties who come to court with a small claims dispute:

- The service is offered to all cases at the allocation stage but only some cases are selected.
- Mediation is entirely voluntary and both parties must agree to take part before the mediator will become involved.
- The mediator is not a judge but is trained to conduct mediations.
- The parties themselves must both contact the mediator and only then will the mediator fix an appointment.
- While almost all mediations are by telephone, occasionally it will be conducted face to face.
- When mediations take place they are usually successful in the sense that the case settles and there is no court hearing; this saves the cost of the hearing fee, which is between £25 and £335.
- The process is confidential to the parties.
- The judge is told nothing of what is said or what occurs during a mediation.

This scheme is administered and paid for out of the Courts Service budget. This chapter equips the reader with the information needed to make the most of the scheme or to decide if it is not suitable for a particular case. Paragraph 7.9 discusses some of the background to the scheme, including the historical perspective. Table 7.1 sets out the stages of mediation. Paragraph 7.3 considers which cases are suitable for mediation.

Table 7.1   Procedural table – small claims mediation

Before allocation	The parties are sent information about the small claims mediation service with the directions questionnaire (see para 7.3)
At the allocation stage	The parties are invited to take up the mediation option or the district judge can select the case for mediation
If mediation is selected, the case is usually put on hold for 6 weeks (sometimes a hearing date is fixed)	
	The court staff notify the mediator about the case (see para 7.4.1)
	The parties must ask the mediator to set an appointment (see para 7.4.2)
	The parties are sent information about mediation and sign an agreement to mediate
The mediation takes place by telephone but sometimes in person or by email – the appointment is no more than an hour	
If mediation succeeds (settlement reached)	The parties sign a settlement agreement or a *Tomlin* order is made (see para 7.6.1)
If mediation fails	The case returns to the system for a hearing before a district judge (see para 7.6.2)

7.2   DEFINITION OF MEDIATION[1]

Mediation is a voluntary, non-binding and private dispute resolution process in which a neutral person helps the parties try to reach a negotiated settlement, the contents of which remain confidential and without prejudice[2] unless or until a settlement is achieved.

The concept of encouraging out of court settlement is integral to the duty of the court to manage cases (see CPR rule 1.4(2)(e) which is reproduced at Appendix 6).

---

[1]   Mediation is a category of 'Alternative Dispute Resolution', which covers any method of settling a dispute without going to court. It is not the same as 'Arbitration' since the mediator has no power to impose a decision. Any decision rests entirely with the parties. Please refer to the glossary if you are interested in the technical difference.

[2]   Please refer to the glossary for the definition of 'without prejudice'.

7.3   SELECTING CASES FOR MEDIATION

The directions questionnaire asks the parties to indicate if they want to take part in the mediation scheme (see Chapter 4, para 4.8). Parties are sent a Courts Service leaflet about mediation with the directions questionnaire, which will help them decide if they want to take this route.

7.3.1   Selection by category of case

Many different types of cases are suitable for mediation. For example, where there is a claim for unpaid charges for any sort of service and the defendant disputes payment because he or she is not happy with the service provided. This includes disputes between individuals, between individuals and businesses and disputes between businesses. The range of cases which fall into this category is vast and will include, for example, claims by computer experts, musicians, double glazing companies, plumbers, electricians and builders; non-payments for the supply of goods are also suitable. The mediator may also assist the parties in reaching a settlement which involves something other than money – for example replacement goods or a discount on future purchases – where the court may not be able to.

There is no referral to the small claims mediation service in cases concerning road traffic accidents, personal injury or housing disrepair.

Only a judge, not a mediator, is qualified to determine the amount of a claim if the quantum of compensation for a personal injury claim is in dispute. Mediation may not be suitable where there is a legal point to be determined or if there is a disagreement about the interpretation of written documents, including terms and conditions of a contract.

At the small claims level of jurisdiction, government agencies including HM Revenue and Customs and the Child Support Agency will be interested only in a judgment for the full amount owed, rendering mediation in these cases unlikely to be desirable by at least one side.

7.3.2   Selection by willingness to negotiate through mediation

Whatever the type of case, if both parties indicate in their directions questionnaire that they want the case to be referred to mediation, the case is likely to be suitable for mediation. The decision about referral is made by the district judge but it is unlikely that a unanimous request for referral to mediation would be ignored.

7.3.3   Selection by the district judge

The district judge may wish to give the parties a second chance to consider mediation even if only one of them or neither of them ticks the 'mediation box'. If this occurs, the parties will be told of the judge's decision to refer the matter to mediation.

7.4   PROCEDURE BETWEEN SELECTION FOR MEDIATION AND MEDIATION

7.4.1   What the court does

Firstly, the court refers the case to mediation:

STANDARD ORDER (STAY OF PROCEEDINGS FOR SETTLEMENT AND MEDIATION)

Having considered the papers in your case, the court believes that your case is suitable for mediation. This is a very simple process designed to give you the opportunity to resolve your dispute without having to attend a court hearing. You are therefore encouraged to contact the Small Claims Mediation Service to arrange a mediation appointment. The mediation service is free. Mediation appointments are conducted by telephone and so do not involve you having to attend court. The mediation appointment is limited to one hour, is confidential and can be done anytime up to 10 working days before the final hearing. Further information on mediation is contained in the attached information sheet or can be found at www.gov.uk.

To accept the offer of this service and arrange your mediation appointment both parties should contact HMCTS by telephone on 01604 795511 or email on scmreferrals@hmcts.gsi.gov.uk within 7 days of receipt of this order. If you contact the Small Claims Mediation Service by email please ensure you include a return telephone number, and the case number. Please note that if you wish to undertake mediation, you must contact the Small Claims Mediation Service. If both parties confirm they wish to undertake mediation, the Small Claims Mediation Service will contact you to arrange an appointment. If you require any further information about mediation please contact the Small Claims Mediation Service by email at scmenquiries@hmcts.gsi.gov.uk.

Secondly, a judge will decide whether to put the case on hold for up to 6 weeks for the mediation to take place or whether to fix a final hearing date with the proviso that the hearing date will be vacated if the case is settled. The first option (putting the case on hold) results in the whole case being delayed if the mediation fails. The second option secures the onward progress of the case to a final hearing whether or not the mediation is successful. There is no uniform procedure in this regard – the option chosen varies from court to court and from case to case.

In addition, the court will make provision for what to do next in the event that mediation does not take place or that mediation fails.

Thirdly, if the mediation route is chosen, information is sent to the parties about the mediation (see para 7.4.2) and the mediator receives information about the case (see para 7.4.3).

7.4.2   What the parties do next

The parties receive a court order plus details of the mediation scheme in their particular area including information about how to contact the mediator.

It is important to note that the parties must prompt the mediation themselves. If they do not contact the mediator and ask for a hearing date it is unlikely that the mediation will take place. The key to the process is that it is voluntary and this means that the parties must volunteer themselves to the mediator and ask for an appointment. If one party still does not want to progress with mediation then there can be no mediation; courtesy alone would suggest that the party who changes their mind about mediation should let the mediator, if not the other side, know of their decision.

The parties may individually contact the mediator by phone or email to ask for clarification of the mediation process – although the leaflets provided are comprehensive and are designed to answer most questions about the process.

7.4.3   What the mediator does next

The mediator receives the details of the case from the court. The scheme has been established on the understanding that this will be the form of the computer printout of the case from the court computer (the 'Caseman' print out). This document contains a brief summary of the claim, details of the parties and the dates for filing of the court documents. In some areas the mediator will rely in addition, or instead, on the information in the 'small claims mediation service reply form' (see para 7.4.2).

It is not usual for the mediator to take the initiative to contact the parties; usually, the mediator waits to hear from one or other of them. The mediator will answer queries made by phone or by email about the mediation process. If one party confirms that they want mediation to go ahead the mediator may, time permitting, contact the other party to clarify if they wish to proceed.

The mediator will then set a time for the mediation to take place, and, if it is to be face to face, its location.[3] The venue for mediation will be rooms made available for that purpose at a local county court, but not necessarily the court which would be the hearing venue for the hearing before the judge.

7.5   MEDIATION APPOINTMENT

- The time allowed for the mediation appointment is only one hour.
- The mediator has only the most basic information about the case and does not usually have any papers; information is gained by gathering information and suggestions from each side verbally.
- Everything the mediator is told is confidential and the mediator will only tell the other side strictly what the other side agrees they want to have passed on.
- The mediator will emphasise to the parties that mediators do not take sides or decide who is right or wrong and cannot give advice. Their role is neutral, to help the parties come to an agreed settlement of the whole dispute.
- The format of the mediation will be shuttle diplomacy by telephone – passing messages on and hopefully narrowing the gap to achieve a settlement.
- Parties who approach mediation with an open mind will be more likely to achieve a settled result than those who do not.
- The outcome of the mediation can be something other than money – possibly an apology or an agreement to correct the faulty work.
- Most mediations involve the litigants themselves as litigants in person but the parties may instruct a legal representative to speak on their behalf.

7.5.1   Role of the mediator

The parties will have received material from the Courts Service about the mediation process.

For the hearing itself, the mediator will ensure that both parties are aware that the process is not a judicial hearing and that the mediator will not take sides but take a neutral role. The mediator will collect confidential information from both sides individually, keeping it to himself or herself, and so establish what offers each party will make to settle the matter.

---

[3]   The mediation will almost always take place by telephone.

The parties may instruct their solicitor, a barrister or a friend to speak on their behalf. If the person doing the talking is a friend and is not legally qualified, the mediator should ensure that the litigant is with the friend and approves of what is being said on his or her behalf.

The mediation appointment is time limited to one hour and the mediator will ensure that parties keep their discussions within sensible time limits.

7.5.2   Preparation for mediation

The parties should ensure in advance that they are clear about what they are hoping to achieve by the court process and whether they are prepared to compromise for less. They will need to be ready to set out their case clearly and it can be helpful to prepare a short script of what they want to tell the mediator. If the script includes information they do not want disclosed to the other side, this should be set out separately and they will have to be clear what is confidential and what is not. Where it is essential for the mediator to read key documents before the hearing, they must be sent to the mediator in advance. It is helpful to calculate in advance what the cost in time and money will be of the mediation failing and the case having to go to a judge's hearing. This should be taken into account when deciding how much to settle for at mediation.

7.5.3   Telephone mediations

The parties may send written material to the mediator before the telephone mediation, but usually the information in the hands of the mediator is simply the written material set out in the Caseman printout or the 'small claims mediation service reply form' completed by the parties (see paras 7.4.2 and 7.4.3). The mediator will conduct the mediation by way of telephone calls individually to the parties, in order to collect information from each party. The parties should not be asked to go head to head in a three-way telephone call unless they expressly agree to such a format.

7.5.4   Face-to-face mediations

These are not the usual format of a small claims mediation. The parties plus any legal adviser or supporting friend will be invited to attend a court venue. They can expect to see the mediator individually and only to see the other party in a face-to-face meeting if they agree. They may be asked by the mediator to sit in the room with the other party at the start of the process so that the format of the mediation can be explained to both parties at the same time. The format of a face-to-face mediation makes it easier to exchange information which is set out in documents or to look at other material; for example if the goods are allegedly defective, the goods themselves.

Hints for a successful mediation

- Prepare what you want to say – write down what you want to say to the mediator in advance
- Listen to the mediator carefully and in particular to what he or she tells you the other side is prepared to offer
- When deciding what to settle for, factor in the cost in time and money of attending a judge's hearing

---

7.6   OUTCOME OF THE MEDIATION

7.6.1   If the outcome of the mediation is a settlement

The mediator has no power to bind the parties by a judgment or decision. For the outcome to be binding it must be set out in either a binding contract signed by both parties or by a consent order.

Usually, because the agreement is reached over the phone and the parties are not represented, the responsibility for drafting the settlement contract (agreement) falls to the mediator. This is unlike most mediation processes, where the parties' representatives would be expected to draft the agreement. The mediator should read out the wording of the agreement and then explain that it needs to be signed by both parties. The agreement can be sent by email, fax or post. A standard form settlement agreement is used (Form N182,[4] set out at Appendix 11).

7.6.2   If no settlement is reached on mediation

In the event of the mediation failing, the case will go back into the system to be dealt with at a judge's hearing. Chapters 8 to 12 set out the procedure to be followed. There should be no need for the parties to take active steps to promote the movement of the case to a final hearing. If the case has been put on hold then the case will be automatically revived at the end of the mediation process. If the case has already been given a hearing date, that date will go ahead (see para 7.4.1).

---

[4]   Available on the Courts Service website at www.justice.gov.uk/forms/hmcts.

7.6.3   Other matters

Whether or not the outcome of the mediation has been successful, the parties will be asked to complete a customer feedback form.

7.7   MEDIATION – FREQUENTLY ASKED QUESTIONS

Can I be forced to go to mediation against my wishes?	No – but bear in mind if you refuse to try and settle and the hearing judge considers you have behaved unreasonably you may be ordered to pay costs (see Chapter 9, para 9.3).
I have a really good case and I do not want to settle for less than I am entitled to – must I accept less just to reach a settlement?	No – the mediation process is not meant to be a way of making parties accept less than their legal entitlement
I want to use my lawyer to represent me at the mediation appointment – is that allowed?	Yes
Is mediation cheaper than going to a small claims hearing?	A claimant who takes the mediation route saves the hearing fee, but if the case is won at a hearing then the other side may be ordered to pay this expense by the judge. A mediation by telephone will be less time consuming than attending a hearing in person before the district judge and there will be no travel and parking expenses. Claims by the Courts Service that the mediation process is free are not the full picture as the court fees paid to start the court case and the allocation fee are not refunded if the mediation is successful
Is mediation faster than going to a judge's hearing?	It depends – a mediation will take place within 6 weeks of referral to mediation. A hearing before a judge is likely to take place more than 6 weeks in the future. If the case is put on hold for the mediation to take place and the mediation fails, this holds up the whole process by 6 weeks
What do other litigants say about mediation?	They are overwhelmingly positive about the process. Customer feedback forms show that over 90% of participants praise the professional and helpful approach of the mediators and express happiness with the outcome. They are happy with the information provided about the mediation process by the courts. For parties who do not want to go to a hearing, the advantages of sorting the case out by telephone are very attractive

What are the chances of the mediation being successful?	Of the cases which actually go to a mediation, on average about 70% result in a settlement. This figure does not include cases which are referred to mediation and where no mediation takes place. It is important to note that the parties who engage in mediation are, by definition, willing to settle
I am acting for myself and will do so at a mediation appointment. Will I be at a disadvantage if the other side is supported by a lawyer?	You may well be. However, this also applies if you go to a judge's hearing. Judges and mediators alike will be sensitive to you feeling at a disadvantage

7.8   FINDING A CIVIL MEDIATION PROVIDER OUTSIDE THE COURT SYSTEM

The parties to a small claims case might wish to pay a private mediator to help them reach a settlement. For cases of higher value and where there is likely to be a repeat of similar claims (e.g. if the parties regularly do business with each other), this may be a sensible alternative to court action. There is an online directory of mediation providers at the Ministry of Justice website.[5]

7.9   THE PAST AND FUTURE OF SMALL CLAIMS MEDIATION

In order to prepare this chapter, we have spoken to mediators, courts' staff, district judges and customers. We have been impressed by the enthusiasm and dedication of the mediators who are encouraged and supported in their work by the high degree of customer satisfaction in the feedback information. There is broad support for the scheme amongst the judges. The scheme has been fully operational since 2009. Over the past 5 years, more administrative support has been provided to enable mediators to spend more time mediating. The results have been encouraging. Since 2009, approximately 11,800 users of the small claims mediation service have given their views about the service in a survey.

The vast majority of respondents to the survey (over 90%) said that they would use the small claims mediation service again. This figure has remained the same for the last 3 years. Even about 85% of those whose cases did not settle said that they would be prepared to use the small claims mediation service again; only 5% said that they would not use the service again, and 9% indicated 'Don't know'.

---

[5]   www.civilmediation.justice.gov.uk.

Prior to the introduction of the CPR in 1998, claims of limited financial value were dealt with by a process termed 'arbitration'. This was a simple procedure presided over by the district judge and involved an informal hearing with only a very limited right of appeal. This historic procedure was not a true arbitration and was not consensual. This procedure thrived at a time when there were no allocation questionnaires and hearing fees. CPR Part 27 incorporated the best bits of this arbitration procedure but in the last decade the small claims track has become burdened by so many reforms and improvements that it increasingly resembles the fast track procedure. The most significant steps in this direction have been the introduction of the appeals process, the introduction of directions questionnaires and the imposition of hearing fees. The introduction of the mediation process in 2005 heralded a move back to simplicity for at least some of these cases of relatively small value.

It is clear that not all cases are suitable for mediation but of those which are selected, often self-selected by the parties, customer feedback indicates a high level of satisfaction. If parties feel 'short changed' by their case being diverted to a mediator and them not seeing a judge, then it appears that this is more than balanced by the satisfaction gained by not having to come to a court for a court hearing, which can be stressful and where the outcome will not be certain.[6]

There is only circumstantial evidence at this stage as to whether the mediation process will have the result of significantly reducing the time spent by district judges presiding over small claims hearings. It is well known that parties who are willing to settle often do so at the door of the court anyway. The process of small claims mediation may offer the customers satisfaction but, so far, only scratches the surface in comparison to the number of small claims hearings.[7] It is to be hoped that this scheme will thrive. Parties should be encouraged to settle and this scheme does just that. Provided that reference to this scheme remains by consent, parties are not so much being deprived of access to a judge as being given access to another option to resolve their case.

---

[6] Satisfaction rates consistently run at approximately 95%, a rate which drops only to 86% when asking only those whose cases did *not* settle.

[7] The number of cases allocated to the small claims track during the years 2009 to 2012 varied between about 93,000 and 75,000 annually.

Part 3

Hearings

Chapter 8

Steps between Allocation and the Hearing, and Checklist for Preparation for the Hearing

8.1 INTRODUCTION

This chapter assumes that mediation has not been attempted or has not resulted in agreement and that any attempt between the parties to settle has failed.

The district judge will now set out the exact steps each side must take to prepare the case for a hearing. The objective is to get the case to a hearing with the minimum of fuss and expense, and to ensure that both sides have prior warning of the details of the other side's case so there are no surprises at the final hearing.

Each party will each receive a notice which sets out:

- the fact that the case has been allocated to the small claims track;
- the date and place of the hearing;
- any directions which the parties must follow;
- the time estimate for the hearing;
- information about payment of the hearing fee (payable by the claimant only).

The court will give the parties at least 21 days' notice of the date of the hearing unless they agree to accept shorter notice (CPR rule 27.4(2)(a)).

Basics

- The district judge will give standard directions in a range of different types of cases but may give special directions
- In some cases there will be a preliminary appointment
- The court will give both sides at least 3 weeks' notice of the date of the hearing of the case
- Both parties must send copies of their documents to the other side, usually 14 days before the hearing
- The district judge may require a party to provide further information at any time but the parties themselves are not allowed to serve Part 18 requests (see Chapter 5, para 5.12)

8.2   STANDARD DIRECTIONS

PD 27 sets out the standard directions in a small claims case plus standard directions for four of the most usual types of small claims disputes. The district judge may also order 'special directions' which are in addition to or instead of the standard directions:

- FORM A – the standard directions.
- FORM B – claims arising out of road accidents.
- FORM C – claims arising out of building disputes, vehicle repairs and similar contractual claims.
- FORM D – tenants' claims for the return of deposits; landlords' claims for damage caused.
- FORM E – holiday and wedding claims.
- FORM F – some special directions.

See the overview table (Table 8.1).

Every case is reviewed by the district judge at the time of allocation and, where appropriate, directions will be tailored to the needs of the particular case.

The basic standard directions are (Appendix A to PD 27):

- Fourteen days before the hearing (or on such other date as the court directs), send copies of documents that are to be relied on to the other side.
- Original documents are to be brought to the hearing.

- The court must be informed immediately if the case is settled by agreement before the hearing date.
- The parties are told the date of the hearing and the time allowed by the court.

8.3   FINAL DECISION ABOUT THE HEARING VENUE

> See Chapter 5, para 5.7 for the rules about cases being sent from one court to another on the filing of a defence

8.3.1   Transfer by court order

The district judge has discretion to decide where a case should be managed or heard, irrespective of the automatic transfer rules. For example, a party who is disgruntled with where the case is going to be heard due to the operation of the preferred court provisions (as explained at Chapter 2, para 2.3.17) can apply to have the case transferred to another court. The parties may apply by agreement to have the case transferred by consent to another court, possibly a court part way between the two of them.

For the preparation of the application, follow the guidelines about applications generally (see Chapter 5, para 5.4). The district judge may feel able to make the order by consent or upon the application of one party without a hearing.

The matters which will be taken into account by the district judge in deciding in which court the case will be heard include:

- the financial value of the claim and the amount in dispute;
- whether it would be more convenient or fair for hearings (including the trial) to be held in some other court;
- the facilities available at the court where the claim is being dealt with and whether they may be inadequate because of any disabilities of a party or potential witness (CPR rule 30.3).

In making an order to transfer a case to another court the district judge will also have the overriding objective in mind including dealing with the case in a manner which is proportionate to the amount of money involved and the financial position of each party (CPR rule 1.1(2)); and giving directions to ensure that the trial of the case proceeds quickly and efficiently (rule 1.4(1)).

Table 8.1   Overview of preparation directions in small claims cases (taken from PD 27)

	All cases	*Road traffic*	*Building disputes, vehicle repairs and similar contractual claims*	*Disputes between landlords and tenants about damage caused and deposits*	*Holiday and wedding claims*
	Form A	Form B	Form C	Form D	Form E
Documents	Will include any: • letters • contracts • notes • photographs • witness statements	May include: • experts' reports • medical evidence • witness statements • invoices and estimates for repairs • documents which relate to other losses, such as loss of earnings • sketch plans and photographs	May include: • experts' reports • the contract • witness statements • experts' reports • invoices for work done or goods • photographs • estimates of work to be done	May include: • tenancy agreement and any inventory • rent book/evidence of rent payments • photographs • witness statements • invoices or estimates for work or goods	May include: • any written contract, brochure or booking form • photographs • documents showing payments made • witness statements • letters
When documents are to be sent to the other side	[14 days] before the hearing	[14 days] before the hearing	[14 days] before the hearing	[14 days] before the hearing	[14 days] before the hearing
Bring original documents to the hearing?	Yes	Yes	Yes	Yes	Yes

Parties to try and agree the cost of repairs and other losses subject to blame being decided at the hearing	Party who complains to provide a list of complaints [14 days] before the hearing	Parties to try and agree the cost of repairs/ replacements and other losses subject to the court's decision about any other issue in the case	Any party wanting to rely on video evidence to tell the court in advance (because of equipment)
	A breakdown of the cost of remedial work must be filed at court	Party who complains to provide a list of complaints plus the cost of repair/replacement [14 days] before the hearing	
Signed witness statements to be prepared (including witnesses who will not attend the hearing)	Signed witness statements to be prepared (including witnesses who will not attend the hearing)	Signed witness statements to be prepared (including witnesses who will not attend the hearing)	Signed witness statements to be prepared (including witnesses who will not attend the hearing)

Table 8.1   Overview of preparation directions in small claims cases (taken from PD 27) (*continued*)

	All cases	Road traffic	Building disputes, vehicle repairs and similar contractual claims	Disputes between landlords and tenants about damage caused and deposits	Holiday and wedding claims
	Form A	Form B	Form C	Form D	Form E
		• Parties invited to prepare a sketch plan and photographs • Court may disregard evidence which is not served in advance of the hearing	• Parties invited to produce photographs of the work in question • Court may disregard evidence which is not served in advance of the hearing	• Parties invited to produce photographs of the condition of the property • Court may disregard evidence which is not served in advance of the hearing	• Court may disregard evidence which is not served in advance of the hearing and may disregard video evidence if not warned about it in advance
The court must be informed immediately if the case is settled by agreement before the hearing date	Yes	Yes	Yes	Yes	Yes

Once an order for transfer has been made, an application to set aside that order is to the same court which made the order (PD 30, para 6.1) – contrast the situation where the transfer is to the preferred or other local court (see above), in which case the application must be made to that court.

The best way to ensure that a case is heard in a suitable location is for the parties to co-operate and agree which is the best court for their particular case to be heard in. Although the district judge is not bound by the recommendation of the parties, their views will certainly be taken fully into account.

8.3.2 Last-minute change of venue by the court

County courts are organised into local 'groups' and the court staff who organise hearings (listing managers) co-operate with each other and with their local district judges to make the best use of court space and judicial time. It is therefore possible that any case may be transferred from one hearing centre to another nearby in the same 'group' for the hearing. The court should warn the parties well in advance that there is to be a change in venue and the parties should feel free to ask the court for an explanation if this happens. Reasons for such a transfer may be:

- to give the parties an earlier hearing date;
- to make use of specific facilities needed for the case (e.g. video/DVD equipment);
- to provide specific facilities for disabled parties or witnesses.

8.4 WHAT DOCUMENTS ARE NEEDED FOR THE CASE?

The definition of 'documents' in a small claims case is wide and includes contract documents, letters, photographs and witness statements plus recordings including video recordings, for example CCTV footage, mobile phone recordings including videos taken on mobile phones. The directions in any particular case will set out what documents should usually be included (see Table 8.1).

The formal rules about disclosure do not apply to cases allocated to the small claims track – no list of documents is required (CPR rules 31.1(2) and 27.2(1)(b)). The standard direction is that copies of documents must be sent to the other side at least 14 days before the hearing, although a different time may be specified. The parties do not have to prepare a list of documents, but are required to send to the opposite party copies of documents that they intend to rely upon at the hearing.

One reason frequently given for disregarding this direction is that 'they have the documents anyway, so I didn't send them again'. This is a perverse interpretation of the direction, which requires the documents to be sent again, even if they have been sent to the other side before the court case started.

There is no point in withholding documents and producing them for the first time at the hearing. The element of surprise will not impress the district judge. Litigants who are ambushed by the other side producing documents at the final hearing should consider asking for an adjournment (see Chapter 10, para 10.6.3).

Documents which should be *excluded* from the papers sent to the court are:

- those which are not relevant to the dispute; and
- without prejudice letters: namely, letters which include offers to settle or make an admission with view to settlement (these letters should be headed 'without prejudice').

In court terminology, documents and/or any witness statements which have been collected and then stapled or otherwise bound together are known as the 'bundle'. There will be two bundles – one prepared by each side. This may result in duplication, but that does not matter. The most important thing is that all the documents should have been seen by both sides before the hearing and that all the documents are available for the district judge at the hearing.

It makes sense to keep a record of the documents sent, and this may be done by preparing a schedule. Whether or not a copy of that schedule is sent to the opposite party is purely a matter of choice. The obvious advantage of sending a schedule is that the other party can check that the copies are complete and will not be able to complain at the hearing that vital documents are missing.

Make sure that the copies are legible, and that the reverse of a document is copied especially if it includes any terms and conditions; the district judge is bound to want to see the terms and conditions. It is helpful to put the documents in date order and to add page numbering.

The standard directions require the documents to be sent to the court before the hearing. A direction to bring original documents to the hearing is made in all cases.

If a video or sound recording is to be used at the hearing make sure that the court knows in advance – this will ensure that equipment is available to show the video/DVD or to give the court staff a chance to transfer the case to a court with suitable equipment if necessary. It would be unwise to rely upon the court to have a computer available with suitable software to play a particular video or audio clip, so parties should bring a suitable computer to court to play any electronic media at the hearing.

8.5 DOCUMENTS FOR A SMALL CLAIMS HEARING – FREQUENTLY ASKED QUESTIONS

Do I need to prepare a formal list of documents in the form required by CPR Part 31?	No
The other side has already seen my documents before the case started – do I still need to send copies to them 14 days before the hearing?	Yes; not only is this because this is required by the rules but also to make doubly sure that the other side knows which documents a party wishes to rely on
What happens if I send copies to the other side in advance and at a later date I get extra papers which I want to use at the hearing?	You must send them to the other side and to the court at once – you may not be able to rely on them at the hearing otherwise
Shall I make an extra copy of my documents for use by the district judge at the hearing?	Yes
Should I bring the original documents to court?	Yes
Would it help the district judge at the hearing if my documents were in date order and given page numbers?	Yes
Should documents marked 'without prejudice' be shown to the judge and included in the bundle?	No – not until after the district judge has given the judgment

8.6 WITNESS STATEMENTS (NON-EXPERTS)

A witness is anyone who can help the court with the evidence, which includes the parties themselves. There are two types of witnesses, namely:

(1) expert witnesses (see para 8.8);
(2) non-expert or 'lay witnesses', sometimes called 'witnesses as to fact'.

This paragraph deals with lay witnesses, which includes the parties themselves.

The general rule is that any fact which needs to be proved by the evidence of a witness at a trial (including a small claims hearing) is given orally (CPR rule 32.2). Most litigants write down their evidence before coming to court, and the common use of computers means that it is rarely a burden for a party to produce a typed statement in advance of the hearing.

If a witness sets out evidence in writing before the hearing and sends it to the other side, this has a number of benefits including:

- all the relevant evidence is brought to the attention of the court and nothing is missed out due to courtroom nerves;
- the other side is not taken by surprise by the witness's evidence (which can result in an adjournment);
- reducing the length of the hearing.

The basic 'standard' directions, which are routinely used in small claims cases, usually suggest that witness statements can be used (see Table 8.1). Only if the district judge makes an order that witness statements must be served are they obligatory. If the court has not ordered the service of witness statements, then there is nothing to prevent either party from serving a witness statement.

A well prepared witness statement will:

- be in the witness's own words;
- describe events in date order, with the earliest events described first;
- refer to relevant documents (if possible by the page number in the bundle);
- be set out in short numbered paragraphs;
- be legible (typed if possible).

Sample witness statements can be found at Chapter 6, para 6.7.5, precedents V and W.

Note

The person who calls the witness (whether by summons or otherwise) is responsible for the payment of any expenses and loss of earnings for the witness. The party who wins may recover these sums for expenses from the loser in due course, up to a limit of £90 per day for loss of earnings or loss of leave plus reasonable travel expenses

---

8.7 WITNESS SUMMONS

The rules about issuing a summons which requires a witness to attend court are set out in CPR Part 34.

If a witness is unwilling to attend court, or requires a witness summons to compel attendance in order to get time off work, then the party who wants to call him or her as a witness can issue a witness summons.

Before issuing the summons, consider if the size of the claim and the importance of the matter to the parties justifies compelling a witness to attend court – consider carefully if the use of a witness summons is proportionate to the issues in the case with reference to the amount of money involved and the importance of the matter (CPR rule 1.1(2)(c)).

The summons is issued on Form N20[1] and a fee is payable. The summons must be served no less than 7 days before the hearing. The permission of the district judge is needed to issue a witness summons less than 7 days before the hearing. The summons can be served by the court or by the party issuing it.

At the time of service, the witness must be offered a sum reasonably sufficient to cover his or her expenses for travelling to and from court, and compensation for loss of his or her time. The rates to be offered are equivalent to those offered in the Crown Court. To establish the amount, contact the Crown Court for the details of the current rates. The person in receipt of the summons can apply for the summons to be set aside.

8.8 EXPERT WITNESS EVIDENCE

Expert evidence shall be restricted to that which is reasonably required to resolve the proceedings (CPR rule 35.1).

No expert may give evidence, whether written or oral, at a hearing without the permission of the court (CPR rule 27.5).

Basics

- The district judge has a duty to restrict expert evidence
- The expert has an overriding duty to help the court
- No party can use the written or oral services of an expert without the permission of the court
- If allowed, expert evidence in small claims cases is usually by written report rather than by personal attendance

---

The district judge will only allow an expert in a small claims case if it is necessary. Unless express permission is given to use expert evidence, it cannot be used. If an expert is allowed, the court will want the expert to be jointly instructed by both sides if possible. The duty of the expert is to assist the court

---

[1] Available on the Courts Service website, www.justice.gov.uk/courts/procedure-rules/civil/forms.

impartially and not to promote the interests of one of the parties. The district judge will identify in advance the specialty of the expert which can be used.

A disincentive for the use of experts is expense. Not only will the expense of an expert often be out of proportion to the amount involved, but the winner cannot recover more than £750 towards the costs of instructing an expert.

The rules recognise that in some cases an expert may be needed and the district judge will often allow an expert to be called in disputes about:

- building works;
- vehicle repairs;
- hardware and software faults in computers.

A *medical report* must be attached to the particulars of the case in claims involving personal injury, but only where the claimant relies on medical evidence (PD 16, para 4.3). However, if the injuries are minor and if the claimant does not rely on any future pain and suffering, as may well be the case in a small claims case, then a medical report may not be needed. In a small claims case, the usual format of a medical report is an informal general practitioner's letter.

8.8.1   Single joint experts

The joint instruction of an expert can be tricky. CPR rule 35.8 sets out the ways in which the district judge can control the instructions to a joint single expert in particular by directing who should pay the expert's fees and saying when (and how) the expert can inspect the subject matter in dispute and carry out any tests. Before a single joint expert is instructed the district judge can direct the maximum fee for the expert to charge and make a direction that this money be paid into court in advance by the parties (rule 35.8(4)). The usual rule is that the parties are both liable to pay the fees of a single joint expert (rule 35.8(5)).

8.8.2   What does an expert need to know about preparing a report for a small claims hearing?

For a small claims case, the essential rules that apply are that:

- the overriding duty of the expert is to the court and to help the court on matters within his or her expertise (CPR rule 35.3);
- the district judge can give directions on how to instruct a joint expert (CPR rule 35.7);

- the court has a power to restrict expert evidence (CPR rule 35.4);
- the winner can recover up to £750 for the cost of an expert's report.

The more technical rules about the preparation of experts' reports, which apply in fast track and multi track cases do not apply to small claims cases. However, in addition to the essential rules which apply (see above), there are common-sense and practical matters to be borne in mind when instructing an expert in a small claims case.

For a small claims case the district judge will take a practical and proportionate approach to an expert's report (CPR rule 1.1(2)). The report may be acceptable even if it does not fully comply with the formal requirements usually insisted upon in cases allocated to the fast track and multi track.

In every case the expert should:

- know that the overriding duty of the expert is to the court (CPR rule 35.3);
- understand that the report should not promote the views of one party but inform the court objectively – the purpose of the report is to inform and help the district judge;
- keep any technical language to a minimum;
- make sure he or she fully understands exactly what points should be covered in the report;
- be clear about the deadline for preparing the report and promise to meet it;
- be aware that he or she is unlikely to be given permission to give personal evidence at the hearing, so the written report should be as complete as possible;
- know in advance who is paying for the report (he or she can demand payment before releasing the report);
- summarise his or her experience or qualifications.

The parties are jointly and severally responsible for paying the fees of the single joint expert, which means that the expert can look to either party for the full fee or for contributions from both but can only recover the full cost once. Joint experts usually require the fee to be paid by the parties equally.

The district judge has the power to give directions as to who should pay for the report and may order that a sum of money be paid into court to cover the fees (CPR rule 35.8(4)).

Cross-references

- Expert fees are discussed in Chapter 9, para 9.2.3 (costs)
- Some of the rules applicable to experts are excluded in small claims cases (Chapter 5, para 5.12)
- See also Chapter 10, para 10.9 (evidence at the final hearing)

8.9   LISTS OF DISPUTED ITEMS (OR LIST OF COMPLAINTS)

In cases involving a number of disputed items the district judge will sometimes suggest that the parties prepare a schedule or list of items in dispute. These lists are very useful and, if the facts justify their use, they should be considered by the parties, even if not suggested or ordered by the court.

The advantages of lists of disputed items are:

- all the information is summarised in point form before the hearing;
- they are a convenient way for the parties and the district judge to comment on the individual points;
- they often highlight whether any items are agreed, thus saving time at the hearing.

An example of such a schedule (sometimes called a 'Scott Schedule', after those commonly used in building dispute claims) can be found at Chapter 6, para 6.7.5, precedent Z.

8.10   PHOTOGRAPHS AND SKETCH PLANS

The standard directions in road traffic cases and those involving repairs to vehicles and buildings suggest that photographs may be included in the documents. Under the no costs rule, the cost of the photographs will not be recovered from the loser, but photographs are so useful in many types of case the expense should not be spared. The photographs should be of the scene of a road traffic accident and the damage to the vehicles. In this digital age, the district judge might, quite reasonably, ask a witness producing photographs to confirm at the hearing that the photographs have not been manipulated or altered on a computer.

A sketch plan of the scene of a traffic accident may also be helpful. See Chapter 6, para 6.7.4, prededent P.

The cost of an expert to prepare a plan is unlikely to be justified and permission must be sought before such an expert is instructed (see para 8.8). Every effort must be made to produce photographs and plans which relate to the layout of the road at the time of the accident. Satellite images of road layouts which can be found on the internet have the disadvantage of not being dated but can be useful.

8.11 INFORM THE COURT IF THE CASE IS SETTLED BEFORE THE HEARING

This applies in all cases. Court timetables are very busy and if the hearing slot can be vacated, this may release time for the district judge to do other work. If the hearing can be vacated and the court is notified in writing more than 7 days before the hearing, the hearing fee will be refunded in full (see Appendix 1).

8.12 TIME ESTIMATE

The notice of allocation informs the parties what time estimate has been placed on the case by the district judge. If either of the parties thinks that the estimate is too short, they should inform the court in writing at once.

It is not always easy to give an accurate time estimate for the hearing of a case, even with a properly completed directions questionnaire to assist. The district judge uses experience combined with guesswork and the information on the questionnaire to determine how much time must be set aside to hear the case.

However, as a guide, district judges may give time estimates as follows:

Time estimate	Type of case
½ to 1½ hours	Cases which appear straightforward and where there is to be no expert evidence
1 to 1½ hours	Road traffic accidents – although these cases can take longer if both liability and quantum are at issue
2 to 2½ hours	Apparently complex cases, for example building disputes and cases involving expert evidence or a number of lay witnesses

These time estimates are a rough guide only, time estimates will depend on the nature of each case – for example cases take longer if there are more than one or two witnesses on each side, if there are more than about a dozen documents to consult and if either party needs an interpreter.

8.13 SPECIAL DIRECTIONS

Appendix C to PD 27 contains a battery of special directions that the district judge can use in addition to, or instead of, the standard directions. These include:

- requiring either party to clarify aspects of their case;
- requiring the parties to instruct a joint expert (see para 8.8);
- making arrangements for a site inspection;
- ordering that the item in dispute be brought to court for the hearing.

The possible directions are not limited to those in the practice direction and the district judge will make whatever directions are sensibly needed to bring the case to a hearing.

The district judge usually gives special directions and sets a date for the final hearing but may require that the matter is referred back in up to 28 days for further directions (CPR rule 27.4(1)(c)). If the district judge needs to know more about the case before giving directions or giving a time estimate, he or she may order a party to send their documents or witness statements to the court before a hearing date is set. The court may, of its own initiative, order a party to provide further information if it considers it appropriate to do so (rule 27.2(3)).

8.14 PRELIMINARY HEARING

The district judge will decide whether to list the matter for a preliminary hearing, but only if:

- special directions are needed; and
- it is necessary for the parties to attend court to understand how to comply with the special directions; or
- to dispose of the claim because one side has no real prospect of success or to strike out a hopeless claim or defence.

The court must 'have regard to the desirability of limiting the expense to the parties of attending court' (CPR rule 27.6(2)), and for this reason preliminary hearings are not the norm.

Preliminary hearings are not a formality. The parties must make sure that they are ready to deal with points arising. The parties cannot simply write to the court and say that they have agreed between themselves not to attend. Indeed, some district judges will actively consider striking out the claim or defence of any party who chooses not to attend a preliminary hearing.

The notice of the preliminary hearing will give the reason for the hearing. If either side does not understand the reason for the preliminary hearing, they should write to the court at once for clarification. The purpose of the hearing may be defeated if its purpose is obscure.

At the preliminary hearing the district judge may strike out any claim, defence or counterclaim and may give directions as to how the case will progress. After the preliminary hearing, both sides will be given at least 21 days' notice of the date for the final hearing and written confirmation of the directions, including the time allowed for the hearing (CPR rule 27.6).

8.15   APPLICATIONS FOR DIRECTIONS BY THE PARTIES

In a small claims case there should rarely be the need to apply to the court for directions. The standard directions given at allocation or at the preliminary hearing will usually cover all the steps reasonably needed to prepare the case for a hearing. Many of the procedural devices which are used in cases allocated to the fast track and multi track and which often give rise to pre-hearing applications are excluded in the small claims track. This includes applications for further information and applications concerning disclosure and inspection (see Chapter 5, para 5.12).

There could be some matters of housekeeping which need tidying up in a small claims case. For example:

- to set aside or vary any order or direction made by the district judge at the allocation stage or without a hearing;
- to change the venue of the hearing;
- to request permission to use expert evidence;
- an application for the case to be heard in private;
- an application to change a hearing date.

If any application is necessary, it should be issued as soon as possible after allocation. Chapter 5, para 5.4 deals with rules about applications. Note that, because of the no costs rule, any legal fees incurred in connection with the application will not be recoverable (see Chapter 9).

8.16 CHECKLIST FOR PREPARING FOR A SMALL CLAIMS HEARING

Step 1   Note the date and time
Step 2   Evaluate and consider settlement
Step 3   Prepare and serve copy documents (at least 14 days before the hearing)
Step 4   Prepare and serve witness statements (at least 14 days before the hearing)
Step 5   Prepare a list of items in dispute (if needed or ordered)
Step 6   Obtain expert evidence (but only if permission has been given)
Step 7   Decide whether to attend the hearing (CPR rule 27.9(1)) (at least one week before the hearing)
Step 8   Pay the hearing fee

8.16.1 Note the date and time (step 1)

Practitioners must tell their own client and any witnesses of the hearing date. If the date is not convenient for the parties or any witness, the other side and the court must be told at once that another date is needed. It is far better for the parties to co-operate with each other and agree in principle for the date to be changed – if the parties do not agree on an adjournment, then a formal application must be made on notice for the date to be changed. If the parties agree to the date being changed, then the application will be by consent.

Check the directions and note the date before the hearing when documents are to be sent to the other side (usually 2 weeks before the hearing).

8.16.2 Evaluate and consider settlement (step 2)

The strengths and weaknesses of a case must be considered carefully in response to any defence or counterclaim. The evaluation must be repeated at this stage, as well as when the other side have provided their documents and any witness statements.

Litigants in person can get legal advice from solicitors and Citizens Advice Bureaux. Even if they do not get legal advice, they should discuss the case with a friend who, even though not legally qualified, may be able to give an 'objective view' of the case. Members of motoring organisations and other clubs may be entitled to advice on consumer or other legal problems, free of charge or upon payment of a modest fee. Many house insurance policies and car insurance policies include legal advice as part of the package.

At all stages, both parties should actively consider settlement.

Correspondence which is marked 'without prejudice' and which is written with the intention of trying to reach a settlement cannot be shown to the district judge until after judgment has been given. Therefore, parties can safely write and offer to settle for less than the full amount claimed or offer to make a payment to settle without the fear that the letter will be shown to the district judge as a sign of weakness.

In some types of case, the directions specifically tell the parties to agree aspects of the claim. In motor claims, the actual cost of repairs can usually be agreed, subject to blame. In cases involving repairs to buildings, including disputes with landlords about deposits, the parties should do their best to agree the cost of works; this will of course be subject to blame.

Make any final checks on the legal position and, if the law is unusual or involves cases or statutory references, make copies of the texts and documents which will be used at the hearing to support the case. It is good practice, even if not required by the court, to send copies to the other side in advance of the hearing. Make an additional copy for the use of the district judge at the hearing.

8.16.3 Prepare and serve copy documents (at least 14 days before the hearing) (step 3)

See para 8.4

8.16.4 Prepare and serve witness statements (at least 14 days before the hearing) (step 4)

See para 8.6

8.16.5   Prepare a list of items in dispute (if needed or ordered) (step 5)

See para 8.9

8.16.6   Obtain expert evidence (but only if permission has been given) (step 6)

See para 8.8

8.16.7   Decide whether to attend the hearing (CPR rule 27.9(1)) (at least one week before the hearing) (step 7)

CPR rule 27.9 concerns the non-attendance of parties at a final hearing and states as follows:

Non-attendance of parties at a final hearing
27.9
(1)   If a party who does not attend a final hearing—

(a)   has given written notice to the court and the other party at least 7 days before the hearing date that he will not attend;

(b)   has served on the other party at least 7 days before the hearing date any other documents which he has filed with the court; and

(c)   has, in his written notice, requested the court to decide the claim in his absence and has confirmed his compliance with paragraphs (a) and (b) above,

the court will take into account that party's statement of case and any other documents he has filed and served when it decides the claim.

Note that to use this procedure, a party must inform the other side and the court at least 7 days before the hearing. After the hearing, the district judge will set out the reasons for the decision in writing and these will be sent to both parties by the court (PD 27, para 5.4) (see Chapter 10, para 10.11).

If a party does not intend to attend the hearing, he or she should notify the court *and* the other side in advance, failing which the court may disregard his or her evidence and strike out his or her case (CPR rule 27.9(2), (3) and (4)). See also the provision about awards of costs for unreasonable behaviour (Chapter 9, para 9.3.3. In other words, failure to attend *without prior notice* is likely to give rise to a poor outcome.

8.16.8 Pay the hearing fee (step 8)

The hearing fee is payable upon demand, which will be made within 14 days after the court notifies the parties of a hearing date. In a small claims case this is when the court sends out the allocation directions. This fee is payable on a sliding scale up to a hefty £325 for small claims cases. The claim can be struck out if this fee is not paid. As an incentive to settle, however, this fee will be refunded in full if the court receives notice in writing at least 7 days before the hearing date that the case is settled or discontinued.[2]

8.17 VISITING THE COURT BEFORE THE HEARING DATE

Small claims hearings are held in public, and a litigant who wants to get a flavour of what his or her day in court may be like may wish to visit the court beforehand and watch other cases. The courts do not deal with small claims cases every day, so contact the court in advance to find out when there is a small claims list. On arrival, tell the usher that you want to watch some cases. Since people rarely ask to watch other people's cases, your request is likely to be treated as a novelty and the usher is likely to tell the district judge in advance that you want to sit in. When watching someone else's case, bear in mind that, given the wide range of procedures adopted by different judges and for different cases, the procedure you observe may not be replicated in your own hearing. Even if you do not watch a case, it is worthwhile attending the actual court building in advance of your big day – just to check that you know how to get there and to plan your journey so that you arrive on time.

---

[2] Small claims cases get special treatment here because cases allocated to the fast track or above only get a full refund if a case settles 28 days before the final hearing.

Chapter 9

The No Costs Rule

The no costs rule at a glance

The basic principle is that in small claims cases legal costs are not recovered by the winner

The rules do, however, allow for the winner to be reimbursed for routine expenses namely:

- court fees paid (commencement fee/allocation fees/hearing fees)
- the fixed costs shown on the claim form, if a solicitor issued the proceedings, or up to £260 if it is an injunction case
- expert fees up to £750
- expenses incurred by the party and witnesses, including the reasonable cost of staying away from home for attending the hearing
- loss of earnings for the parties and any witnesses (up to £90 per day)
- any costs awarded are assessed by the summary procedure

Any award for costs is discretionary, and the district judge has the final say on whether costs and expenses are allowed in any particular case. Further sums may be allowed if the district judge comes to the conclusion that a party has behaved 'unreasonably'

The no costs rule also covers appeals against decisions made on the small claims track (CPR rule 27.14(2))

9.1   THE NO COSTS RULE – BASICS

9.1.1   Definition of costs

The term 'costs' means fees, charges, disbursements and expenses, including those paid to a solicitor, barrister or lay representative.

9.1.2 The rule

CPR rule 27.14[1] sets out the costs rules in small claims cases:

(2) The court may not order a party to pay a sum to another party in respect of that other party's costs, fees and expenses, including those relating to an appeal, except—

    (a) the fixed costs attributable to issuing the claim which—

        (i) are payable under Part 45; or

        (ii) would be payable under Part 45 if that Part applied to the claim.

    (b) in proceedings which included a claim for an injunction or an order for specific performance a sum not exceeding the amount specified in the relevant practice direction for legal advice and assistance relating to that claim;

    (c) any court fees paid by that other party;

    (d) expenses which a party or witness has reasonably incurred in travelling to and from a hearing or in staying away from home for the purposes of attending a hearing;

    (e) a sum not exceeding the amount specified in the relevant practice direction [£90] for any loss of earnings or loss of leave by a party or witness due to attending a hearing or to staying away from home for the purpose of attending a hearing;

    (f) a sum not exceeding the amount specified in the relevant practice direction [£750] for an expert's fees;

    (g) such further costs as the court may assess by the summary procedure and order to be paid by a party who has behaved unreasonably;

    (h) the Stage 1 and, where relevant, the Stage 2 fixed costs in rule 45.29 where—

        (i) the claim was within the scope of the Pre-Action Protocol for Low Value Personal Injury Claims in Road Traffic Accidents ('the RTA Protocol');

        (ii) the claimant reasonably believed that the claim was valued at more than the small claims track limit in accordance with paragraph 4.1(4) of the RTA Protocol; and

        (iii) the defendant admitted liability under the process set out in the RTA Protocol; but

        (iv) the defendant did not pay those Stage 1 and, where relevant, Stage 2 fixed costs[2] (rule 27.14(2));

    (i) in an appeal, the cost of any approved transcript reasonably incurred.

---

[1]   The figures in square brackets are specified by PD 27, para 7(3).

[2]   Appendix 7 sets out a very brief commentary on CPR rule 27.14(2)(h), which concerns low value personal injury claims.

9.1.3 Electing to use the small claims track by agreement

If the parties agree (or elect) to use the small claims track, then the case will be treated as a small claims case in all respects including on the issue of costs.

9.1.4 Quantifying the costs

If any costs in small claims cases are awarded for unreasonable conduct, they will be assessed at the hearing by the summary procedure (CPR rule 27.14(2)(g)).

See para 9.6 for more about the summary procedure. Detailed assessment is not available.

9.1.5 Overall discretion

Subject to the general limitations on costs in a small claims case, district judges have overall discretion over costs (CPR rule 44.2) (see para 9.4 for more detail on the topic of discretion).

9.1.6 Offers of settlement and compliance with the practice direction on pre-action conduct

Parties are encouraged to try to settle their cases out of court and without a hearing and should, therefore, make offers to settle. If this is not done or if good offers to settle out of court are rejected, this can amount to unreasonable conduct (see para 9.3).

Both parties must comply with the spirit and terms of the practice direction on pre-action conduct in terms of exchanging information and considering settlement options before the start of a court action. This is discussed in detail at Chapter 1, para 1.4.5. It is clear that litigants who are unreasonable in their actions before the start of court proceedings may attract an adverse order for costs (see para 9.3).

9.2 ROUTINE AWARDS FOR COSTS

9.2.1 Court fees

A winner will, almost as a matter of routine, recover any court fee paid (CPR rule 27.14(3)) (see Appendices 1 and 2 for details of court fees).

Sometimes, if the claimant recovers less than the amount claimed in the claim form, the district judge will abate (i.e. reduce) the fee awarded. An example of abatement is that if a claimant claimed £1,750 and paid court fees of £120 but was only awarded £450, the claimant may, at the discretion of the district judge, be awarded, for example, only £50 towards the court fees paid.

9.2.2   Fixed commencement costs

CPR rule 27.14(2) states that the claimant may recover:

> (a)   the fixed costs attributable to issuing the claim which—
>   (i)   are payable under Part 45; or
>   (ii)   would be payable under Part 45 if that Part applied to the claim.

Fixed costs are only relevant where a solicitor has issued the proceedings; they are not recoverable by a litigant in person (CPR rule 45.1(1)).

Where the claim is for a specified sum, the costs are inserted in the claim form in accordance with the scale set out by the rules (see Chapter 2, para 2.3.15). The scale of costs is set out at Appendix 3.

Where the claim is not specified, the district judge will determine what issue costs are payable by the loser based on the amount awarded at the hearing. The amount awarded will be based on the scale set out at Appendix 3.

The rules do not provide for the reimbursement of any fixed costs on a counterclaim.

9.2.3   Expert fees

The parties must have permission from the district judge to use an expert at the hearing and will almost always be directed to appoint a single joint expert. The district judge will control the amount payable to the expert and who pays the costs – most usually each side will have to pay half in advance.

The district judge may award up to £750 towards the cost of employing each expert (CPR rule 27.14(2)(f) and PD 27, para 7.3(2)). The figure of £750 is meant to be a realistic sum to cover the cost of an expert in a small claims case, and the parties may have to 'shop around' to find someone who will provide the advice within budget. Rules about the engagement of experts are discussed in Chapter 8, para 8.8.

9.2.4 Witness expenses

The expense of attending court for the parties and any witnesses can be reimbursed under two headings: loss of earnings and travelling expenses.

Loss of earnings (limited to £90 per witness per day)

The district judge may award the winner and the winner's witnesses up to £90 per person for loss of earnings, plus the reasonable cost of staying away from home for the purpose of the hearing (CPR rule 27.14(2)(e) and PD 27, para 7.3(1)). The cost of staying away from home could also include, for example, the cost of a babysitter. This means that a person who has to pay someone to cover for him or her at work on the day of the hearing can recover that expense up to the stated maximum. A person who takes leave (holiday) from work to attend court can, subject to the discretion of the hearing judge, recover the lost monetary value of that leave.

The loss must be real and not illusory and is easiest to recover in the case of employed persons working on a daily or hourly rate. Self-employed persons can also recover their losses, but a distinction must be drawn between those self-employed people who lose earnings by attending court, and those who do not. For example, self-employed people working on flexible hours can usually make up for the lost time spent in court, so their earnings have not been lost at all. However, if the self-employed person can demonstrate that he or she lost the chance to earn a fee for a specific job, up to £90 of those losses will be recoverable.

Travelling expenses (limited to a reasonable amount)

The district judge may award the winner reasonable travelling expenses plus the reasonable cost of the party or a witness staying away from home for the purposes of the hearing.

The provision for payment of travelling expenses and overnight expenses, if justified, may add a hefty sum to the loser's bill – something which should have been borne in mind when considering which court a case should be heard in. If it is inevitable that one party will have to travel a considerable distance to a hearing, then the parties should consider choosing a court to hear the matter which is halfway between the claimant and the defendant (see Chapter 4, para 4.7.4).

9.2.5   Lay representatives

The limits on costs covered by this rule also apply to any fee or reward for acting on behalf of a party to the proceedings charged by a person exercising a right of audience by virtue of an order under Courts and Legal Services Act 1990, section 11 (a lay representative) (CPR rule 27.14(4)).

In small claims cases, a party can engage an unqualified lay representative for a fee to act as an advocate. Even if paid, these fees cannot usually be recovered from the loser as they are covered by the no costs rule (CPR rule 27.14(4)).

9.2.6   Injunction cases

In proceedings which included a claim for an injunction or for an order for specific performance or similar relief, a sum not exceeding £260[3] for legal advice and assistance relating to the claim may be awarded (CPR rule 27.14(2)(b) and PD 27, para 7.2).

The award will be in the discretion of the district judge, and will only be made if instructing a solicitor was, in the opinion of the district judge, justified on the facts of the particular case.

9.2.7   Costs of enforcement

The expense of enforcing a judgment is not covered by the no costs rule.

9.2.8   Costs of appeal

The costs on appeal to the circuit judge are covered by the no costs rule (CPR rule 27.14(2)). This includes not only appeals to the circuit judge but also so-called 'second' appeals to the Court of Appeal (*Ashktar v Boland* [2014] EWCA Civ 943, CA).

9.2.9   Photographs and sketch plans

In many types of case, photographs and sketch plans are of great assistance at the hearing; they are routinely suggested in the allocation directions for a variety of cases including road traffic accidents, building disputes and holiday claims. The rules do not allow the costs of plans or photographs to be recovered from the loser.

---

[3]   This figure is specified by PD 27, para 7.

However, if the district judge gives permission in advance to instruct a specialist to prepare sketch plans or take photographs, the fees up to a limit of £750 would be recoverable. For example, it may be reasonable to instruct a specialist to prepare a plan in a boundary dispute, but the court is unlikely to sanction the cost of a specialist takings photographs or drawing a plan for a small claims road traffic case.

9.2.10   Low value personal injury claims

Claims for personal injury arising out of accidents at work and road traffic claims of value between £1,000 and £25,000 are covered by specialist pre-action steps and a special costs regime. A claimant may reasonably believe that a claim is worth more than £1,000 but it is later established that the claim is worth under £1,000. In such cases, the defendant may be liable to pay the costs under 'Stage 1' or 'Stage 2' which are specified by the Pre-Action Protocol for Low Value Personal Injury Claims. The award for costs is limited to the amounts payable under the protocol and are awarded where the defendant fails to admit liability and pay the protocol fixed costs.

9.3   UNREASONABLE BEHAVIOUR

9.3.1   The rule

CPR rule 27.14(2)(g) states that the court may award:

(g)   such further costs as the courts may assess by the summary procedure and order to be paid by a party who has behaved unreasonably;

There is a two-stage process in dealing with costs based on unreasonable behaviour:

- *Stage 1*: deciding whether the behaviour has been unreasonable.
- *Stage 2*: assessing the costs for unreasonable behaviour.

9.3.2   Stage 1: What amounts to unreasonable behaviour?

District judges are used to resisting applications for costs by overenthusiastic practitioners, and are unlikely to make an award for costs unless a losing party has behaved in an exceptional way.

There is no doubt that, from time to time, awards for costs are made, but they are rarely appealed, and in such cases are not often reported. As a result of this, there is a dearth of reported cases on this topic, and those cases which are reported are of limited general application because they involve specific facts from which it is difficult to extract any universal principles.

Often, litigants are not legally represented, and only discover at the hearing that the law is against them. Not knowing the law is not generally interpreted as unreasonable behaviour.

The following sets out some categories of behaviour which district judges may decide are unreasonable:

- pulling out of a case at the last minute when there has been no change in the circumstances;
- the pursuit of a case which is both speculative and unsupportable;[4]
- making unnecessary or disproportionate applications for procedural orders;
- pressing a hopeless case with the ulterior motive of embarrassing or inconveniencing the opposite party;
- adjournments – if these are caused by one side not turning up at the hearing without a reasonable excuse then a district judge may in some cases consider this to be unreasonable behaviour and make an order for costs;
- requesting an adjournment at the last moment because the evidence to substantiate a case has not been prepared for a hearing;[5]
- making a claim which is dishonest;[6]
- ignoring a reasonable offer to settle before the hearing;[7]
- disregarding the practice direction on pre-action conduct.

In summary, whether a party has behaved in an unreasonable way is a matter of fact and degree. The behaviour must be quite serious to attract an order for costs.

Note that costs awarded under this category are not properly described as 'wasted costs' which has a special meaning (see para 9.7).

CPR Part 36 and the no costs rule

Having regard to CPR rule 27.14(3) the district judge may also consider offers of settlement (otherwise known as Part 36 offers) made before the hearing.

---

[4]   *Afzal and Others v Ford Motor Co Ltd and other appeals* [1994] 4 All ER 720, CA.

[5]   *Lacey v Melford CC* [1999] 12 CL 37.

[6]   *Bashir v Hanson CC* [1999] 12 CL 143.

[7]   *Clohessy v Homes* [2004] CL 418, Bristol CC.

What is a Part 36 offer?

A Part 36 offer is an offer made before the case goes to a final hearing which is intended to settle the claim. It is useful in cases where a defendant accepts that it has some liability to the claimant but not to the extent claimed. The facts of a Part 36 offer are kept secret from the final hearing judge until after the judge has made his or her decision; the making of a Part 36 offer therefore does not influence the judge against the party making the offer. Part 36 offers are made in writing and are made without prejudice. They can be made in money cases or in cases where money is not in issue between the parties (e.g. claims for an injunction).

CPR Part 36 and small claims cases

The basic rule is that CPR Part 36 does not apply to small claims cases but the court may make an order otherwise (rule 36.2(5)). In specific cases, therefore, and following an order of the district judge, Part 36 cost consequences can apply in small claims cases.

If a party makes a Part 36 offer which is more generous to the other side than the award made by the judge at the final hearing then, under CPR Part 36, the court may award costs in favour of the party who made the offer out of court. This is a reversal of the usual costs rule which is that usually the successful party is awarded costs.

Is rejection of a Part 36 offer unreasonable conduct?

The answer to this question is 'not automatically'. However, when considering what amounts to unreasonable behaviour, the district judge may take into account the fact of a Part 36 offer and, if it is more generous to the winner than the awards made after a full hearing, may decide that the claimant was unreasonable to press on with the case to a final hearing. Professional advocates should beware of using Part 36 offers to unduly pressurise a litigant in person to settle out of court. If the litigant feels correspondence has been unfair, he can bring this to the attention of the district judge and the relevant disciplinary body of the professional concerned.

9.3.3   Stage 2: Assessing the costs for unreasonable behaviour

The amount of the costs will be determined at the hearing (see para 9.6), and the district judge will have in mind the discretionary factors set out below.

9.4   THE COURT'S DISCRETION ON COSTS

The rules set out guidelines for judges to exercise their discretion on costs, and these rules will guide the district judge when considering how to exercise discretion on the issue of costs.

CPR rule 44.2 defines the judge's discretion on costs. The district judge will decide:

- whether costs should be awarded at all (including consideration of the conduct of the parties);
- the amount of the costs; and
- when they are to be paid.

CPR rule 44.4 emphasises that the conduct of the parties will be taken into account. Obviously, in a small claims case the unreasonable conduct of the parties has been considered in deciding if costs should be awarded at all. The degree of the misconduct and, indeed, the conduct of the winner can also be considered under this heading.

When determining the amount of costs (see para 9.6 for the procedure) the district judge will take into account the factors set out in CPR rule 44.4(3). This involves looking at whether costs are 'proportionate' to the claim and whether the costs are reasonable in amount and have been reasonably incurred.

The concept of proportionality is not simply a mathematical relationship between the amount of money in dispute and the costs awarded.

CPR rule 44.3(5) states that costs incurred are proportionate if they bear a reasonable relationship to:

(a)   the sums in issue in the proceedings;
(b)   the value of anything other than money claimed in the proceedings (e.g. an injunction);
(c)   the complexity of the litigation;
(d)   any additional work generated by the conduct of the paying party; and
(e)   any wider factors involved in the proceedings, such as reputation or public importance.

In a small claims case, this could mean that the costs awarded (if they are awarded at all) could exceed the amount involved in the dispute. The district judge will, however, be reluctant to make an excessive award for costs in a small claims case as this could offend the overriding objective, which emphasises that the court must deal with each case in a way that is proportionate to the amount of money involved, the importance of the case, the complexity of the issues and the financial position of each party (CPR rule 1.2) (see Chapter 5, para 5.2).

9.5   STANDARD BASIS AND INDEMNITY BASIS

The distinction between standard basis costs and indemnity basis costs can be very important in high value cases (i.e. those allocated to the multi track) and of significant value to the winner. In small claims cases, the difference is likely to be insignificant and a full consideration of the technical differences between indemnity and standard basis costs is not relevant to the purpose of this book. In brief, an award of indemnity costs is more generous to the winner than standard basis costs. Where costs are awarded on the small claims track, it is most likely that the district judge will simply consider the amount (the quantum) of costs on the standard basis. The district judge will consider if the costs claimed are of a reasonable amount and if they have been reasonably incurred.

9.6   PROCEDURE FOR SUMMARY ASSESSMENT

'Summary assessment' means that the district judge will put a value on the costs award at the hearing. This will involve considering the amount claimed and giving the paying party a chance to comment on the amount claimed. The small claims rules do not give the district judge the option of referring the costs for detailed assessment at a later hearing.

The party who is awarded costs must be prepared to explain the costs incurred and justify these by reference to the hourly rate, including the seniority of the fee earner and the time spent. A party who has sought legal advice but is not represented at the hearing should bring the solicitor's bill to court; the solicitor should be asked to set out in the bill the hourly rate applied and the time spent. The district judge will also consider the costs claimed relative to the amount in dispute and decide if the costs are proportionate. However, there is no automatic correlation between the amount of the award and the costs recovered, and if the work done was necessary and reasonable, the costs award may exceed the claim.

A litigant in person's costs are assessed at an hourly rate reflecting actual financial loss or, where the litigant does not prove actual financial loss, at the rate of £18 per hour.

In either event, the maximum the litigant can recover for their time spent is two-thirds of the amount they would have been allowed if legally represented. Companies that act without a solicitor and barristers and solicitors who conduct their own cases are treated as litigants in person (CPR rule 48.6(6)).

Solicitors acting against unrepresented parties may want to warn the other side of the costs that are building up, but, of course, will also make it clear that these costs can only be awarded if the district judge makes a finding of unreasonable conduct. It is best to serve any schedule of costs before the hearing, but failure to do so in a small claims case should not be fatal to recovering costs for unreasonable conduct. Although the rules require service of a costs schedule in advance, the district judge has the discretion to consider a costs schedule produced at the hearing or even to assess costs where there is no schedule.

9.7   COSTS TERMINOLOGY

The terms used in court orders to do with costs have specific meanings – those most commonly encountered in small claims cases are as follows:

- *No order for costs*: means that the question of costs has been determined and neither party will be liable to pay the other side's costs. Where the order says nothing about costs, this is the same as no order for costs (CPR rule 44.10).
- *Costs reserved*: means that the costs of that hearing will be dealt with at a later date (often the next hearing date), but if no later order is made, the costs will be the costs in the case.
- *Costs in the case*: means that the party against whom the court makes an order for costs at the end of the case will have to pay the costs of the application in question (this is generally a meaningless order in a small claims case because there is usually no order for costs at the end of the case).
- *Wasted costs*: refers to a special procedure where the court considers whether to make an order for costs against a party's lawyer who has behaved in an improper, unreasonable or negligent manner. It is incorrect to refer to the unreasonable behaviour costs orders made in small claims cases as wasted costs orders.

9.8   COSTS ON THE SMALL CLAIMS TRACK – FREQUENTLY ASKED QUESTIONS

Note the full Rules are set out in para 9.9.

What happens if a case is allocated to the fast track or the multi track and is later reallocated to the small claims track?	Any award for costs already made is not affected. The judge who is making the decision to reallocate must decide whether to make an award of costs and, if so, assess those costs by the summary procedure. If no costs orders were made, then unless the court orders otherwise, the rules about costs applying to the fast track or multi track will apply up to the date of re-allocation; and the rules applying to the small claims track will apply from the date of re-allocation (CPR rule 46.13(2))
What happens if there is a hearing on a case which qualifies for the small claims track before allocation (e.g. the hearing of an application for summary judgment)?	The district judge is not restricted by the no costs rule when deciding how to deal with the costs (PD 46, para 7.1(1)) but will be conscious of the requirement that costs should be proportionate
What happens if there is an initial hearing on a case after allocation to the small claims track (e.g. the preliminary appointment hearing or an application for summary judgment)?	The no costs rule will apply
What happens if the claim is issued for more than the qualifying limit for the small claims track and is then reduced to within the scope of the small claims track because of the defendant's admission?	Any award for costs already made is not affected. The judge who is making the decision to reallocate must decide whether to make an award of costs and, if so, assess those costs by the summary procedure. If no costs orders were made, then unless the court orders otherwise, the rules about costs applying to the fast track or multi track will apply up to the date of re-allocation; and the rules applying to the small claims track will apply from the date of re-allocation (CPR rule 46.13(2))
What about orders for costs made before allocation to the small claims track?	The orders are not affected (PD 46, para 7.1(2))
When do the costs have to be paid?	Although the district judge can specify when costs are to be paid, if no period is mentioned, the costs are payable within 14 days (CPR rule 44.7)
The claim is worth over £10,000 but both parties want to use the small claims track – will the no costs rule apply?	Yes – unless the parties agree otherwise (see para 9.1.3)
What about the costs before the allocation to the small claims track?	Except in the circumstances set out in the first and fourth FAQs above, the costs of the case from the beginning will be those covered by the small claims rules about costs (PD 46, para 7.1(2))
Does the no costs rule apply to appeals against decisions on the small claims track?	Yes
What happens if a claimant starts proceedings for a personal injury claim under the procedure for low value road traffic personal injury claims and then settles for under £1,000?	Stage 1 or Stage 2 of the special fixed costs may be recoverable if the claimant reasonably believed the claim to be above £1,000 in value (see CPR rule 27.14(2), set out at Appendix 7)

9.9   COSTS FOLLOWING ALLOCATION, RE-ALLOCATION AND NON-ALLOCATION: THE RULES

The effect of these rules is summarised in para 9.8.

CPR rule 46.13 states as follows:

(1)   Any costs orders made before a claim is allocated will not be affected by allocation.

(2)   Where—
    (a)   claim is allocated to a track; and
    (b)   the court subsequently re-allocates that claim to a different track,
    then unless the court orders otherwise, any special rules about costs applying—
    (i)   to the first track, will apply to the claim up to the date of re-allocation; and
    (ii)   to the second track, will apply from the date of re-allocation.

(3)   Where the court is assessing costs on the standard basis of a claim which concluded without being allocated to a track, it may restrict those costs to costs that would have been allowed on the track to which the claim would have been allocated if allocation had taken place.

PD 46, para 7.1 states as follows:

(1)   Before a claim is allocated to either the small claims track or the fast track the court is not restricted by any of the special rules that apply to that track but see paragraph 8.2 below.

(2)   Where a claim has been so allocated, the special rules which relate to that track will apply to work done before as well as after allocation save to the extent (if any) that an order for costs in respect of that work was made before allocation.

(3)   Where a claim, issued for a sum in excess of the normal financial scope of the small claims track, is allocated to that track only because an admission of part of the claim by the defendant reduces the amount in dispute to a sum within the normal scope of that track; on entering judgment for the admitted part before allocation of the balance of the claim the court may allow costs in respect of the proceedings down to that date.

PD 46, para 8.1 states as follows:

8.1 Before reallocating a claim from the small claims track to another track, the court must decide whether any party is to pay costs to the date of the order to re-allocate in accordance with the rules about costs contained in Part 27. If it decides to make such an order the court will make a summary assessment of those costs in accordance with that Part.

PD 46, para 8.2 states as follows:

> 8.2 Where a settlement is reached or a Part 36 offer accepted in a case which has not been allocated but would, if allocated, have been suitable for allocation to the small claims track, rule 46.13 enables the court to allow only small claims track costs in accordance with rule 27.14. This power is not exercisable if the costs are to be paid on the indemnity basis.

9.10   COSTS SCHEDULE

> For suggested layout of a costs schedule, see Appendix 10

Chapter 10

The Hearing

Basics

The key elements of the small claims hearing are:

- informality
- the strict rules of evidence do not apply
- the district judge will ensure that the parties are on an equal footing

---

10.1 OVERVIEW

There is a great deal of flexibility and unpredictability in small claims hearings, but the overall objectives are clear: the district judge will aim to get to the heart of the matter and then to reach a fair decision with the minimum fuss.

10.2 DEALING WITH CASES JUSTLY

The overriding objective is to deal with cases justly (see Chapter 5, para 5.2). CPR Part 1 is reproduced at Appendix 6

The small claims hearing will be conducted with the overriding objective in mind. The amount of money involved, plus the importance of the case and the complexity of the issues will govern a proportionate approach to the case (CPR rule 1.1(2)).

As well as ensuring that the case is dealt with fairly, the district judge at the hearing will ensure that the parties are on an equal footing (CPR rule 1.1(2)(a)) and will have an eye on saving expense (rule 1.1(2)(b)).

There are specific provisions in CPR Part 27 which govern the conduct of a small claims hearing. The district judge will, in addition, further the overriding objective by the management of the case at the hearing. This is done by:

- encouraging the parties to co-operate with each other and helping them to come to an agreement about the case (i.e. to settle the case);
- identifying the issues at an early stage;
- deciding the order in which issues are to be resolved;
- ensuring that the trial (final hearing) proceeds quickly and efficiently (rule 1.4).

10.3 RIGHTS OF AUDIENCE (ADVOCACY)

Basics

- Qualified lawyers have full rights of representation in small claims hearings
- Parties can be represented by lay representatives at small claims hearings
- A company can be represented by any of its employees or officers
- Individuals can represent themselves alone or with the support of a McKenzie friend

---

A party can present his or her own case at a hearing, or a lawyer or lay representative may present it on the party's behalf (PD 27, para 3.2(1)). A qualified solicitor or barrister can conduct the case in the absence of the party, but a lay representative may only do so if the party is present.

10.3.1 Lawyers

In fast track and multi track cases advocacy rights can only be exercised by those professionally qualified and permitted to do so. Such advocates have not only studied law and procedure for some years, of course, but are governed by the codes and rules of their professional bodies. See the Glossary under the definitions of barrister, legal executive, advocate and solicitor.

The district judge will not prevent one party using a professional advocate if the other is acting in person. There is a fundamental right of citizens to be represented by counsel or solicitors of their own choice. CPR rule 1.1, which includes the provision that the parties should be on an equal footing, is not interpreted to reduce or remove that right. However, the unrepresented litigant faced with a big firm of lawyers representing the other side may need concessions to make sure he or she is not at a disadvantage, for example extra time to provide copy documents.[1]

10.3.2 Lay representatives

A lay representative actually presents the case to the court as an advocate. This is not the same as the so-called 'McKenzie friend' who merely assists the litigant in person in court whilst the party speaks to the judge directly (see para 10.6.6).

The function of a lay representative is to give individuals confidence to pursue or defend their cases in court. A lay representative does not need to be particularly skilled, and standards of competence vary. Anyone can be a lay representative.

A lay representative may not exercise any right of audience where the client does not attend the hearing unless the court gives permission (see PD 27, para 3.2(2)).

Although a lay representative can speak in court, this right does not extend to conducting the litigation generally; the claim, the defence and all correspondence with the court must be signed by the litigant in person personally. The right of audience of a lay representative does not extend to any steps after judgment or to any appeal (PD 27, para 3.2(2)).

10.3.3 Companies

A company can be represented in court by any of its officers or employees (PD 27, para 3.2(4)).

---

[1] *Dulce Maltez v Damien Lewis and Anr* (1999) *The Times*, 4 May, ChD, [1999] All ER (D) 425.

10.4 HEARINGS ARE IN PUBLIC

Basics

- Small claims hearings are normally open to the public
- The parties can agree to a private hearing
- In some cases the court can direct a private hearing
- Hearings which take place other than at the court are not in public

The general rule for all civil cases is that the trial is to be in public, and there is no exception for small claims cases (CPR rule 39.2 and PD 27, para 4.1(1)). This is consistent with ECHR, Article 6.[2]

Anyone contemplating a small claims case should not be deterred from pursuing or defending the claim by the fact that the case will be heard in public. It is very rare for any outside observers to turn up to hear a small claims case, which almost always involve no more than the parties, the district judge and perhaps an observer or two invited by the parties themselves. Journalists rarely, if ever, turn up to listen to small claims cases.

CPR rule 39.2 and PD 39A set out the circumstances under which a hearing can be in private. For example, a hearing may be in private if publicity would defeat the object of a hearing or if a private hearing is necessary to protect the interests of a child. The court can order the hearing to be in private if it is necessary in the interests of justice. Almost without exception, small claims hearings are public hearings.

Even if the hearing is in private, the decision is not. The judgment itself can, with the permission of the district judge, be available to the public (PD 39A, para 1.12).

The fact that the hearing is open to the public does not impose on the court a duty to make special arrangements for accommodating members of the public

---

[2] **Article 6. Right to a fair trial**
1. In the determination of his civil rights and obligations or of any criminal charge against him, everyone is entitled to a fair and public hearing within a reasonable time by an independent and impartial tribunal established by law. Judgment shall be pronounced publicly but the press and public may be excluded from all or part of the trial in the interests of morals, public order or national security in a democratic society, where the interests of juveniles or the protection of the private life of the parties so require, or to the extent strictly necessary in the opinion of the court in special circumstances where publicity would prejudice the interests of justice.

(CPR rule 39.2(2)). This probably does not mean that lack of suitable accommodation is a reason for the hearing not being in public. If the public turn up in numbers, and the case is listed for hearing in a small room, then a decision on how to deal with such a situation would obviously be taken carefully by the district judge, having due regard to all relevant provisions of the rules and the ECHR. One option could be for the case to be put back (adjourned) to another day when a larger court room can be made available for the case (PD 39A, para 1.10).

The district judge may decide to hold the hearing in private if both parties agree (PD 27, para 4.1(2)).

If the hearing, or part of a hearing, takes place other than at the court, for example at the home or business address of a party, that part of the hearing will not be in public (PD 27, para 4.1(3)).

> Those concerned with privacy should consider the mediation route; the small claims mediation service offered by the court is private (see Chapter 7)

10.4.1 It is never too late to settle

Parties attending a final hearing should bear in mind that a negotiated settlement may bring them more satisfaction than the result of a contested hearing. Parties attending a final hearing should not be surprised if the district judge invites them to make one last attempt to settle. Bear in mind that if the settlement is reached at the door of the court, the district judge can be asked to set out the terms of settlement in a court order which is then fully enforceable by the court if the terms are not adhered to.

10.5 RECORDING THE HEARING – TAPES AND NOTES

> **Summary**
>
> The hearing will be recorded by the court and private recordings are not allowed

All rooms used by district judges for small claims hearings are equipped with sound recording equipment.

The district judge does not have to write anything down or take notes if the proceedings are recorded, but will probably take notes.

The parties must pay for the cost of any transcript if they want one. The fee is paid to the court reporter who prepares the note and not to the court. The rate charged is a commercial one, based on the number of words, so the cost is variable. As a guide, a transcript of a judgment of about an hour would be about £150 plus VAT.

Professional advocates are under a duty to take notes at the hearing. It is practical and sensible for litigants conducting their own cases to bring pen and paper to the hearing to make notes.

The parties cannot, except with the permission of the court, make personal sound recordings of the case – to do so would be a contempt of court (PD 39A, para 6.2).

10.6   LAYOUT OF THE COURT AND COURTROOM ETIQUETTE

There is no standard size, shape or layout for the room in which the hearing will be held. If the hearing takes place at court it will usually be held in the judge's hearing room (formerly called 'chambers') but it may take place in a courtroom. If the hearing takes place in the judge's room and the door is shut, this does not make the hearing private; the hearing is a public hearing.

The district judge can direct that the hearing can take place outside the court, for example at the home or business premises of a party, in which case the hearing will not be in public.

If the judge's room is used the parties may sit round a table, but some district judge's rooms are set up in a formal way. Sometimes a district judge may use a large courtroom for a small claims hearing.

In formal trials, it is conventional in many courts for the claimant to sit to the left (facing the judge) with the defendant to the right. This formality should be adopted unless the district judge or usher indicates otherwise. Sometimes the question 'Where do I sit?' is answered by labels or signs, or the usher or district judge may say where everyone should sit.

It is usual for the lawyer or representative to sit closest to the district judge with the client or witnesses behind or to the side. Witnesses and observers should sit at the back.

Neither the advocates nor the district judge will be robed.

Mobile phones and computer devices must not be used to make or receive telephone calls in court and must not be used to record hearings. However, there is no legal restriction against tweeting during a public hearing.

10.6.1 Addressing the court and the district judge

A female district judge should be addressed as 'madam', a male as 'sir'. There is no need to stand when addressing the district judge unless the district judge directs otherwise. When addressing the district judge, it is important that everyone in the room, especially the other side, should be able to hear what is said. Courtroom microphones are for recording purposes and usually do not amplify sound.

10.6.2 Documents

The district judge will have the court file, which includes:

- the claim and defence plus any court orders (including directions) and correspondence on the court file;
- the directions questionnaires;
- any documents, notes or statements (including experts' reports) lodged at court before the hearing by the parties (when bound together for use at a hearing, usually called 'bundles').

District judges will review the court file before the hearing and, if the file is complete, will be able to start the case with an overall understanding of what the case is about.

Wise practitioners may wish to take a spare copy of their bundle of documents and witness statements (see Chapter 8, para 8.4) for use in court by the district judge – it is not unknown for bundles sent to the court not to be on the judge's desk at the start of a hearing.

10.6.3 Introduction of new documents at the final hearing

Proper preparation for the final hearing will have involved each side sending copies of documents to the other in advance (see Chapter 8, para 8.4). Note, however, there is no default rule that if the other side has not complied with the order to send documents before the hearing that the other side automatically wins. The claimant still has to prove the case and the district judge has discretion to allow the introduction of documents at a late stage. Where a party is ambushed by new documents at the final hearing, the district judge will have to decide whether to press on with the hearing, allowing the new documents to be used, or whether to adjourn the case to another date. An alternative course is for the hearing to proceed without the additional documents.

This is an area of considerable difficulty for both professional advocates and litigants in person. A decision will have to be taken under pressure, and allowing a few moments for reflection will assist the party on the receiving end of the new papers to take a sensible decision. It is good practice for the party who is seeing new documents for the first time to have permission to leave the hearing room to consider the documents in private before deciding what to ask the judge to do. A balance has to be struck between, on the one hand, the understandable desire to get on with a case and avoid the inconvenience of adjourning the case to another date and, on the other hand, the possible unfairness of proceeding when one party might not have had a proper opportunity to consider all the evidence.

Sometimes, the additional documents do not contain material which is unexpected. If, however, the documents come as a true surprise and the party seeing them for the first time needs time to reconsider their case or prepare fresh evidence themselves, the interests of justice may well require the case be adjourned, or for the case to proceed without them. If an adjournment is requested and refused, and that refusal is unfair, this would be grounds for appeal. If the documents are truly new and come as a real blow to one party's case then it could be considered unreasonable conduct for them to be produced, without good reason, at such a late stage – in such a case the costs consequences should be considered (see Chapter 9 and especially para 9.3).

10.6.4   Interpreters in various languages and hearings in Welsh

Litigants who have difficulty with the English language can usually be assisted with interpretation at a small claims hearing by friends or family members. If for some reason informal interpretation is not sufficient, a professional language interpreter can be used. In cases where a litigant is unrepresented and cannot understand the language of the court well enough to take part in the hearing and cannot afford to pay for an interpreter, the Courts Service will provide one without charge. Enquiries should be made with the court manager well in advance of the hearing so that arrangements can be made.

In Wales, the English and Welsh languages are treated equally. All court hearings, including small claims hearings, may be conducted in Welsh, if this is the choice of the parties. Certain district judges are able to conduct the hearings in Welsh. Arrangements for coordinating the Welsh-speaking parties with a suitable district judge are made by the county court, and the parties should have notified the court no later than at the allocation stage that a hearing in Welsh is required.

10.6.5 Witnesses

There are two types of witness namely:

- *witnesses as to fact*: who tell the story as it happened but do not give any opinion of a technical nature;
- *experts*: who have a special qualification and give a considered opinion on technical aspects of the case. Experts can only give evidence (either in writing or in person at the hearing) with the prior permission of the district judge; this may be sought at the allocation stage or at a preliminary hearing (see Chapter 8, para 8.8).

All witnesses need to know what the case is about and the procedure to be followed, and therefore some judges will invite witnesses in to hear the preliminaries (see para 10.7.2). Witnesses as to fact will sometimes sit in the hearing room and wait until their evidence is needed. In some cases, however, especially where the truthfulness of the parties is in issue, the witnesses may be asked to leave after the preliminaries have been completed and wait outside the hearing room until they are called. The parties should not hesitate to discuss with the district judge whether or not the witnesses should wait outside the room.

10.6.6   Friends and observers, including McKenzie friends

People who are not involved with the case, including reporters, can listen to the hearing because the hearing is in public (see para 10.4).

Apart from an advocate or lay representative, a litigant in person may invite a friend into the hearing to 'quietly make suggestions, take notes and give advice'; this is the so-called 'McKenzie friend'.[3] The McKenzie friend does not address the court; contrast the lay representative who does address the court (see para 10.3.2).

The judge will decide whether or not to allow a McKenzie friend in accordance with the guidance given by senior judges in 2010.[4] The guidance also clarifies the role of the McKenzie friend.

---

[3] *R v Leicester City Justices ex parte Barrow and another* [1991] 3 All ER 935, CA.
[4] See *Guidance for McKenzie Friends (Civil and Family Courts)* [2010] 4 All ER 272.

The relevant principles are as follows:

(1) litigants have the right to have reasonable assistance from a McKenzie friend; however, litigants assisted by a McKenzie friend remain litigants in person and a McKenzie friend has no independent right to provide assistance, act as an advocate or carry out the conduct of litigation;

(2) a McKenzie friend may provide moral support for a litigant, take notes, help with case papers and quietly give advice on any aspect of the conduct of the case;

(3) a McKenzie friend may not act as the litigant's agent in relation to the proceedings, manage litigants' cases outside court (e.g. by signing court documents), address the court, make oral submissions or examine witnesses;

(4) while litigants ordinarily have a right to receive reasonable assistance from a McKenzie friend, the court retains the power to refuse to permit such assistance and may do so where it is satisfied that, in that case, the interests of justice and fairness do not require the litigant to receive such assistance;

(5) a litigant who wishes to exercise the right to appoint a McKenzie friend should inform the judge as soon as possible, indicating who the McKenzie friend will be;

(6) the proposed McKenzie friend should produce a short CV or other statement setting out relevant experience, confirming that he or she has no interest in the case and understands the McKenzie friend role and the duty of confidentiality;

(7) the proposed McKenzie friend should not be excluded from the courtroom or chambers while the application is made, and should ordinarily be allowed to assist the litigant in person to make the application;

(8) if the court considers that there might be grounds for circumscribing the right to receive such assistance, or a party objects to the presence of, or assistance given by, a McKenzie friend, it is not for the litigant to justify the exercise of the right but for the court or the objecting party to provide sufficient reasons why the litigant should not receive such assistance;

(9) if an application to appoint a McKenzie friend is refused, the reasons for the decision should be explained carefully and fully to both the litigant in person and the proposed McKenzie friend. While the litigant in person may appeal that refusal, the McKenzie friend has no standing to do so.

In practice, particularly in cases allocated to the small claims track, the judge will almost always give permission for a party to be assisted by a McKenzie friend.

10.6.7 Parties with special needs or concerns about their personal safety

Parties should contact the court in advance to find out about any special facilities. Courts have special facilities, for example hearing loops and special parking spaces for those with disabled badges. Most courts have security staff on duty, but parties must tell the court in advance if they are concerned for their personal safety so that suitable arrangements can be made. The courts do not have child-minding facilities and children will not usually be allowed in the hearing room. Some courts have children's rooms where children and a carer can wait during or before a hearing.[5]

10.7 PROCEDURE AT SMALL CLAIMS HEARINGS

CPR rule 27.8 sets out the procedure, as follows:

(1) The court may adopt any method of proceeding at a hearing that it considers to be fair.
(2) Hearings will be informal.
(3) The strict rules of evidence do not apply.
(4) The court need not take evidence on oath.
(5) The court may limit cross examination.
(6) The court must give reasons for its decision.

10.7.1 A fair hearing method

CPR rule 27.8 allows the court to adopt any method of proceeding that it considers to be fair and to limit cross examination.

The judge may in particular (PD 27, para 4.3):

(1) ask questions of any witnesses himself before allowing any other person to do so;
(2) ask questions of all or any of the witnesses himself before allowing any other person to ask questions of any witnesses;
(3) refuse to allow cross examination of any witness until all of the witnesses have given evidence in chief;
(4) limit cross examination of a witness to a fixed time or to a particular subject or issue, or both.

---

[5] See www.justice.gov.uk/about/hmcts/.

CPR rule 27.8 and PD 27 are the key to the flexibility of a small claims hearing and allow district judges to be adaptable in approach. They will decide on the day how the hearing of each case is to be organised, asking the questions, helping the parties and generally adopting a much more interventionist role than at a normal trial.

10.7.2   At the start of the hearing (preliminaries)

When everyone has settled down, and before the start of the case itself, it is usual for the district judge to:

- check who everyone is and deal with introductions;
- explain the procedure to be followed including the order in which everyone will speak;
- decide whether the witnesses should listen to the whole hearing or wait until their evidence is to be heard;
- summarise what he or she understands to be the apparent issues in the case; if the issues are clear at the outset, he or she will explain the relevant law;
- state whether he or she has a view on the issues *and* what that view is.

All this can take quite a while, and the influx of information from the district judge may be overwhelming. Questions should be asked to clarify anything said by the district judge, but if a point is not clear then questions can be asked later. Throughout the hearing, the district judge should ensure that everyone knows what is going on.

At this point in the proceedings the minimum information which the parties should know is:

- who everyone in the room is and why they are there;
- in what order everyone is going to speak;
- whether the district judge has a view on what the issues are *and* what that view is.

10.8   ORGANISATION OF THE HEARING

Before looking at the possible methods of proceeding at any particular small claims hearing, it will be useful to look at the sequence that is usually followed in civil trials.

10.8.1   Usual sequence in civil trials

When the claimant and defendant are both going to call evidence, the procedure is as follows:

Step 1	Claimant explains what the case is about from his or her point of view and what evidence is to be put before the court ('opens')
Step 2	Claimant's witnesses (each witness is cross examined by the defendant's advocate in turn immediately after giving evidence)
Step 3	Defendant opens
Step 4	Defendant's witnesses (each witness is cross examined in turn by the claimant's advocate immediately after giving evidence)
Step 5	Defendant finally explains to the district judge why his or her case should succeed in the light of the evidence ('closes')
Step 6	Claimant closes
Step 7	Decision
Step 8	Winner applies for costs
Step 9	Loser may apply for permission to appeal

The advocates will decide in what order their clients' witnesses are to be called, and nearly all the questions will be asked by the advocates with only minimum interruption from the judge.

10.8.2   Order of hearing for small claims cases

The district judge may adopt the usual sequence of a civil trial and may have this method in mind as the template for the hearing.

However, different methods may be adopted – entirely at the discretion of the district judge – in accordance with his or her personal preferences and the circumstances of the particular case. Some district judges habitually adopt an unstructured approach and will not follow a set routine. The district judge may interject and make comments, and may take over the questioning at any stage. (see para 10.7.1).

Here are some possible methods that may be used.

Method 1

This method is suitable in cases where the district judge can roughly identify the issues at the start of the case. This method is very similar to that for a traditional trial:

Step 1	Claimant is not asked to open the case, the district judge summarises issues at the outset and asks the claimant and defendant to comment on whether or not the summary is correct and explains any relevant aspects of the law
Step 2	Claimant's evidence (including any witnesses)
Step 3	Defendant cross examines claimant's witnesses
Step 4	Defendant's evidence (including any witnesses)
Step 5	Claimant cross examines defendant's witnesses
Step 6	Defendant says how the district judge should decide the case and why
Step 7	Claimant says how the district judge should decide the case and why
Step 8	District judge gives decision
Step 9	If appropriate, winner asks for costs on grounds of unreasonable behaviour
Step 10	If appropriate, loser may ask for permission to appeal

Method 2 (all the evidence in chief goes first)

This second method differs from the sequence at a traditional trial mainly because all the cross questioning is dealt with at the end of all the examination in chief. This considerably lessens the burden of cross examination and cuts out duplicated questions:

Step 1	Claimant is not asked to open the case, the district judge summarises issues at the outset and asks the claimant and defendant to comment on whether or not the summary is correct and explains any relevant aspects of the law
Step 2	Claimant's evidence (including any witnesses)
Step 3	Defendant's evidence (including any witnesses)
Step 4	Defendant cross examines claimant's witnesses
Step 5	Claimant cross examines defendant's witnesses
Step 6	Defendant says how the district judge should decide the case and why
Step 7	Claimant says how the district judge should decide the case and why
Step 8	District judge gives decision
Step 9	If appropriate, winner asks for costs on grounds of unreasonable behaviour
Step 10	If appropriate, loser may ask for permission to appeal

Method 3 (quick method)

This third method is applicable in cases where most of the evidence is in writing and the district judge has had an opportunity to read the papers in detail before the hearing and where the only witnesses are the parties themselves:

Step 1	District judge explains what has been deduced from reading the papers and explains any relevant questions of law
Step 2	Claimant gives any additional evidence orally
Step 3	Defendant gives any additional evidence orally
Step 4	Claimant and defendant each given opportunity to cross examine the other party
Step 5	Each party addresses the district judge in turn on how the case should be decided and why
Step 6	District judge gives decision
Step 7	If appropriate, winner may ask for costs and loser may apply for permission to appeal

10.8.3 Informality

The concept of 'informality' is relative to the conduct of fast track and multi track trials, and thus has very little meaning to litigants who are not accustomed to the conduct of civil cases. The usual television courtroom drama depicts a criminal trial so is an unhelpful reference point.

A litigant who has been told the hearing is informal may well be surprised by how formal it actually is. Although some small claims hearings may be quite relaxed, they are often quite serious affairs and will feel quite formal to most people – perhaps as formal as a job interview.

The district judge will determine for each individual case how informal any particular hearing will be, bearing in mind factors including whether the parties are legally represented and the layout of the hearing room being used.

10.8.4 Contempt of court

The informality of the proceedings should not lull any party or their representatives into forgetting where they are. They are still in court, and insulting or threatening a witness, or the district judge, either in the hearing room or close by, will amount to contempt. The use of recording equipment in court, including devices which are part of computers and mobile phones, except with the permission of the district judge, will be a contempt (see para 10.5).

Members of the public who attend the hearing may be held in contempt if they disrupt the proceedings. The punishment may be a prison sentence (County Courts Act 1984, section 118). Professional advocates will be bound by the standards of their professional bodies.

10.8.5   Where a party has given notice that they are not coming to court

A party may choose not to attend a hearing and to tell the court and the other side 7 days in advance that he or she does not intend to appear. In this case, the district judge will take that party's written evidence and any documents into account before taking a decision (CPR rule 27.9(1)) (see Chapter 8, para 8.16.7). The party who does not attend will be sent a written note of the reason for the judge's decision (see para 10.11.1).

10.8.6   Consequences of not attending where no notice has been given

If the party has *not* given notice under CPR rule 27.9(1), then the district judge can disregard his or her evidence and documents, and decide the case on the basis of the evidence of the party who turns up at the hearing (rule 27.9(2) and (3)).

If neither party turns up, the district judge can strike out the claim, any counterclaim, or both (CPR rule 27.9(4)).

10.9   EVIDENCE AND THE SMALL CLAIMS HEARING (INCLUDING THE BURDEN AND STANDARD OF PROOF)

Basics

- Be practical about evidence – the more important it is, the better it must be
- Witness statements will be useful, but are not always obligatory
- The court must give permission if expert evidence is to be called
- The case must be proved on balance

10.9.1   Proof – a burden and a standard

The *standard* of proof in a civil case is that the case must be proved 'on the balance of probabilities'; whether one explanation of events is more likely than another.

The *burden*, or responsibility, of proving the case to that standard is on the claimant for the claim and the defendant for the counterclaim; it is said that 'he who asserts must prove'. A party who succeeds in proving his or her case is said to have discharged the burden of proof.

The civil standard and burden of proof will be applied in a small claims case. When making the final decision, the district judge will first look at all the evidence and then weigh it in the balance. The district judge will consider how likely it is that matters occurred as alleged. If, and only if, the district judge considers the claimant's version to be more likely than not, the claimant will win.

10.9.2 Rules of evidence

The strict rules of evidence do not apply (CPR rule 27.8(3)).

This rule of CPR Part 27, possibly above any other, makes the professional advocate apprehensive of a small claims hearing. What exactly are the formal rules that do not apply? What rules apply?

What follows is a practical summary of how evidence is treated in small claims cases.

10.9.3 The usual rules of evidence

In order to understand how evidence is treated at small claims hearings, it is necessary to note the 'strict rules' that usually apply at a civil court hearing:

- *Documents*: the originals must be in court and, unless a document is agreed as being authentic by the other side, the person who produced the document will have to appear in court to 'prove' it.
- *Witness evidence is given in person* and the witness must attend court to be cross examined.
- *Expert evidence* can only be given with the permission of the court by properly qualified experts; also, only experts and not witnesses as to fact can express technical opinions.
- *There are restrictions on circumstantial and similar fact evidence.*

The starting point at a small claims hearing is that none of these rules applies (CPR rule 27.8(3)); a case will not necessarily fail because these strict rules are not followed.

However, it does not follow that parties can expect to produce documents and call witnesses to give evidence without prior notice to the other party and the court: there are some rules (summarised below) which the district judge is likely to enforce simply to ensure a fair hearing.

10.9.4 Documents

Copies of all the documents to be used at the hearing should have been sent to the other side 2 weeks beforehand, or at such other time as directed by the court. The usual directions remind the parties that the originals should be brought to court for the trial. The person who makes the document will only be needed to prove that the document itself is authentic if the case is about the authenticity of that particular document. In any event, it makes sense to bring the originals to court.

10.9.5 Witness evidence

> 'Witness' means any person giving evidence about the case, including the parties themselves

Witnesses will give oral evidence, but probably not on oath (CPR rule 27.8(4)). In many cases, if the standard directions have been given, a written summary of the witnesses' evidence in the form of a witness statement will have been sent to or exchanged with the opposite party before the hearing. The advantages of preparing a good witness statement are clear:

- The other side will have full notice of the evidence they expect to face; this minimises the risk of an adjournment.
- The witness may be allowed to read out his or her written statement (helpful for nervous witnesses).
- The district judge may allow witness statements to stand as their evidence, even without being read out (even more helpful for nervous witnesses).
- In any case where the parties have difficulty with English, it will certainly help matters and speed up the hearing if written statements can be prepared and translated before the hearing.

One of the parties may have notified the court in advance that he or she does not intend to attend the hearing under CPR rule 27.9(1). The district judge will take that person's written evidence and submissions into account.

Often, a witness will not be able to attend a small claims case to give evidence in person: witness allowances are not generous and the amount of money at stake may not justify the cost of attending and losing a day off work, or paying a babysitter. District judges will take into account a letter or written statement from an absent witness.

However, the regard or weight that is give to that statement or letter will almost certainly not be as great as the impact of the witness attending in person. An absent witness is not able to answer questions about his or her evidence or have it tested by cross examination.

A common-sense decision will have to be taken for each witness and for every case. The following questions must be asked:

- How important is the evidence?
- What will be the expense of the witness attending?
- How effective will the evidence be if it is simply written down?
- Is the evidence likely to be controversial?
- Will the other side be able to complain about not being able to ask the absent witness questions about the evidence?

10.9.6 Do not tell the judge about settlement discussions outside court

The district judge must not be told the details of any settlement negotiations before the hearing, including those at mediation, or outside the court before judgment: this information must not be included in any witness statements or mentioned when the witness gives evidence. If the district judge hears about these offers, he or she may have to adjourn the case to a different date for it to be heard by a different judge.

10.9.7 Expert evidence

A party can only call expert evidence with the prior permission of the district judge, which should be sought at the allocation stage or at the preliminary hearing (see Chapter 8, para 8.8). (Normally, where permission is given in a case allocated to the small claims track, it will be for a single expert, jointly instructed by the parties (CPR rule 35.4(3A).) Such an expert will be directed to produce a written report to be used at the trial. The expert will not usually be directed to attend the trial in person.

10.9.8   Categories of prohibited evidence

The district judge will hesitate to allow similar-fact and circumstantial evidence into the case. However, if the evidence is introduced, or included in a witness statement, then it may be difficult to ignore completely. Tread carefully, a blatant attempt to poison the mind of the district judge with statements which cannot be supported by other evidence is only going to make him or her slow to accept evidence relating to other parts of the case.

10.9.9   Taking evidence on oath

The district judge need not take evidence on oath (CPR rule 27.8(4)). However, the parties may well be reminded that the hearing is in a court of law and they are expected to tell the truth. A district judge can require evidence to be taken on oath and will do so if, for example, it is clear that the conscience of the witness to tell the truth will not be bound unless he or she is put on oath.

10.9.10 Limiting cross examination

The theme here is that the judge is in charge, and will not allow a disproportionate amount of time in questioning witnesses (CPR rule 27.8(5)). Cross examination is considered in detail in the following paragraph.

10.10 ADVOCACY SKILLS AND THE SMALL CLAIMS HEARING – MAKING THE MOST OF YOUR TIME IN COURT

A hearing in the judge's room is meant to be less daunting than a hearing in a large courtroom. The district judge will try to put the parties and their witnesses at ease and will assist inexperienced advocates and litigants alike. The district judge may adopt an interventionist approach, for example by asking questions, limiting cross examination and generally assisting the parties.

In practice, this means that the district judge may well sideline the professional advocate but should not do so to such an extent that the advocate takes no part.

How, then, can the chances of winning be improved by effective advocacy?

10.10.1 Opening speech

In a formal trial, the claimant's advocate will probably set the scene for the case at the outset by giving a summary of the apparent issues. In small claims cases, this is often done by the district judge.

There is no harm in the claimants or their advocates preparing the points which they would like to be covered in a formal opening. When the district judge gives the opening summary (see para 10.8.2, step 1 in methods 1, 2 and 3), the points can be ticked off, and any points not noted by the district judge can then be politely added. It is, of course, possible that the claimant will be asked to open anyway – it depends on what method of hearing is adopted on the day.

The points which should be covered at the opening (whether by the claimant or by the district judge) are:

- introductions of all the advocates;
- a summary of the facts;
- a summary of the apparent issues.

10.10.2 Asking questions of your own witnesses (examination in chief)

The district judge may ask many of the questions and the advocate may be left to fill in the gaps. The advocate should, therefore, prepare a checklist of the points that need to be covered, and these should be checked off to determine what additional points need to be made.

Here are some hints on how to get the best out of a witness giving oral evidence:

- Remember where you are (it is not a formal trial, but it is a trial).
- Keep your questions short.
- Keep your language simple.
- Make sure the district judge can hear you and your witness.
- Make sure that the district judge can keep up with his or her notes (do not let the witness go too fast).
- Let the witness tell the story – do not interrupt; the evidence will be much more convincing if given without prompting.
- Stop your witness if he or she strays from the point.
- Ask questions in a logical order.
- Ask specific questions – avoid vague questions which may tempt your witness to stray into irrelevant or unhelpful areas of evidence
- Make sure you know what answers to expect.
- Make your last question your best, and be doubly sure that you are confident that the witness will give a helpful answer.

The key is thoughtful preparation:

- all witnesses should have seen a written statement of their evidence and read it over before the hearing;
- prepare a list of questions and use it at the hearing.

Questions put to a witness which suggest a particular answer are called 'leading questions'. An example of this is, 'Is it correct that you were driving at only 15 mph?'. The same question not put in a leading way would be, 'At what speed were you travelling?', where the witness has the freedom to answer in an open manner. In formal trials, a judge will prevent the use of questions which lead a witness, unless the evidence which is led is not controversial. Since the strict rules of evidence do not apply, it can be expected that the district judge at a small claims hearing will be fairly tolerant of leading questions on aspects of evidence which are not central to the dispute – after all, they may well speed up the hearing. However, there is a trap here for the unwary: if a witness's evidence consists of words that have been put into his or her mouth, that evidence may not be convincing. It follows that leading questions should be avoided where key issues are at stake.

10.10.3 Asking questions of the other party and his or her witnesses (cross examination)

The object of cross examination is to test your opponent's case by:

- putting the other side's evidence in doubt if it damages your case;
- giving the witness a chance to comment on your theory of the case (i.e. what you say happened, and why).

It follows that if the witness has not damaged your case, there may be no need to cross examine. It can be quite difficult to discredit a witness, and the district judge will intervene to stop an aggressive line of questioning (CPR rule 27.8(4)) (see para 10.7.1). In formal trials, putting the case ensures that no party is taken by surprise and has a chance to comment on any theory advanced by the other side. In a small claims case, it will sometimes be unnecessary to put the case to the witness; the order of witnesses can be flexible and if something new does turn up, then the witness can easily be recalled and asked about the new point later.

As a rule of thumb, it is useful to limit any questions in cross examination to those where you are fairly sure of the answer that will be given. In cross examination, you should never ask the other side's witness to give you his or her theory about the case – you know it will not be favourable to you.

The rule forbidding leading questions does not apply to cross examination, even in formal trials.

10.10.4 Re-examination

Following the cross examination of a witness, the advocate who originally called the witness has a final opportunity to ask him or her more questions. This is called 're-examination'. It is usually limited to one or two questions and may not be necessary at all. The purpose of re-examination is to clarify points which have arisen in cross examination. The advocate is not allowed to ask questions in re-examination unless they are on topics which were raised in cross examination. If, for example, the witness was asked about the cost of repairing his bumper and could not recall that figure, the advocate may have found the receipt for the repairs in the bundle and may direct the witness to that page. This is strictly not an opportunity to ask questions which were missed out during the examination in chief. It is sometimes thought that if a party is re-examined at length, this may suggest to the district judge that the cross examination has damaged the party's case. Thus, as a matter of strategy, re-examination may be avoided completely or at least minimised in order to give an impression that the case has not been dented by cross examination. It is, however, an opportunity to leave as the last impression in the judge's mind points favourable to you, rather than to your opponent. In that sense, you should think about whether to waste such an opportunity if you think you need it.

10.10.5 Closing speech

At the end of the case, each party will be asked to say how the case should be decided and why – this is where a well-prepared litigant or advocate can really shine.

You should emphasise only the evidence which has helped you. If the evidence against you has been unhelpful, this is a chance to put it into context and show that the good evidence in your client's favour outweighs the negative evidence.

You may suspect that the district judge has sympathy with the other side, for example if the other side is unrepresented or apparently less powerful than your client. If so, the best you can do is to emphasise the objective things which help your case – the relevant law and any independent or expert evidence. You should consider the points that tip the balance in your client's favour – never forget that to succeed, the burden of proof must be discharged (see para 10.9).

10.10.6 Legal points

The district judge must and will apply the law in small claims cases.

Although the district judge may be familiar with the relevant law, the judge's legal knowledge on a particular topic cannot be taken for granted, and professional advocates must come prepared to set out the law clearly and without using complicated language. If previously decided cases are to be relied on, make copies – enough for yourself, the other side and the district judge.

10.10.7 Practical tips

For road traffic cases, it is useful to bring toy cars to court so that the scene of the accident can be reconstructed as a tableau on the district judge's table, plus a copy of the Highway Code. Always bring a calculator – and if using the calculator on your phone or tablet, make sure that the telephone mode is disabled.

Effective advocacy at the small claims hearing

- Remember where you are – be brief and use simple language
- Prepare checklists of what you want to say
- Prepare a checklist of what you hope your witnesses will say
- Bring copies of case reports and relevant legal texts to the hearing

---

10.10.8 Taking a note

Legal professionals are under a duty to take a note of the evidence at the hearing. Even if it is not possible to write everything down as it is said, it is useful to note down the main points of evidence and in particular any points which are likely to be useful when making a final summary of the case to the district judge.

Litigants in person will find invaluable the assistance of a friend or supporter to take notes for them and manage their papers.

10.11 THE JUDGMENT

- The district judge may give reasons as briefly or simply as the nature of the case allows (PD 27, para 5.3(1)).
- Judgment will normally be given orally at the hearing but the decision may be given later, either in writing or at another hearing (PD 27, para 5.3(2)).

- Where the hearing was conducted in the absence of both parties or where a party who has given notice in advance that he or she is not attending the hearing, the judge will prepare a summary of reasons (PD 27, para 5.4) (see Chapter 8, para 8.16.7).
- Professional advocates must make a note of the judgment and litigants in person are recommended to jot the reasons down.

10.11.1 A reasoned decision

The judgment will contain the result of the case and brief reasons for the decision. The detail in the judgment will be proportionate to the nature of the case, and the reasons given may be brief.

The decision will be reasoned (CPR rule 27.8(6)) but the judge will produce a written note of the reasons for the decision only if:

- there was no recording; or
- the case was decided without a hearing under rule 27.10 or either side notified the court under rule 27.9(1) that they did not propose to attend the hearing.

The district judge's reasons will be considered by the circuit judge in the event of an appeal – if a reasonable note has been made, this may save the cost of a transcript of the judgment.

10.11.2 Costs and witness expenses

Decisions on what expenses and costs are to be allowed are taken after the award has been given, and the district judge will make a note of the sums awarded. The parties and their representatives should have their calculators ready and be prepared to assist the district judge with:

- interest calculations;
- witness expenses;
- arithmetical calculations.

Costs are dealt with in detail in Chapter 9

See in particular:

- routine awards for costs – para 9.2
- unreasonable behaviour – para 9.3
- discretion on costs – para 9.4

Although the rules governing without prejudice correspondence between the parties are sometimes ignored or forgotten, strictly speaking, correspondence written without prejudice may not be used after the trial even on the issue of costs.[6] Check with the district judge before producing correspondence, even at this stage. However, if correspondence is marked, 'Without prejudice, save as to costs', the parties are entitled to use it after the trial.

10.11.3 Time to pay

If the loser needs time to pay the sum awarded, the district judge will consider whether the judgment should be paid by instalments. If the judgment is to be paid in one lump sum, the district judge will decide when the payment is to be made. If no time period is set, the judgment must be paid in full within 14 days (CPR rule 40.11). Note that if the loser is granted time to pay, then the instalment order is registered as a judgment in the register of county court judgments (see Chapter 12).

Even if the district judge does not give the loser time to pay at the hearing, an application can be made at a later date. The party requesting time to pay contacts the court and the staff will send him or her a form to complete enabling the party to set out his or her income and liabilities. The court staff then work out an appropriate rate of payment using standard guidelines. The debtor and creditor are then both notified of the rate of payment which has been so determined. If either the judgment debtor or creditor is unhappy with the rate determined by the court, the matter is, at their request, referred to the district judge who can confirm the order or set it aside and make such new order as he or she thinks fit. The judgment creditor does not have to accept a payment by instalments, for example, if the debtor has assets which could be sold to meet the judgment immediately then the district judge may, at the request of the judgment creditor, set aside the instalment order.

10.11.4 Permission to appeal

The loser can ask the district judge at the end of the hearing for permission to appeal. No formalities or fee are involved and if the request is refused, this does not affect the loser's right to make an application for permission to appeal to the circuit judge within 21 days of the hearing. Permission to appeal will be given only if the appeal has a real prospect of success. If permission to appeal is requested and refused, the district judge will inform the parties that any further request for permission to appeal must be to the circuit judge.

---

[6]   *Reed Executive plc v Reed Business Information Ltd* [2004] EWCA Civ 887, [2004] 4 All ER 942.

> See Chapter 11 for more about appeals

10.11.5 Court order

The district judge makes a note of the decision and the money award on the court file. The file is returned to the court office where the court staff 'enter the judgment', which comprises setting out the decision details on the court's computer (Caseman). A formal order is prepared, sealed and sent to both parties as a record of the result.

10.12 SMALL CLAIMS HEARING – FREQUENTLY ASKED QUESTIONS

Can I bring a friend to support me?	Yes
Will I have to wait?	Probably – contact the court to find out how many cases are listed at the same time – you may have to wait for some time for your case to be called. Hesitate before parking your car on a meter – you may be in court for well over 2 hours
What do I call the judge?	'Sir' if male or 'madam' if female On an appeal or before a circuit judge, 'your honour'
How formal is the hearing?	The parties will probably sit around a table but the atmosphere will be about as formal as a job interview
What will the courtroom look like?	Hearings are generally held in the judge's room and the parties will sit around a table, but the arrangements in courts vary; more modern courts tend to have more formal hearing rooms for the district judges
Will the hearing be in public?	Yes – but strangers or court reporters are unlikely to attend unless invited by the parties themselves
Can I make my own recording of the hearing?	No. It is a contempt of court to make a tape recording of any part of the hearing without the permission of the district judge (Contempt of Court Act 1981, section 9)
If I lose, can I appeal?	Yes – if the district judge or circuit judge decides the appeal has a real prospect of success (see Chapter 11)

Chapter 11

Appeals and Applications to Set Aside Judgment

11.1 INTRODUCTION

> **Basics**
>
> - Appeal – the loser must first get permission to appeal, which will be given if the appeal has a real prospect of success
> - The no costs rule applies to the appeal process for small claims cases
> - The appeal is usually not a re-hearing but a review of the decision of the district judge
> - A party who, for good reason, fails to attend a hearing may be able to get a re-hearing
> - A judgment in default (without a hearing) can sometimes be set aside

This chapter considers three types of situation where the losing party may want a further hearing, namely:

- the appeal route (para 11.2);
- setting aside and re-hearing (para 11.3);
- setting aside a judgment in default (para 11.4).

A party dissatisfied with the final result of the case can appeal, but only with permission, which must be obtained from a judge; either the district judge who heard the case or a circuit judge will grant permission if the appeal has a real prospect of success. A summary is set out in Table 11.1. The rules about appeals are set out in CPR Part 52 (see para 11.2).

Table 11.1 Summary table – appeals

Appeals in bold type are heard by a *circuit judge* – all other applications are heard by a *district judge*.

	Circumstances	*Complaint*	*Action*	*Timescale*
Judgment after hearing	Both parties attend the hearing	**Decision was wrong and the loser has a real chance of success on appeal**	**Apply for permission to appeal. Appeal will be heard by a circuit judge**	**Apply for permission at the hearing to the district judge or within 21 days to the circuit judge**
		Loser unhappy, but the decision was not wrong	No action can be taken	
	One party does not turn up at the hearing having given notice in advance under CPR rule 27.9 of absence	**The absent party considers the decision was wrong and has real chance of success on appeal**	**Apply for permission to appeal. Appeal will be heard by a circuit judge**	**Application for permission must be made to the circuit judge within 21 days of the decision**
	Loser fails to attend the hearing (no notice having been given under CPR rule 27.9)	Loser's case has a reasonable prospect of success, and loser has a good reason for non-attendance	Application to set aside (CPR rule 27.11) – will be heard by the district judge	No more than 14 days after receipt of the judgment notice
Judgment in default	No acknowledgment or defence	Judgment entered too soon or after the whole of the claim was paid in full (CPR rule 13.2)	Application to set aside or vary default judgment (CPR Part 13)	No specific timescale (note that the district judge must set aside the judgment and will not impose conditions) (CPR rule 13.2)
	Failure to file defence or acknowledgment	Judgment debtor has real prospect of defending or there is other good reason why the judgment should be set aside	Application to set aside or vary default judgment (CPR Part 13)	Promptly (note that the district judge may set aside the judgment and if he or she does so may impose conditions) (CPR rule 13.3)

There is also a procedure to set aside a judgment delivered in the absence of one of the parties. If a party had a good reason for not attending, and his or her case had a reasonable prospect of success, the district judge may allow a re-hearing (see para 11.3).

This chapter also deals with situations where there has been a default judgment and the judgment debtor wishes to have the judgment set aside. In such cases, the applicant must usually be able to establish that he or she has a real prospect of successfully defending the case or there is some other good reason to set aside the judgment (see para 11.4).

On appeal, the loser will only be ordered to pay costs on the basis of the usual rules applicable to the small claims track, including those governing unreasonable behaviour.

11.1.1 Terminology

* *Appellant*: the party making the appeal.
* *Appeal court*: the court which hears the appeal (not to be confused with the Court of Appeal; appeals from decisions of district judges in small claims are made to a circuit judge who sits in the county court).
* *Respondent*: the party responding to the appeal.

11.2 APPEALS

The important time limits in relation to appeals are as follows:

Within 21 days of the decision	Appellant must lodge notice of appeal (including application for permission to appeal if not granted by the district judge at the hearing)
Within 7 days of the appellant filing notice of appeal	Appellant must serve a copy of the notice of appeal on the other side (no need to serve the notice until permission to appeal has been given)
Within 14 days of the respondent being notified of the appeal	Respondent may lodge notice of appeal

11.2.1 The appeal rules

The rules which apply to appeals in small claims cases are the same as those that apply to appeals from decisions made in cases allocated to the fast track and multi track, although the paperwork needed on the appeal is slightly reduced for appeals against small claims decisions. A full discussion of all the rules relevant to appeals is outside the scope of this book and what follows is a working summary relevant to appeals in small claims cases.

11.2.2 Grounds for appeal

CPR rule 52.11(3) states that the appeal court will allow an appeal where the decision of the lower court was:

(a) wrong; or

(b) unjust because of a serious procedural or other irregularity in the proceedings in the lower court.

The circuit judge will only interfere with decision if it is wrong or unjust; this is not the same as a decision with which the loser disagrees.

Ask the following questions when considering an appeal. In making the original decision, did the district judge:

(1) make a critical finding of fact against the weight of the evidence; or

(2) make a critical finding of fact which was totally unsupported by evidence; or

(3) misinterpret a statute and thus come to a wrong decision; or

(4) get any aspect of law wrong and thus come to a wrong decision; or

(5) fail to give reasons for the decision.

If the answer to any one of these questions is 'yes', an appeal may be possible.

Since the circuit judge will generally not re-hear the case but will review the original decision, he or she is interested in the reasons given for the original decision. The rules require the circuit judge to be provided with a suitable record of the district judge's reasons or judgment (see para 11.2.6).

A practitioner who is presenting a case at a small claims hearing will no doubt have heeded the advice given elsewhere in this book to research the law thoroughly and to provide the district judge with copies of any relevant legal authorities. If the decision is wrong because the district judge got the law wrong, this should be thoroughly researched before an appeal is mounted and the correct legal analysis set out in the appeal document.

In considering a possible procedural irregularity, remember that the small claims hearing is, by its nature, a simple affair and that the district judge can conduct the case in any manner provided is fair (CPR rule 27.8(1)). A failure to give reasons for a judgment decision is itself grounds for appeal. Reasons are necessary in order for a party to consider if he or she has grounds for appeal. Justice must be seen to be done.[1]

11.2.3 Permission to appeal

CPR rule 52.3(6) states that permission to appeal will *only* be given where:

(a)   the court considers that the appeal would have a real prospect of success; or

(b)   there is some other compelling reason why the appeal should be heard.

There can be no appeal without permission. Permission to appeal will be given if the appeal has a real, not a fanciful, prospect of success.[2] However, in very rare cases, even if the appeal is likely to fail, permission will be given to appeal if the court identifies some other compelling reason why the appeal should be heard. Such reasons may exist in cases of general public importance or where an issue of human rights is involved.

The prospective appellant has two opportunities to apply for permission: at the hearing itself and later to a circuit judge.

The loser can ask the district judge at the hearing for permission to appeal. No formalities or fee are involved, and if the request is refused, this does not affect the right to make a written application to the circuit judge after the hearing. The district judge will consider whether the appeal has a real prospect of success, and if the request is refused, the district judge will note the reasons on the court file. The failure to apply for permission to appeal at the hearing does not prejudice a party's right to apply later.

If an application for permission to appeal is made after a hearing has been completed, the application cannot be made to the district judge who heard the case but must be to a circuit judge. The application is made in writing and must be made within 21 days of the date of decision (CPR rule 52.4(2)(b)), although the district judge who made the decision may specify a different period. The application is lodged at the county court where the original decision was made.

If an application for permission to appeal is made more than 21 days after the final decision or any extended time granted by the district judge at the final hearing, a separate application must be made for permission to appeal out of

---

[1]   *English v Emery Reimbold & Strick Ltd* [2002] EWCA Civ 605, [2002] 3 All ER 385.

[2]   For more detail on the appellate approach and the appeal court's powers, see *Tanfern Ltd v Cameron-Macdonald* [2000] 2 All ER 801.

time. Late applications will not be granted without good reason and are often refused if the delay is more than a few days.

The application for permission to appeal is combined with the appeal document (Form N164[3]), and the separate fee for making an application for permission to appeal no longer exists.

The application for permission is reviewed, in the first instance, by a circuit judge as boxwork. Permission to appeal may be given there and then, but if it is refused on paper, the prospective appellant has a right to have that decision reviewed at a face-to-face hearing before the circuit judge (CPR rule 52.3(4)). Where the circuit judge has refused permission to appeal in writing and had not altered that decision following a hearing, the loser can take the case no further. The effect of the refusal of permission to appeal is final.[4]

In any case, where permission to appeal is given, the permission may limit the issues to be heard and may be given subject to conditions (CPR rule 52.3(7)).

An outline of the appeal process is set out in the appeal flowchart in para 11.2.10

11.2.4   Review and not re-hearing

CPR rule 52.11(2) states that, unless ordered otherwise, the appeal court will not receive:

(a)   oral evidence;
(b)   evidence which was not before the lower court.

The appeal is not a chance for the loser to start again and present the case once more to a fresh judge. The appeal is strictly a review of the original hearing. There is no new evidence and oral evidence is not called. Argument is based solely on whether the original judge reached a decision that was wrong.

In rare cases, the circuit judge can consider fresh evidence on the appeal, where it could not have been obtained with reasonable diligence for use at the original hearing.[5]

---

3   Available on the Courts Service website, www.justice.gov.uk/forms/hmcts.
4   See *Moyse v Regal Partnerships Ltd* [2004] EWCA Civ 1269.
5   See *Ladd v Marshall* [1954] 3 All ER 745, CA.

11.2.5 Appeals against case management decisions

A case management decision is a decision made to prepare the case for a final hearing, for example an order refusing permission to call an expert or directions about the timetabling of the case.

The procedure for an appeal against a case management decision is the same as for the appeal against a final decision as described above. However, in considering whether permission to appeal is to be granted, the court will consider not only the requirement in para 11.2.3 but also if the issue is of 'sufficient significance' to justify the cost of the appeal and whether the issue would be more conveniently dealt with at the final hearing (PD 52A, para 4.6). Given the relatively low value of most small claims cases and the high costs of an appeal, permission to appeal against a case management decision in a small claims case is rarely requested or granted.

11.2.6 Paperwork for the appeal

PD 52B, para 4.2 states that where the appeal relates to a claim allocated to the small claims track, the appellant must file the following documents with three copies of the appellant's notice:

(1) a sealed copy of the order being appealed;
(2) any order giving or refusing permission to appeal, together with reasons for that decision;
(3) a list of the grounds of (i.e. reasons for) appeal.

Form N164[6] must be fully and properly completed; special permission will be needed to rely on any matter that is not included in the form (CPR rule 52.11(5)). The form is fairly lengthy, but comes with helpful notes.

The appellant against a small claims decision only needs to file a 'suitable record' (e.g. a note or transcript) of the decision of the district judge if required to do so by the circuit judge (PD 52B, para 6.2). In practice, a circuit judge considering a possible appeal will ask for a 'suitable record' in most cases and this will usually take the form of a transcript of the judgment and possibly the whole hearing.

Legal representatives should have made a written note of the judgment given by the district judge (see Chapter 10, para 10.11) and must agree the note, if possible. All small claims hearings are recorded, and the appellant can obtain a

---

6   Available on the Courts Service website, at www.justice.gov.uk/forms/hmcts.

transcript of the recording of the judgment (PD 27, para 5.1) if necessary. The cost of providing the transcript will be about £100 for a half hour judgment. A transcript of the judgment may take several weeks to obtain, and will often not be available to lodge with Form N164. In such cases, Form N164 should contain a coherent summary of the district judge's reasons and a request that the circuit judge allow sufficient time for a full transcript of the judgment to be obtained.

The documents required to support an appeal from a small claims case are slightly fewer in number than the documents needed to support an appeal from a decision made in a case allocated to one of the other case management tracks. However, the small claims appellant may, if he or she chooses, add to the documents strictly required, a skeleton argument, a bundle of documents relevant to the appeal and copies of relevant witness statements

The notice of appeal must be served on the other side promptly and in any event no less than 7 days after it has been filed at the court; this is done by the appellant and not by the court.

Documents needed for a small claims appeal

- Fully completed Form N164 (a fee is payable)
- Sealed copy of the original order
- Any order giving/refusing permission to appeal

Plus (optional):

- Suitable record of the original judgment (note or transcript of tape recording)
- Skeleton argument
- Witness statements
- Documents to support the appeal

Plus:

- Documents which the judge orders the appellant to file in a particular case

---

11.2.7 Respondent's cross appeal

The respondent to the appeal who wishes to ask the appeal court to vary the order of the district judge in any way must also appeal; permission is needed. The respondent's notice is prepared on Form N164. The time limit is 14 days after being notified that the appellant has obtained permission to appeal (CPR rule 52.5).

11.2.8   Hearing of the appeal

The appeal hearing will be before a circuit judge. Whereas many district judges deal with the open court hearings of small claims cases in the relatively informal setting of a hearing room (see Chapter 10, para 10.6), the circuit judge will always hear the case in a traditional court room. Advocates must expect to be robed. The procedure is formal.

A litigant in person may be assisted by a friend at the hearing – the so-called McKenzie friend (see Chapter 10, para 10.6.6) but cannot be assisted by an unqualified lay representative on an appeal (PD 27, para 3.2(2)), unless the circuit judge specifically gives permission. The only advocates who are usually allowed at an appeal hearing are those formally qualified so to act (see Chapter 10, para 10.3.1).

Although the appeal papers are lodged in the court where the case was heard by the district judge, the appeal hearing may be in a different town, in the same court group. The reason for this is that smaller county courts do not always have facilities for circuit judges to hear cases. The staff at the local county court will be able to advise the prospective appellant where the appeal is likely to be heard.

Orders for costs on appeal are restricted by the rules applicable to small claims cases: under CPR rule 27.14 the no costs rule applies to appeals. Chapter 9 considers the no costs rule in detail.

It is usually sensible for the respondent to the appeal to attend the appeal hearing but, even if they do not, the appeal may still be dismissed in their absence. In deciding the merits of the appeal, the circuit judge will have to be satisfied that the appeal should be granted having regard to the factors previously discussed (see para 11.2.2).

11.2.9   Second appeals

The CPR impose severe restrictions on second-tier appeals. The rejection of the appeal by the circuit judge is the effective end of the appeal process. The Court of Appeal itself must give permission for any second appeal and this will only be given if the appeal would raise an important point of principle or practice, or if there is some other compelling reason for the court to hear it (rule 52.13).

As to costs on second appeals, these are covered by the no costs rule (see Chapter 9, para 9.2.8).

11.2.10 Small claims appeal flowchart

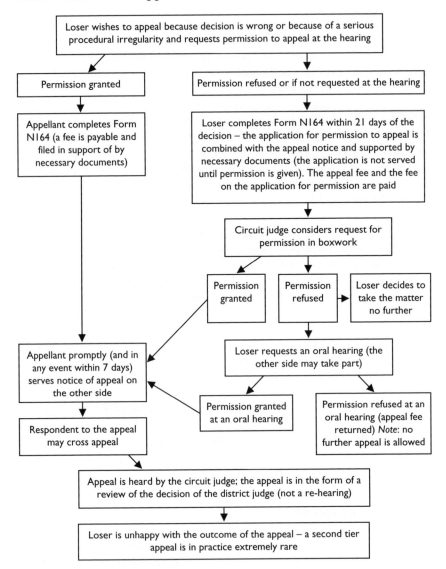

Loser wishes to appeal because decision is wrong or because of a serious procedural irregularity and requests permission to appeal at the hearing

Permission granted

Permission refused or if not requested at the hearing

Appellant completes Form N164 (a fee is payable and filed in support of by necessary documents)

Loser completes Form N164 within 21 days of the decision – the application for permission to appeal is combined with the appeal notice and supported by necessary documents (the application is not served until permission is given). The appeal fee and the fee on the application for permission are paid

Circuit judge considers request for permission in boxwork

Permission granted

Permission refused

Loser decides to take the matter no further

Appellant promptly (and in any event within 7 days) serves notice of appeal on the other side

Loser requests an oral hearing (the other side may take part)

Permission granted at an oral hearing

Permission refused at an oral hearing (appeal fee returned) *Note:* no further appeal is allowed

Respondent to the appeal may cross appeal

Appeal is heard by the circuit judge; the appeal is in the form of a review of the decision of the district judge (not a re-hearing)

Loser is unhappy with the outcome of the appeal – a second tier appeal is in practice extremely rare

11.3 SETTING JUDGMENT ASIDE AND RE-HEARING

CPR rule 27.11 sets out the rules for applying for a small claims decision to be set aside where the loser did not attend the hearing.

A party who did not attend the final hearing and gave the court notice under CPR rule 27.9(1) in advance cannot use this procedure, but if challenging the decision he or she must make an appeal.

A party who was neither present nor represented at the hearing of the claim, and who has not given written notice to the court under CPR rule 27.9(1), may apply for an order that a judgment under Part 27 be set aside and the claim re-heard.[7] The court may grant an application to set aside the judgment only if the applicant:

(a) had a good reason for not attending or being represented at the hearing or giving written notice to the court under rule 27.9(1); and
(b) has a reasonable prospect of success at the hearing.

The party must give a good reason for not attending. It will be for the district judge who hears the application to decide on what is a good reason, but a district judge may be sympathetic to reasons relating to sudden illness or unforeseen circumstances such as transport difficulties. A body of case law has grown up under the heading 'failure to attend the trial' applicable to cases allocated to the fast and multi track (CPR rule 39.3). Those cases offer guidance to the appropriate exercise of judicial discretion when considering applications under rule 27.11(2).[8]

In addition to having a good reason for not attending, the party must show that his or her case had a reasonable prospect of success so, on the hearing of the application, the strength of the case will be considered. Determining whether a case has a reasonable prospect of success is quite a high threshold to cross. The district judge will not only look at the case in some detail but may also consider whether the case is supported by sufficient evidence.

11.3.1 Procedure

Any application must be made within 14 days after the party was served with the notice of judgment; see Chapter 5, para 5.6 as to when the court order will be deemed to have been served.

The court has power to extend time to allow an application to be brought after the 14-day deadline (CPR rule 3.1(2)(a)). However, the district judge to whom

---

7   Unless the aggrieved party gave notice under CPR rule 27.9(1), it is *not* appropriate to challenge a decision given in his or her absence by way of *appeal* (see *Bank of Scotland v Pereira & Pain & Pain* [2011] EWCA Civ 241).

8   *Kenny v Abubaker* [2012] EWCA Civ 1962.

the application to extend time is made will have to bear in mind the obligation to enforce compliance with the rules (rule 3.1(2)(f)) and will usually require a good explanation for the delay.

Chapter 5, para 5.4 deals with the general procedure on applications. The party applying must complete a form and pay a court fee. The form must set out the reason for the application in as much detail as possible. The reasons must cover not only the reason for missing the hearing but also why the party has a reasonable prospect of success. The statement of truth on the application should be signed.

The application will be listed for hearing with a time estimate to cover the time needed to deal with the application (typically 20 or 30 minutes). The parties should not expect the court to hear the whole case again on the day of the application; a further attendance at court will be needed for any re-hearing.

The district judge may use the court's case management powers to attach conditions to setting a new hearing date. These conditions must be expressed clearly and must be capable of being complied with – for example, making it a condition that the party pays a sum of money into court until the case is re-heard (CPR rule 3.1(3)), although an order that funds must be paid into court pending an application will not be made unless the applicant has funds to pay into court.

11.4 SETTING ASIDE A JUDGMENT IN DEFAULT

The relevant rules are found in CPR Part 13.

A judgment in default means a judgment entered because a defence (including a defence to counterclaim) or acknowledgment has not been filed. It follows that the case will not yet have been allocated to the small claims track and the application is not protected by the no costs rule.

11.4.1 Mandatory grounds

The court must set aside a judgment in default if it was wrongly entered (sometimes called an irregular judgment) (CPR rule 13.2). Examples of irregular judgments are those entered before the time for filing a defence had expired or a judgment entered after an application had been made for summary judgment. Where the court is satisfied that the claim form has not been served on the defendant at all, the judgment must be set aside without regard to the defendant's promptness or the prospects of success.[9]

---

[9]   See *Credit Agricole Indosuez v Unicof Ltd* [2002] EWHC 77 (Comm), (2003) LTL, 4 February.

11.4.2 Discretionary grounds

The court has discretion to set aside a default judgment if the defendant has a real prospect of successfully defending the claim or it appears to the court that there is some other good reason why the judgment should be set aside or varied or the defendant should be allowed to defend the claim.

So, although the quality of the proposed defence will usually be the key to success, the district judge can also set the judgment aside for an alternative good reason.

The defence must be something more than an illusion. The district judge will look at the matter in the round, and all the circumstances considered. This may include examining any evidence that the defendant may use to support the defence and considering whether any legal argument has substance.

11.4.3 Procedure

There is no set time limit on making the application – although the rules specify that the application must be made promptly. The district judge will take every case on its own merits. Inevitably, opinions as to what is prompt enough will vary from judge to judge. As a rule of thumb, we suggest that if there is a delay of more than one week before issuing the application, there must be a special explanation for the delay. For example, in *Regency Rolls Ltd and Another v Carnall*,[10] where a party who did not attend trial but did not apply for a re-hearing until 26 days after receiving the adverse judgment, the Court of Appeal decided that the application had not been made promptly enough. In *Bank of Credit and Commerce International (in liq) v Zafar*,[11] a delay of 30 days by a party who needed to obtain representation was described as 'dangerously close' to the margin.

Since the changes to the CPR made on 1 April 2013, the need for promptness has even greater significance than it had previously and relief will be granted much more sparingly.[12]

Chapter 5, para 5.4 deals with the general procedure on applications. The judgment debtor must complete an application and pay a court fee. The application must set out the reason for the application in as much detail as possible and be supported by evidence (CPR rule 13.4(3)).

---

[10] *Regency Rolls Ltd and Another v Carnall* [2000] EWCA Civ 379, (2000) LTL, 16 October.

[11] *Bank of Credit and Commerce International (in liq) v Zafar* [2001] All ER (D) 21 (Nov),

[12] See *Samara v MBI & Partners UK Ltd and Another* [2014] EWHC 563 (QB).

A district judge will hear the application. The judgment debtor must be prepared to show evidence to explain why the original time limits were not adhered to, and any reason for a delay in making the application.

If the judgment is set aside for one of the mandatory grounds, the district judge will not attach any conditions. If the judgment is set aside on a discretionary ground then the district judge can attach conditions – for example making the judgment debtor pay a sum of money into court to await the outcome of the case. These conditions must be expressed clearly and must be capable of being complied with; a party should not be ordered to bring money into court as such a condition unless it is likely he can raise the necessary funds.

11.5   CREDIT REPAIR APPLICATIONS

A judgment debtor may discover years or months after a hearing which he or she did not attend, or after a default judgment, that his or her credit record is blighted. If the judgment debtor was genuinely unaware of the proceedings and would have had a good prospect of defending, then a valid application can be made to set aside the judgment. The application is made as explained above.

Individuals are sometimes tempted by misleading adverts from companies which promise to repair their credit record without them having to pay off the judgment debt. The only legal way of repairing the credit record is to pay the debt or to wait for 6 years when the registration will lapse. District judges are always aware of the possibility that some applications to set aside judgments may be a credit repair application in disguise. Such applications will fail and may open the applicant to criminal charges for perjury[13] (see Chapter 12, para 12.4 for more about the register of county court judgments).

---

[13]   On the grounds that the statement of truth signed with the claim form will be confirming a dishonest reason for the judgment being in existence.

Chapter 12

Enforcement of Small Claims Judgments in the County Court

12.1 PRELIMINARY

Although this short chapter on enforcement appears at the end of the book, there would be a respectable argument for placing it at the beginning. There is no point in pursuing a case through the small claims procedure, securing a judgment, and then being frustrated because the defendant has insufficient funds to meet the judgment. A party embarking on litigation should find out in advance if the other side has funds with which to pay.

This chapter offers some practical tips on how to investigate the ability of a company or an individual to meet a judgment – most of which can be done before starting the case. It also offers a simple overview of the most useful methods of securing payment through the court system. The initiative for enforcement comes from the judgment creditor and not from the judge or the court. All the steps for enforcement involve payment of court fees, filling out forms and some delay.

The Courts Service offers leaflets which will assist with the procedural steps to be followed and these are available on its website.[1]

This chapter is, therefore, not a procedural guide, rather an overview of the options available.

---

[1] www.justice.gov.uk/about/hmcts.

12.2 FINDING OUT ABOUT A DEBTOR'S ASSETS

There are a number of sources of information available to members of the general public. The most important are set out in Table 12.1.

Table 12.1 Sources of information

Name of organisation	Source of information about	Contact details	Fees payable
Companies House	Information about a company, including filed accounts and whether or not a company is in liquidation	www.companieshouse.gov.uk Crown Way Cardiff CF14 3UZ 0303 1234 500	Reports delivered electronically start at £1 each; basic reports online are free
DVLA (Driver and Vehicle Licensing Agency)	Registered keeper of vehicle *Note*: this may not be the legal owner if the car is on finance (see HPI (below))	www.gov.uk/government/organisations/driver-and-vehicle-licensing-agency Enquiries in writing only on Form V888, available on the DVLA website	Starts at £2.50
Electoral Roll	Current residents at a given address	Local town hall upon personal attendance	Free
HPI	Whether a vehicle is stolen, has been written off or is on finance	www.hpicheck.com Enquiries by telephone on 0845 300 8905 and online	£24.99 by telephone and £19.99 online
Individual Insolvency Register	Search here to discover if a person is bankrupt	www.gov.uk/government/organisations/insolvency-service	Free
Land Registry including Land Charges Department	The name of the registered owner of any house or land and details of any mortgages	www.landregistry.gov.uk FAO Citizen Centre Land Registry Wales Office Ty Cwn Tawe Phoenix Way Llansamlet Swansea SA7 9FQ 0844 892 1111	Fees start at £3.00
Local bankruptcy county court	Whether a bankruptcy petition has been issued against a judgment debtor	Contact the bankruptcy county court relevant to the address of the judgment debtor	Free

Name of organisation	Source of information about	Contact details	Fees payable
Local county court	Existing attachment of earnings orders	Apply in writing to the county court on Form N336, available at www.justice.gov.uk/forms/hmcts	Free
Local county court (only available after judgment)	Debtor's assets	Application for order to obtain information, see para 12.3	£50 (see EX50)
Trust Online	Register of judgments, orders and fines	www.trustonline.org.uk 153–157 Cleveland Street London WIT 6QW 020 7380 0133	Searches may be made online, or by post. The fee structure is based on a search against a single name or trading name at an address or against a limited company. The basic charge is £4 per search but there are discounts for frequent users

12.3 ORDER TO OBTAIN INFORMATION

This is not a direct method of enforcement, but a way in which the court can assist in investigating the assets of the judgment debtor. The judgment debtor is summonsed to court to be questioned by a senior court officer or the district judge about his or her assets. A manager of a company can be summonsed to answer questions about the company's assets. If the judgment debtor does not co-operate, the matter may be referred to a circuit judge, who can make an order for the judgment debtor's committal to prison.

The procedure is effective for investigating the judgment debtor's assets, and the inconvenience it can cause to the judgment debtor is sometimes enough to prompt him or her into payment.

See CPR Part 71.

12.4 REGISTER OF JUDGMENTS, ORDERS AND FINES

This is not an enforcement method, but the threat of registration or the desire to get a credit record cleared can result in payment to the creditor. Defendants are warned, in the response pack which they receive with the claim form, about the possibility of a judgment being registered, and this warning may in some cases be sufficient to prompt a debtor to settle a claim. The process of registration is automatic in the cases mentioned below.

The Register of judgments, orders and fines is not operated by the courts but by Trust Online, which has a helpful and well laid out website.[2] A search of the Register will alert a claimant in advance that the debtor has a history of bad debts (see Table 12.1). A charge of £4 is made for each search. The effect of registration is to make it difficult for the judgment debtor to get credit, for example to get a loan to buy a car or to get a mortgage. A judgment debtor may decide to pay a judgment so that it is marked as 'satisfied' on the register and to help him or her get credit.

Judgments which are registered include:

- any default judgment (including a judgment on admission);
- a judgment after a hearing which is payable by instalments;
- a judgment after a hearing when the money is not paid or if the judgment creditor issues enforcement or oral examination.

A registration is cancelled if judgment is set aside and is marked as satisfied when it is paid in full. A fee of £15 is payable to the court for a certificate of satisfaction. If the debt is paid within one month of the entry of the debt on the register it can be cancelled and will not appear on the register; the court charges a fee of £15 for a request for cancellation. Debts which are satisfied remain on the register but are shown as satisfied. Judgment debts remain on the register for 6 years.

12.5 BANKRUPTCY AND COMPANY INSOLVENCY

Although bankruptcy is available for debts of £750 and more, it rarely results in payment to ordinary creditors. A judgment creditor, even the creditor who starts the insolvency action is not a preferential creditor and must take a share in any assets with other ordinary creditors, but only after those with security (e.g.

---

[2]   www.trustonline.org.uk.

mortgagees) have been paid, and after payment of outstanding tax and the fees and expenses of the receiver in bankruptcy.

A statutory demand is the first step to bankruptcy against an individual and this is prepared and served without any court involvement. A statutory demand can be served as soon as the debt is due, and a judgment is not necessary. If the debtor who is an individual disputes the claim, he or she can apply for the statutory demand to be set aside. The bankruptcy court will halt the bankruptcy if there is any real dispute about the sum outstanding. It can be relatively easy for a debtor to have a statutory demand set aside and the process can result in an order for costs being made against the creditor.

The winding up procedure against companies also starts with a statutory demand. There is no set procedure to set aside a statutory demand against a company, and if the debt is disputed, the case is argued after the presentation of the petition.

The court fees and sums payable to the official receiver by way of deposit are considerable and will deter most creditors pursuing a small claims judgment via the bankruptcy or insolvency route.

12.6   WARRANT OF CONTROL

The county court bailiffs can enforce any judgment up to £5,000 by the seizure and sale of the judgment debtor's goods. Permission to issue a warrant of execution is needed if the judgment debt is more than 6 years old.

The warrant itself remains valid for 12 months, after which it may be renewed by order of the court.

Unless the district judge orders otherwise, the bailiff gives the judgment debtor 7 days' notice of execution action. Thereafter, the bailiff attends at the judgment debtor's premises and usually invites the judgment debtor to sign a controlled goods agreement. The judgment debtor promises not to remove the goods in exchange for being given a chance to pay the debt in full. If the debt is then not paid, the goods are removed and sold at auction.

If anyone else claims that the goods seized belong to them and not to the judgment debtor, they can make a claim for the goods under CPR Part 85. The bailiff cannot execute the warrant against items which are on hire purchase, including cars and household furniture. The bailiffs also cannot remove any exempt goods, for example domestic items such as beds and bedding, cooker, fridge, washing machine, medical aids, and office equipment for the debtor's personal business such as computers, tools, telephones – even vehicles – as long as they do not together exceed a value of £1,350 (see Taking Control of Goods Regulations 2013,[3] regulation 4).

If the judgment is £600 or more, the enforcement can be transferred to the High Court for enforcement by the High Court Enforcement Officers.

See CPR Parts 83, 84 and 85.

12.7   THIRD PARTY DEBT ORDER

This is an action to intercept a debt owed to the judgment debtor by someone else and to get the money paid to the judgment creditor direct.

The most usual debts intercepted in this way are credit balances in bank and building society accounts and trade debts owed to the judgment debtor. The method of enforcement is not available against an account or debt due to the judgment debtor jointly with someone else.

The order to obtain information procedure can be used to obtain details about a person's bank and building society accounts. If the judgment debtor has previously paid by a cheque which was not met on presentation, this may be a clue that the account does not hold sufficient funds. Any third party holding the debtor's funds can deduct their own expenses of searching their own records for the debtor's funds before handing the money over to the judgment creditor.

See CPR Part 72.

12.8   ATTACHMENT OF EARNINGS

This method of enforcement is available against judgment debtors who are in employment.[4] A sum of money is sent weekly or monthly straight to the judgment creditor direct by the judgment debtor's employer. The procedure is in two parts. The court requires the judgment debtor to fill out a form setting out details of his or her earnings and outgoings (a statement of means). If this is not completed, the judgment debtor can be ordered to attend court to give the

---

[3]   Taking Control of Goods Regulations 2013 (SI 2013/1894).

[4]   But is not available against members of the army, navy or air force or where the judgment debtor is a merchant seaman.

information. Failure to co-operate completely in this process could result in the judgment debtor being fined or imprisoned.

The second part involves making the order for the employer to deduct a suitable monthly or weekly sum from the judgment debtor's wages. The court sets a protected earnings threshold, which allows the judgment debtor to cover his or her basic home expenses in priority to any payment to the judgment creditor.

Once an attachment of earnings order is in place, the judgment creditor must bring to the attention of the court the existence of the order before commencing any other enforcement steps.

Overall, this can be an effective, if often slow, method of ensuring that the judgment debt is paid.

Generally, see CCR Order 27, set ou in CPR Schedule 2.

12.9   CHARGING ORDER ON LAND

This method of enforcement gives the judgment creditor the equivalent of a mortgage over the judgment debtor's land. The charging order remains on the land registry records and the judgment debtor will have to clear the judgment debt before the land can be sold. Since the judgment does not attract interest and the wait before sale may be several years, the delay in payment may significantly reduce the value of this method to the judgment creditor.

The usual way of proving that the debtor owns the land is to produce a copy of the entry at the Land Registry (see Table 12.1).

12.9.1   Charging order on securities

The charging order procedure can also be used against stocks and shares including government stock and dividends.

12.9.2   Order for sale

A judgment creditor who has registered a charging order against land may apply to the court for an order for sale. The procedure depends on whether the land is jointly owned or is in the sole name of the judgment debtor. The district judge has a discretion whether or not to make the order and if the judgment debt is small, then the order for sale may not be made.

Where a charging order was made to secure a debt owed under a regulated agreement within Consumer Credit Act 1974, section 189(1), the court will not allow it to be enforced to recover an amount which is less than £1,000 (Charging Orders (Orders for Sale: Financial Thresholds) Regulations 2012[5]).

See CPR Part 73.

12.10 TIMESCALE FOR ENFORCEMENT AND INTEREST

A judgment debt can be enforced at any time after judgment. However, a registration of judgment debt runs out after 6 years, and the permission of the district judge is required to issue a warrant of execution after 6 years (CPR rule 83.2). Confusingly, if a fresh action is started by way of enforcement (e.g. an application for an order for sale following a charging order), it must be commenced within 6 years.

Interest does not run on judgment debts enforced in a county court for £5,000 or less.

12.11 STEPS AFTER A SMALL CLAIMS JUDGMENT – OVERVIEW

		Available against the following assets	
Enforcement method	Bankruptcy/company insolvency	An unsecured creditor will share the debtor's assets with all other unsecured creditors	An up-to-date list of fees can be found at www.justice.gov.uk/about/hmcts/
	Warrant of control (bailiffs seizing goods)	Personal possessions (excluding domestic necessities and possessions needed for the judgment debtor to earn a living)	
	Third party debt proceedings	Trade debts Bank and building society accounts which are in credit	

---

[5]   Charging Orders (Orders for Sale: Financial Thresholds) Regulations 2012 (SI 2012/491).

		Available against the following assets	
Enforcement method	Attachment of earnings	The wages of an employed (not self-employed) person insofar as they exceed the protected earnings rate	An up-to-date list of fees can be found at www.justice.gov.uk/ about/hmcts/
	Charging order	Land Stocks and shares Government securities	
Also	Order to obtain information	A method of determining the judgment debtor's assets (not a method of enforcement)	
	Registration of the judgment	Applies to default judgments and judgments after a hearing if payment is made by instalments or enforcement action is taken (not a method of enforcement)	

Appendices

1	Court Fees Payable in Small Claims Cases – Commencement and Hearing Fees	235
2	Court Fees Payable in Small Claims Cases – Applications and Appeals	237
3	Fixed Commencement Costs (CPR Rule 45.2)	239
4	Fixed Costs on Entry of Judgment	241
5	Practice Direction (Pre-Action Conduct), Extracts	243
6	Civil Procedure Rules, Part 1	255
7	Civil Procedure Rules, Part 27	257
8	Civil Procedure Rules, Practice Direction 27	265
9	Directions Questionnaire (Small Claims Track), Form N180	273
10	Costs Schedule	277
11	Mediation Settlement Agreement, Form N182	279

Appendix 1

Court Fees Payable in Small Claims Cases – Commencement and Hearing Fees

Amount stated in the claim/fee payable on counterclaim	Fee payable on commencement (figures in brackets are when the proceedings are issued online)	Hearing fee	
Does not exceed £300	£35 (£25)	£25	The hearing fee is refunded if the case is withdrawn 7 days or more before the final hearing
£300.01 and does not exceed £500	£50 (£35)	£55	
£500.01 and does not exceed £1,000	£70 (£60)	£80	
£1,000.01 and does not exceed £1,500	£80 (£70)	£115	
£1,500.01 and does not exceed £3,000	£115 (£105)	£170	
£3,000.01 and does not exceed £5,000	£205 (£185)	£335	
£5,000.01 and does not exceed £15,000[1]	£455 (£410)	£335	
Any claim for a remedy other than the payment of money (rare in the small claims track)	£280 (£250 for recovery of land online)		

---

[1] Of course, any claim for more than £10,000 will not normally be allocated to the small claims track.

Appendix 2

Court Fees Payable in Small Claims Cases – Applications and Appeals

Any application requiring the attendance of both sides, including applications under CPR Parts 23 and 24	£155
Application to vary a judgment, suspend enforcement or an application by consent	£50
Appeal (including fee for permission to appeal)	£120
Fee payable on making *Tomlin* order at the end of a successful mediation – if applied for at least 14 days before the date of hearing (treated as a request to vacate the final hearing)	0

Appendix 3

Fixed Commencement Costs[1] (CPR Rule 45.2)

These costs can only be claimed if a solicitor drafts the claim.

Value of claim	Where the claim form is served by the court	Where the claim form is served by the claimant personally and there is only one defendant[2]
Not more than £25	Nothing	Nothing
£25.01 to not more than £500	£50	£60
£500.01 to not more than £1,000	£70	£80
£1,000.01 to £5,000	£80	£90
Exceeding £5,000.01	£100	£110

[1] These fixed costs are applicable only where the claim is for a specified sum. If the claim is unspecified, the fixed costs can be added depending on the sum actually awarded.

[2] Add £15 for each defendant personally served.

Appendix 4

Fixed Costs on Entry of Judgment

These costs are only allowed if the judgment is in default of defence or acknowledgement and do not apply following allocation to the small claims track when the no costs rule applies. The sum in brackets applies if the judgment is for a sum in excess of £5,000.

Judgment in default of defence	£25 (£35)
Judgment in default of acknowledgment of service	£22 (£30)
Judgment on admission for whole or part and the parties decide the date or times of payment	£40 (£55)
Judgment on admission of whole or part and the court decides the date or times of payment	£55 (£70)
Summary judgment or case struck out	£175 (£210)

Appendix 5

Practice Direction (Pre-Action Conduct), Extracts

These are the extracts which are relevant to small claims:

- Exchanging information before starting proceedings.
- Alternative Dispute Resolution.
- Annex A: guidance on pre-action procedure where no pre-action protocol applies.
- Annex B: information to be provided in debt claims where the claimant is a business and the defendant is an individual.
- Compliance.

7. Exchanging information before starting proceedings

7.1
Before starting proceedings –

(1) the claimant should set out the details of the matter in writing by sending a letter before claim to the defendant. This letter before claim is not the start of proceedings; and

(2) the defendant should give a full written response within a reasonable period, preceded, if appropriate, by a written acknowledgment of the letter before claim.

7.2
A 'reasonable period of time' will vary depending on the matter. As a general guide –

(1) the defendant should send a letter of acknowledgment within 14 days of receipt of the letter before claim (if a full response has not been sent within that period);

(2) where the matter is straightforward, for example an undisputed debt, then a full response should normally be provided within 14 days;

(3) where a matter requires the involvement of an insurer or other third party or where there are issues about evidence, then a full response should normally be provided within 30 days;

(4) where the matter is particularly complex, for example requiring specialist advice, then a period of longer than 30 days may be appropriate;

(5) a period of longer than 90 days in which to provide a full response will only be considered reasonable in exceptional circumstances.

7.3

Annex A sets out detailed guidance on a pre-action procedure that is likely to satisfy the court in most circumstances where no pre-action protocol applies and where the claimant does not follow any statutory or other formal pre-action procedure.

7.4

Annex B sets out the specific information that should be provided in a debt claim by a claimant who is a business against a defendant who is an individual.

8. Alternative Dispute Resolution

8.1

Starting proceedings should usually be a step of last resort, and proceedings should not normally be started when a settlement is still actively being explored. Although ADR is not compulsory, the parties should consider whether some form of ADR procedure might enable them to settle the matter without starting proceedings. The court may require evidence that the parties considered some form of ADR (see paragraph 4.4(3)).

8.2

It is not practicable in this Practice Direction to address in detail how the parties might decide to resolve a matter. However, some of the options for resolving a matter without starting proceedings are –

(1) discussion and negotiation;

(2) mediation (a form of negotiation with the help of an independent person or body);

(3) early neutral evaluation (where an independent person or body, for example a lawyer or an expert in the subject, gives an opinion on the merits of a dispute); or

(4) arbitration (where an independent person or body makes a binding decision), many types of business are members of arbitration schemes for resolving disputes with consumers.

8.3

The Legal Services Commission has published a booklet on 'Alternatives to Court', CLS Direct Information Leaflet 23 (www.clsdirect.org.uk) which lists a number of organisations that provide alternative dispute resolution services. The National Mediation Helpline on 0845 603 0809 or at www.nationalmediationhelpline.com can provide information about mediation.

8.4

The parties should continue to consider the possibility of reaching a settlement at all times. This still applies after proceedings have been started, up to and during any trial or final hearing.

ANNEX A

Guidance on pre-action procedure where no pre-action protocol or other formal pre-action procedure applies

1. General

1.1

This Annex sets out detailed guidance on a pre-action procedure that is likely to satisfy the court in most circumstances where no pre-action protocol or other formal pre-action procedure applies. It is intended as a guide for parties, particularly those without legal representation, in straightforward claims that are likely to be disputed. It is not intended to apply to debt claims where it is not disputed that the money is owed and where the claimant follows a statutory or other formal pre-action procedure.

2. Claimant's letter before claim

2.1

The claimant's letter should give concise details about the matter. This should enable the defendant to understand and investigate the issues without needing to request further information. The letter should include –

(1) the claimant's full name and address;
(2) the basis on which the claim is made (i.e. why the claimant says the defendant is liable);
(3) a clear summary of the facts on which the claim is based;
(4) what the claimant wants from the defendant;
(5) if financial loss is claimed, an explanation of how the amount has been calculated.

2.2

The letter should also –

(1) list the essential documents on which the claimant intends to rely;
(2) set out the form of ADR (if any) that the claimant considers the most suitable and invite the defendant to agree to this;
(3) state the date by which the claimant considers it reasonable for a full response to be provided by the defendant; and
(4) identify and ask for copies of any relevant documents not in the claimant's possession and which the claimant wishes to see.

2.3

Unless the defendant is known to be legally represented the letter should –

(1) refer the defendant to this Practice Direction and in particular draw attention to paragraph 4 concerning the court's powers to impose sanctions for failure to comply with the Practice Direction; and

(2) inform the defendant that ignoring the letter before claim may lead to the claimant starting proceedings and may increase the defendant's liability for costs.

3. Defendant's acknowledgment of the letter before claim

3.1

Where the defendant is unable to provide a full written response within 14 days of receipt of the letter before claim the defendant should, instead, provide a written acknowledgment within 14 days.

3.2

The acknowledgment –

(1) should state whether an insurer is or may be involved;

(2) should state the date by which the defendant (or insurer) will provide a full written response; and

(3) may request further information to enable the defendant to provide a full response.

3.3

If the date stated under paragraph 3.2(2) of this Annex is longer than the period stated in the letter before claim, the defendant should give reasons why a longer period is needed.

3.4

If the defendant (or insurer) does not provide either a letter of acknowledgment or full response within 14 days, and proceedings are subsequently started, then the court is likely to consider that the claimant has complied.

3.5

Where the defendant is unable to provide a full response within 14 days of receipt of the letter before claim because the defendant intends to seek advice then the written acknowledgment should state –

(1) that the defendant is seeking advice;

(2) from whom the defendant is seeking advice; and

(3)   when the defendant expects to have received that advice and be in a position to provide a full response.

3.6
A claimant should allow a reasonable period of time of up to 14 days for a defendant to obtain advice.

4. Defendant's full response

4.1
The defendant's full written response should –

(1)   accept the claim in whole or in part; or
(2)   state that the claim is not accepted.

4.2
Unless the defendant accepts the whole of the claim, the response should –

(1)   give reasons why the claim is not accepted, identifying which facts and which parts of the claim (if any) are accepted and which are disputed, and the basis of that dispute;
(2)   state whether the defendant intends to make a counterclaim against the claimant (and, if so, provide information equivalent to a claimant's letter before claim);
(3)   state whether the defendant alleges that the claimant was wholly or partly to blame for the problem that led to the dispute and, if so, summarise the facts relied on;
(4)   state whether the defendant agrees to the claimant's proposals for ADR and if not, state why not and suggest an alternative form of ADR (or state why none is considered appropriate);
(5)   list the essential documents on which the defendant intends to rely;
(6)   enclose copies of documents requested by the claimant, or explain why they will not be provided; and
(7)   identify and ask for copies of any further relevant documents, not in the defendant's possession and which the defendant wishes to see.

4.3
If the defendant (or insurer) does not provide a full response within the period stated in the claimant's letter before claim (or any longer period stated in the defendant's letter of acknowledgment), and a claim is subsequently started, then the court is likely to consider that the claimant has complied.

4.4

If the claimant starts proceedings before any longer period stated in the defendant's letter of acknowledgment, the court will consider whether or not the longer period requested by the defendant was reasonable.

5. Claimant's reply

5.1

The claimant should provide the documents requested by the defendant within as short a period of time as is practicable or explain in writing why the documents will not be provided.

5.2

If the defendant has made a counterclaim the claimant should provide information equivalent to the defendant's full response (see paragraphs 4.1 to 4.3 above).

6. Taking Stock

6.1

In following the above procedure, the parties will have a genuine opportunity to resolve the matter without needing to start proceedings. At the very least, it should be possible to establish what issues remain outstanding so as to narrow the scope of the proceedings and therefore limit potential costs.

6.2

If having completed the procedure the matter has not been resolved then the parties should undertake a further review of their respective positions to see if proceedings can still be avoided.

ANNEX B

Information to be provided in a debt claim where the claimant is a business and the defendant is an individual

1.

Where paragraph 7.4 of the Practice Direction applies the claimant should –

(1)   provide details of how the money can be paid (for example the method of payment and the address to which it can be sent);

(2)   state that the defendant can contact the claimant to discuss possible repayment options, and provide the relevant contact details; and

(3)   inform the defendant that free independent advice and assistance can be obtained from organisations including those listed in the table below.

INDEPENDENT ADVICE ORGANISATIONS

Organisation	Address	Telephone number	Email address
National Debtline	Tricorn House 51–53 Hagley Road Edgbaston Birmingham B16 8TP	FREEPHONE 0808 808 4000	www.nationaldebtline.co.uk
Consumer Credit Counselling Service (CCCS)		FREEPHONE 0800 138 1111	www.cccs.co.uk
Citizens Advice	Check your local Yellow Pages or Thomson local directory for address and telephone numbers		www.citizensadvice.org.uk
Community Legal Advice (formerly Community Legal Services Direct)		0845 345 4345	www.clsdirect.org.uk

2.

The information set out in paragraph 1 of this Annex may be provided at any time between the claimant first intimating the possibility of court proceedings and the claimant's letter before claim.

3.

Where the defendant is unable to provide a full response within the time specified in the letter before claim because the defendant intends to seek debt advice then the written acknowledgment should state –

(1) that the defendant is seeking debt advice;
(2) who the defendant is seeking advice from; and
(3) when the defendant expects to have received that advice and be in a position to provide a full response.

4.

A claimant should allow a reasonable period of time of up to 14 days for a defendant to obtain debt advice.

5.

But the claimant need not allow the defendant time to seek debt advice if the claimant knows that –

(1) the defendant has already received relevant debt advice and the defendant's circumstances have not significantly changed; or
(2) the defendant has previously asked for time to seek debt advice but has not done so.

4. Compliance

4.1

The CPR enable the court to take into account the extent of the parties' compliance with this Practice Direction or a relevant pre-action protocol (see paragraph 5.2) when giving directions for the management of claims (see CPR rule 3.1(4) and (5)) and when making orders about who should pay costs (see CPR rule 44.2(5)(a)).

4.2

The court will expect the parties to have complied with this Practice Direction or any relevant pre-action protocol. The court may ask the parties to explain what steps were taken to comply prior to the start of the claim. Where there has been a failure of compliance by a party the court may ask that party to provide an explanation.

Assessment of compliance

4.3

When considering compliance the court will –

(1) be concerned about whether the parties have complied in substance with the relevant principles and requirements and is not likely to be concerned with minor or technical shortcomings;
(2) consider the proportionality of the steps taken compared to the size and importance of the matter;
(3) take account of the urgency of the matter. Where a matter is urgent (for example, an application for an injunction) the court will expect the parties to comply only to the extent that it is reasonable to do so. (Paragraph 9.5 and 9.6 of this Practice Direction concern urgency caused by limitation periods.)

Examples of non-compliance

4.4

The court may decide that there has been a failure of compliance by a party because, for example, that party has –

(1) not provided sufficient information to enable the other party to understand the issues;
(2) not acted within a time limit set out in a relevant pre-action protocol, or, where no specific time limit applies, within a reasonable period;

(3) unreasonably refused to consider ADR (paragraph 8 in Part III of this Practice Direction and the pre-action protocols all contain similar provisions about ADR); or

(4) without good reason, not disclosed documents requested to be disclosed.

Sanctions for non-compliance

4.5

The court will look at the overall effect of non-compliance on the other party when deciding whether to impose sanctions.

4.6

If, in the opinion of the court, there has been non-compliance, the sanctions which the court may impose include –

(1) staying (that is suspending) the proceedings until steps which ought to have been taken have been taken;

(2) an order that the party at fault pays the costs, or part of the costs, of the other party or parties (this may include an order under rule 27.14(2)(g) in cases allocated to the small claims track);

(3) an order that the party at fault pays those costs on an indemnity basis (rule 44.3(3) sets out the definition of the assessment of costs on an indemnity basis);

(4) if the party at fault is the claimant in whose favour an order for the payment of a sum of money is subsequently made, an order that the claimant is deprived of interest on all or part of that sum, and/or that interest is awarded at a lower rate than would otherwise have been awarded;

(5) if the party at fault is a defendant, and an order for the payment of a sum of money is subsequently made in favour of the claimant, an order that the defendant pay interest on all or part of that sum at a higher rate, not exceeding 10% above base rate, than would otherwise have been awarded.

Appendix 6

Civil Procedure Rules, Part 1

Contents of this Part
The overriding objective	Rule 1.1
Application by the court of the overriding objective	Rule 1.2
Duty of the parties	Rule 1.3
Court's duty to manage cases	Rule 1.4

The overriding objective

1.1

(1) These Rules are a new procedural code with the overriding objective of enabling the court to deal with cases justly and at proportionate cost.

(2) Dealing with a case justly and at proportionate cost includes, so far as is practicable –

    (a) ensuring that the parties are on an equal footing;

    (b) saving expense;

    (c) dealing with the case in ways which are proportionate –

        (i) to the amount of money involved;

        (ii) to the importance of the case;

        (iii) to the complexity of the issues; and

        (iv) to the financial position of each party;

    (d) ensuring that it is dealt with expeditiously and fairly;

    (e) allotting to it an appropriate share of the court's resources, while taking into account the need to allot resources to other cases; and

    (f) enforcing compliance with rules, practice directions and orders.

Application by the court of the overriding objective

1.2

The court must seek to give effect to the overriding objective when it –

(a) exercises any power given to it by the Rules; or

(b) interprets any rule subject to rules 76.2 and 79.2 and 80.2 and 82.2.

Duty of the parties
1.3
The parties are required to help the court to further the overriding objective.

Court's duty to manage cases
1.4
(1) The court must further the overriding objective by actively managing cases.

(2) Active case management includes –

(a) encouraging the parties to co-operate with each other in the conduct of the proceedings;

(b) identifying the issues at an early stage;

(c) deciding promptly which issues need full investigation and trial and accordingly disposing summarily of the others;

(d) deciding the order in which issues are to be resolved;

(e) encouraging the parties to use an alternative dispute resolution procedure if the court considers that appropriate and facilitating the use of such procedure;

(f) helping the parties to settle the whole or part of the case;

(g) fixing timetables or otherwise controlling the progress of the case;

(h) considering whether the likely benefits of taking a particular step justify the cost of taking it;

(i) dealing with as many aspects of the case as it can on the same occasion;

(j) dealing with the case without the parties needing to attend at court;

(k) making use of technology; and

(l) giving directions to ensure that the trial of a case proceeds quickly and efficiently.

Appendix 7

Civil Procedure Rules, Part 27

Contents of this Part
Scope of this Part   Rule 27.1
Extent to which other Parts apply   Rule 27.2
Court's power to grant a final remedy   Rule 27.3
Preparation for the hearing   Rule 27.4
Experts   Rule 27.5
Preliminary hearing   Rule 27.6
Power of court to add to, vary or revoke directions   Rule 27.7
Conduct of the hearing   Rule 27.8
Non-attendance of parties at a final hearing   Rule 27.9
Disposal without a hearing   Rule 27.10
Setting judgment aside and re-hearing   Rule 27.11
Costs on the small claims track   Rule 27.14
Claim re-allocated from the small claims track to another track   Rule 27.15

Scope of this Part
27.1
(1) This Part –

    (a) sets out the special procedure for dealing with claims which have been allocated to the small claims track under Part 26; and

    (b) limits the amount of costs that can be recovered in respect of a claim which has been allocated to the small claims track.

(Rule 27.14 deals with costs on the small claims track)

(2) A claim being dealt with under this Part is called a small claim.

(Rule 26.6 provides for the scope of the small claims track. A claim for a remedy for harassment or unlawful eviction relating, in either case, to residential premises shall not be allocated to the small claims track whatever the financial value of the claim. Otherwise, the small claims track will be the normal track for –

- any claim which has a financial value of not more than £5,000 subject to the special provisions about claims for personal injuries and housing disrepair claims;
- any claim for personal injuries which has a financial value of not more than £5,000 where the claim for damages for personal injuries is not more than £1,000; and
- any claim which includes a claim by a tenant of residential premises against his landlord for repairs or other work to the premises where the estimated cost of the repairs or other work is not more than £1,000 and the financial value of any other claim for damages is not more than £1,000).

Extent to which other Parts apply
27.2
(1) The following Parts of these Rules do not apply to small claims –

(a) Part 25 (interim remedies) except as it relates to interim injunctions;
(b) Part 31 (disclosure and inspection);
(c) Part 32 (evidence) except rule 32.1 (power of court to control evidence);
(d) Part 33 (miscellaneous rules about evidence);
(e) Part 35 (experts and assessors) except rules 35.1 (duty to restrict expert evidence), 35.3 (experts – overriding duty to the court), 35.7 (court's power to direct that evidence is to be given by single joint expert) and 35.8 (instructions to a single joint expert);
(f) Subject to paragraph (3), Part 18 (further information);
(g) Part 36 (offers to settle); and
(h) Part 39 (hearings) except rule 39.2 (general rule – hearing to be in public).

(2) The other Parts of these Rules apply to small claims except to the extent that a rule limits such application.
(3) The court of its own initiative may order a party to provide further information if it considers it appropriate to do so.

Court's power to grant a final remedy
27.3
The court may grant any final remedy in relation to a small claim which it could grant if the proceedings were on the fast track or the multi-track.

Preparation for the hearing
27.4
(1) After allocation the court will –

    (a) give standard directions and fix a date for the final hearing;
    (b) give special directions and fix a date for the final hearing;
    (c) give special directions and direct that the court will consider what further directions are to be given no later than 28 days after the date the special directions were given;
    (d) fix a date for a preliminary hearing under rule 27.6; or
    (e) give notice that it proposes to deal with the claim without a hearing under rule 27.10 and invite the parties to notify the court by a specified date if they agree the proposal.

(2) The court will –

    (a) give the parties at least 21 days' notice of the date fixed for the final hearing, unless the parties agree to accept less notice; and
    (b) inform them of the amount of time allowed for the final hearing.

(3) In this rule –

    (a) 'standard directions' means –
        (i) a direction that each party shall, at least 14 days before the date fixed for the final hearing, file and serve on every other party copies of all documents (including any expert's report) on which he intends to rely at the hearing; and
        (ii) any other standard directions set out in the relevant practice direction; and
    (b) 'special directions' means directions given in addition to or instead of the standard directions.

Experts
27.5
No expert may give evidence, whether written or oral, at a hearing without the permission of the court.

(Rule 27.14(3)(d) provides for the payment of an expert's fees)

Preliminary hearing
27.6
(1) The court may hold a preliminary hearing for the consideration of the claim, but only –

(a) where –
   (i)   it considers that special directions, as defined in rule 27.4, are needed to ensure a fair hearing; and
   (ii) it appears necessary for a party to attend at court to ensure that he understands what he must do to comply with the special directions; or
(b) to enable it to dispose of the claim on the basis that one or other of the parties has no real prospect of success at a final hearing; or
(c) to enable it to strike out a statement of case or part of a statement of case on the basis that the statement of case, or the part to be struck out, discloses no reasonable grounds for bringing or defending the claim.

(2) When considering whether or not to hold a preliminary hearing, the court must have regard to the desirability of limiting the expense to the parties of attending court.
(3) Where the court decides to hold a preliminary hearing, it will give the parties at least 14 days' notice of the date of the hearing.
(4) The court may treat the preliminary hearing as the final hearing of the claim if all the parties agree.
(5) At or after the preliminary hearing the court will –

   (a) fix the date of the final hearing (if it has not been fixed already) and give the parties at least 21 days' notice of the date fixed unless the parties agree to accept less notice;
   (b) inform them of the amount of time allowed for the final hearing; and
   (c) give any appropriate directions.

Power of court to add to, vary or revoke directions
27.7
The court may add to, vary or revoke directions.

Conduct of the hearing
27.8
(1) The court may adopt any method of proceeding at a hearing that it considers to be fair.
(2) Hearings will be informal.
(3) The strict rules of evidence do not apply.
(4) The court need not take evidence on oath.
(5) The court may limit cross-examination.
(6) The court must give reasons for its decision.

Non-attendance of parties at a final hearing

27.9

(1) If a party who does not attend a final hearing –

    (a) has given written notice to the court and the other party at least 7 days before the hearing date that he will not attend;

    (b) has served on the other party at least 7 days before the hearing date any other documents which he has filed with the court; and

    (c) has, in his written notice, requested the court to decide the claim in his absence and has confirmed his compliance with paragraphs (a) and (b) above,

the court will take into account that party's statement of case and any other documents he has filed and served when it decides the claim.

(2) If a claimant does not –

    (a) attend the hearing; and

    (b) give the notice referred to in paragraph (1),

the court may strike out the claim.

(3) If –

    (a) a defendant does not –
        (i) attend the hearing; or
        (ii) give the notice referred to in paragraph (1); and

    (b) the claimant either –
        (i) does attend the hearing; or
        (ii) gives the notice referred to in paragraph (1),

the court may decide the claim on the basis of the evidence of the claimant alone.

(4) If neither party attends or gives the notice referred to in paragraph (1), the court may strike out the claim and any defence and counterclaim.

Disposal without a hearing

27.10

The court may, if all parties agree, deal with the claim without a hearing.

Setting judgment aside and re-hearing
27.11
(1)   A party –

    (a)   who was neither present nor represented at the hearing of the claim; and

    (b)   who has not given written notice to the court under rule 27.9(1),

    may apply for an order that a judgment under this Part shall be set aside and the claim re-heard.

(2)   A party who applies for an order setting aside a judgment under this rule must make the application not more than 14 days after the day on which notice of the judgment was served on him.

(3)   The court may grant an application under paragraph (2) only if the applicant –

    (a)   had a good reason for not attending or being represented at the hearing or giving written notice to the court under rule 27.9(1); and

    (b)   has a reasonable prospect of success at the hearing.

(4)   If a judgment is set aside–

    (a)   the court must fix a new hearing for the claim; and

    (b)   the hearing may take place immediately after the hearing of the application to set the judgment aside and may be dealt with by the judge who set aside the judgment.

(5)   A party may not apply to set aside a judgment under this rule if the court dealt with the claim without a hearing under rule 27.10.

Rules 27.12 and 27.13 are revoked.

Costs on the small claims track
27.14
(1)   This rule applies to any case which has been allocated to the small claims track unless paragraph (5) applies.

(Rules 44.9 and 44.11 make provision in relation to orders for costs made before a claim has been allocated to the small claims track)

(2) The court may not order a party to pay a sum to another party in respect of that other party's costs, fees and expenses, including those relating to an appeal, except –

   (a) the fixed costs attributable to issuing the claim which –
      (i) are payable under Part 45; or
      (ii) would be payable under Part 45 if that Part applied to the claim;
   (b) in proceedings which included a claim for an injunction or an order for specific performance a sum not exceeding the amount specified in the relevant practice direction for legal advice and assistance relating to that claim;
   (c) any court fees paid by that other party;
   (d) expenses which a party or witness has reasonably incurred in travelling to and from a hearing or in staying away from home for the purposes of attending a hearing;
   (e) a sum not exceeding the amount specified in the relevant practice direction for any loss of earnings or loss of leave by a party or witness due to attending a hearing or to staying away from home for the purposes of attending a hearing;
   (f) a sum not exceeding the amount specified in the relevant practice direction for an expert's fees;
   (g) such further costs as the court may assess by the summary procedure and order to be paid by a party who has behaved unreasonably;
   (h) the Stage 1 and, where relevant, the Stage 2 fixed costs in rule 45.29 where—
      (i) the claim was within the scope of the Pre-Action Protocol for Low Value Personal Injury Claims in Road Traffic Accidents ('the RTA Protocol');
      (ii) the claimant reasonably believed that the claim was valued at more than the small claims track limit in accordance with paragraph 4.1(4) of the RTA Protocol; and
      (iii) the defendant admitted liability under the process set out in the RTA Protocol; but
      (iv) the defendant did not pay those Stage 1 and, where relevant, Stage 2 fixed costs.

(3) A party's rejection of an offer in settlement will not of itself constitute unreasonable behaviour under paragraph (2)(g) but the court may take it into consideration when it is applying the unreasonableness test.

(4) The limits on costs imposed by this rule also apply to any fee or reward for acting on behalf of a party to the proceedings charged by a person exercising a right of audience by virtue of an order under section 11 of the Courts and Legal Services Act 1990[1] (a lay representative).

(5)   Where –

  (a)   the financial value of a claim exceeds the limit for the small claims
        track; but
  (b)   the claim has been allocated to the small claims track in accordance
        with rule 26.7(3),

  the small claims track costs provisions will apply unless the parties agree
  that the fast track costs provisions are to apply.

(6)   Where the parties agree that the fast track costs provisions are to apply, the
      claim and any appeal will be treated for the purposes of costs as if it were
      proceeding on the fast track except that trial costs will be in the discretion
      of the court and will not exceed the amount set out for the value of claim in
      rule 46.2 (amount of fast track trial costs).

Claim re-allocated from the small claims track to another track
27.15
Where a claim is allocated to the small claims track and subsequently re-
allocated to another track, rule 27.14 (costs on the small claims track) will cease
to apply after the claim has been re-allocated and the fast track or multi-track
costs rules will apply from the date of re-allocation.

Appendix 8

Civil Procedure Rules, Practice Direction 27

PRACTICE DIRECTION – SMALL CLAIMS TRACK

This Practice Direction supplements CPR Part 27.

Judges

1

The functions of the court described in Part 27 which are to be carried out by a judge will generally be carried out by a district judge but may be carried out by a circuit judge.

Case Management Directions

2.1

Rule 27.4 explains how directions will be given, and rule 27.6 contains provisions about the holding of a preliminary hearing and the court's powers at such a hearing.

2.2

Appendix A sets out details of the case that the court usually needs in the type of case described. Appendix B sets out the Standard Directions that the court may give. Appendix C sets out Special Directions that the court may give.

2.3

Before allocating the claim to the Small Claims Track and giving directions for a hearing the court may require a party to give further information about that party's case.

2.4

A party may ask the court to give particular directions about the conduct of the case.

2.5

In deciding whether to make an order for exchange of witness statements the court will have regard to the following –

(a) whether either or both the parties are represented;

(b) the amount in dispute in the proceedings;

(c) the nature of the matters in dispute;

(d) whether the need for any party to clarify his case can better be dealt with by an order under paragraph 2.3;

(e) the need for the parties to have access to justice without undue formality, cost or delay.

Representation at a Hearing

3.1

In this paragraph:

(1) a lawyer means a barrister, a solicitor or a legal executive employed by a solicitor, and

(2) a lay representative means any other person.

3.2

(1) A party may present his own case at a hearing or a lawyer or lay representative may present it for him.

(2) The Lay Representatives (Right of Audience) Order 1999 provides that a lay representative may not exercise any right of audience:–

(a) where his client does not attend the hearing;

(b) at any stage after judgment; or

(c) on any appeal brought against any decision made by the district judge in the proceedings.

(3) However the court, exercising its general discretion to hear anybody, may hear a lay representative even in circumstances excluded by the Order.

(4) Any of its officers or employees may represent a corporate party.

Small Claim Hearing

4.1

(1) The general rule is that a small claim hearing will be in public.

(2) The judge may decide to hold it in private if:

(a) the parties agree, or

(b) a ground mentioned in rule 39.2(3) applies.

(3)   A hearing or part of a hearing which takes place other than at the court, for example at the home or business premises of a party, will not be in public.

4.2
A hearing that takes place at the court will generally be in the judge's room but it may take place in a courtroom.

4.3
Rule 27.8 allows the court to adopt any method of proceeding that it considers to be fair and to limit cross-examination. The judge may in particular:

(1)   ask questions of any witness himself before allowing any other person to do so,
(2)   ask questions of all or any of the witnesses himself before allowing any other person to ask questions of any witnesses,
(3)   refuse to allow cross-examination of any witness until all the witnesses have given evidence in chief,
(4)   limit cross-examination of a witness to a fixed time or to a particular subject or issue, or both.

Recording Evidence and the Giving of Reasons
5.1
A hearing that takes place at the court will be tape recorded by the court. A party may obtain a transcript of such a recording on payment of the proper transcriber's charges.

5.2
Attention is drawn to section 9 of the Contempt of Court Act 1981 (which deals with the unauthorised use of tape recorders in court) and to the Practice Direction ([1981] 1 WLR 1526) which relates to it.

5.3
(1)   The judge may give reasons for his judgment as briefly and simply as the nature of the case allows.
(2)   He will normally do so orally at the hearing, but he may give them later at a hearing either orally or in writing.

5.4
Where the judge decides the case without a hearing under rule 27.10 or a party who has given notice under rule 27.9(1) does not attend the hearing, the judge will prepare a note of his reasons and the court will send a copy to each party.

5.5
Nothing in this practice direction affects the duty of a judge at the request of a party to make a note of the matters referred to in section 80 of the County Courts Act 1984.

Non-attendance of a Party at a Hearing
6.1
Attention is drawn to rule 27.9 (which enables a party to give notice that he will not attend a final hearing and sets out the effect of his giving such notice and of not doing so), and to paragraph 3 above.

6.2
Nothing in those provisions affects the general power of the court to adjourn a hearing, for example where a party who wishes to attend a hearing on the date fixed cannot do so for a good reason.

Costs
7.1
Attention is drawn to Rule 27.14 which contains provisions about the costs which may be ordered to be paid by one party to another.

7.2
The amount which a party may be ordered to pay under rule 27.14(2)(b) (for legal advice and assistance in claims including an injunction or specific performance) is a sum not exceeding £260.

7.3
The amounts which a party may be ordered to pay under rule 27.14(3)(c) (loss of earnings) and (d) (experts' fees) are:

(1) for the loss of earnings or loss of leave of each party or witness due to attending a hearing or staying away from home for the purpose of attending a hearing, a sum not exceeding £90 per day for each person, and

(2) for expert's fees, a sum not exceeding £750 for each expert.

(As to recovery of pre-allocation costs in a case in which an admission by the defendant has reduced the amount in dispute to a figure below £10,000, reference should be made to paragraph 7.4 of Practice Direction 26 and to paragraph 7.1(3) of Practice Direction 46.)

Appeals
8.1
Part 52 deals with appeals and attention is drawn to that Part and Practice Direction 52.

8A
An appellant's notice in small claims must be filed and served in Form N164.

8.2
Where the court dealt with the claim to which the appellant is a party:

(1)   under rule 27.10 without a hearing; or
(2)   in his absence because he gave notice under rule 27.9 requesting the court to decide the claim in his absence,

an application for permission to appeal must be made to the appeal court.

8.3
Where an appeal is allowed the appeal court will, if possible, dispose of the case at the same time without referring the claim to the lower court or ordering a new hearing. It may do so without hearing further evidence.

Appendix A: Information and Documentation the Court usually Needs in Particular Types of Case

Road accident cases (where the information or documentation is available)

- witness statements (including statements from the parties themselves);
- invoices and estimates for repairs;
- agreements and invoices for any car hire costs;
- the Police accident report;
- sketch plan which should wherever possible be agreed;
- photographs of the scene of the accident and of the damage.

Building disputes, repairs, goods sold and similar contractual claims (where the information or documentation is available)

- any written contract;
- photographs;
- any plans;
- a list of works complained of;
- a list of any outstanding works;

- any relevant estimate, invoice or receipt including any relating to repairs to each of the defects;
- invoices for work done or goods supplied;
- estimates for work to be completed;
- a valuation of work done to date.

Landlord and tenant claims (where the information or documentation is available)

- a calculation of the amount of any rent alleged to be owing, showing amounts received;
- details of breaches of an agreement which are said to justify withholding any deposit itemised showing how the total is made up and with invoices and estimates to support them.

Breach of duty cases (negligence, deficient professional services and the like)
Details of the following:

- what it is said by the claimant was done negligently by the defendant;
- why it is said that the negligence is the fault of the defendant;
- what damage is said to have been caused;
- what injury or losses have been suffered and how any (and each) sum claimed has been calculated;
- the response of the defendant to each of the above.

Appendix B: Standard Directions (For use where the district judge specifies no other directions)

The court directs:
1
Each party must deliver to every other party and to the court office copies of all documents on which he intends to rely at the hearing no later than [ ] [14 days before the hearing]. (These should include the letter making the claim and the reply.)

2
The original documents must be brought to the hearing.

3
[Notice of hearing date and time allowed.]

4

The parties are encouraged to contact each other with a view to trying to settle the case or narrow the issues. However the court must be informed immediately if the case is settled by agreement before the hearing date.

5

No party may rely at the hearing on any report from an expert unless express permission has been granted by the court beforehand. Anyone wishing to rely on an expert must write to the court immediately on receipt of this Order and seek permission, giving an explanation why the assistance of an expert is necessary.

NOTE: Failure to comply with the directions may result in the case being adjourned and in the party at fault having to pay costs. The parties are encouraged always to try to settle the case by negotiating with each other. The court must be informed immediately if the case is settled before the hearing.

Appendix C: Special Directions

The　　　　　　　　　　must clarify his case.
He must do this by delivering to the court office and to the　　　　　　no later than
[a list of　　　　　　　　　　]
[details of　　　　　　　　　　]

The　　　　　　　　　　must allow the　　　　　　　　　　to inspect by appointment within　　　　　　days of receiving a request to do so.

The hearing will not take place at the court but at　　　　　　　　　.

The　　　　　　　　　　must bring to court at the hearing the　　　　　　.

Signed statements setting out the evidence of all witnesses on whom each party intends to rely must be prepared and copies included in the documents mentioned in paragraph 1. This includes the evidence of the parties themselves and of any other witness, whether or not he is going to come to court to give evidence.

The court may decide not to take into account a document [or video] or the evidence of a witness if these directions have not been complied with.

If he does not [do so] [   ] his [Claim][Defence] [and Counterclaim] will be struck out and (specify consequence).

It appears to the court that expert evidence is necessary on the issue of   and that that evidence should be given by a single expert to be instructed by the parties jointly. If the parties cannot agree about who to choose and what arrangements to make about paying his fee, either party MUST apply to the court for further directions. The evidence is to be given in the form of a written report. Either party may ask the expert questions and must then send copies of the questions and replies to the other party and to the court. Oral expert evidence may be allowed in exceptional circumstances but only after a further order of the court. Attention is drawn to the limit of £750 on expert's fees that may be recovered.

If either party intends to show a video as evidence he must –

    (a)   contact the court at once to make arrangements for him to do so, because the court may not have the necessary equipment, and

    (b)   provide the other party with a copy of the video or the opportunity to see it at least   days before the hearing.

Appendix 9

Directions Questionnaire (Small Claims Track), Form N180

> ▶ Print form   ▶ Reset form

Directions questionnaire (Small Claims Track)

In the	Claim No.

To be completed by, or on behalf of,

who is [1st][2nd][3rd][   ][Claimant][Defendant][Part 20 claimant] in this claim

You should note the date by which this questionnaire must be returned and the name of the court it should be returned to since this may be different from the court where the proceedings were issued.

If you have settled this claim (or if you settle it on a future date) and do not need to have it heard or tried, you must let the court know immediately.

A Settlement/Mediation

Under the Civil Procedure Rules parties should make every effort to settle their case. At this stage you should still think about whether you and the other party(ies) can settle your dispute without going to a hearing.

You may seek to settle the claim either by direct discussion or negotiation with the other party or by mediation. If settlement is reached parties may enter into a binding agreement which can be enforced if the terms of the agreement were to be breached.

Mediation is a way of resolving disputes without a court hearing, where the parties are assisted in resolving their dispute with the help of an impartial mediator. If the claim is settled at this stage the parties can avoid further court fees, costs and time involved in preparing and attending a hearing.

You may use any mediation provider. However, HMCTS provide a **free confidential** Small Claims Mediation Service which is available to parties in most small claims cases which are for less than £10,000.

Mediation is usually carried out by telephone in one hour time limited appointments convenient to the parties and is quicker than waiting for a court hearing before a judge. There is no obligation to use the Small Claims Mediation Service nor are you required to settle if you do. If you are unable to reach agreement with the other party at mediation, the claim will proceed to a small claims hearing.

You can get more information about mediation from www.gov.uk

If all parties agree, this case will be referred to the Small Claims Mediation Service. In any event the court may order the service to contact you to explore mediation.

A1 Do you agree to this case being referred to the Small Claims Mediation Service?   ☐ Yes   ☐ No

Please give your contact details below – If all parties agree to mediation your details will be passed to the small claims mediation team who will contact you to arrange an appointment.

You must complete the remainder of the form regardless of your answer to A1

B Your contact details

Your full name

Address for Service

Telephone number   Mobile

Email

Notes

It is essential that you provide this information, particularly if you have requested mediation. Staff will contact you within office hours (9am - 5pm).

N180 Directions questionnaire (small claims track) (04.14)   © Crown copyright 2014

C Track

C1 Do you agree that the small claims track is the appropriate track for this case?   ☐ Yes   ☐ No

If No, say why not and state the track to which you believe it should be allocated

Notes

Track
The small claims track – generally for lower value and less complex claims with a value under £10,000. You can get more information by reading leaflet **EX306 'The small claims track in civil courts'**. You can get this leaflet online from hmctsformfinder.justice.gov.uk

D About the hearing

Hearing venue

D1 At which County Court hearing centre would you prefer the small claims hearing to take place and why?

Location
If your claim is a designated money claim the case will usually be transferred to the claimants preferred court or the defendants home court as appropriate. However, there is no guarantee of transfer to this court. For further information see CPR Parts 3, 12, 13, 14 and 26.

Expert evidence

D2 Are you asking for the court's permission to use the written evidence of an expert?   ☐ Yes   ☐ No

If Yes, state why and give the name of the expert (if known) and the area of expertise and the likely cost if appointed.

Expert evidence
The court must grant you permission to use an expert witness. Your notice of allocation will tell you if permission has been granted. Please note the upper limit for experts' fees that can be recovered is £750. You can get more information by reading leaflet **EX306 'The small claims track in civil courts'**. You can get this leaflet online from hmctsformfinder.justice.gov.uk

Witnesses
Witnesses may be asked to give evidence by either party. The court needs to have notice that you intend to call a witness. Witness expenses for travel accommodation and loss of earning should be met by the party requesting their attendance. You can get more information by reading leaflet **EX342 'Coming to a court hearing'**. You can get this leaflet online from hmctformfinder.justice.gov.uk

Witnesses

D3 How many witnesses, including yourself, will give evidence on your behalf at the hearing?

Hearing

D4 Are there any days within the next six months when you, an expert or a witness will not be able to attend court for the hearing?   ☐ Yes   ☐ No

Hearing
Dates to avoid: You should enter those dates where you, your expert or an essential witness will not be able to attend court because of a holiday or other commitments.

If Yes, please give details

	Dates **not** available
Yourself	
Expert	
Other essential witness	

Will you be using an interpreter at the hearing either for yourself or for a witness?   ☐ Yes   ☐ No

If Yes, please specify the type of interpreter

Interpreters: In some circumstances the court will arrange for, and meet the cost of an interpreter. If you require an interpreter, you should contact the court immediately. Further details visit our website www.justice.gov.uk under 'guidance'.

Signature

You must sign this form

[Legal representative for the][1ˢᵗ][2ⁿᵈ][3ʳᵈ][   ]
[Claimant][Defendant][Part 20 claimant]

▶ Print form   ▶ Reset form

Once you have completed this form please return it to the court at the address shown on
the form N149A, notice of proposed allocation to Small Claims Track

Appendix 10

Costs Schedule

IN THE [ ] COUNTY COURT   **CASE NUMBER [ ]**

Name of claimant [ ]

Name of defendant [ ]

Costs claim by the claimant/defendant

Date of hearing [ ]

Level of fee earner [ ]

Hourly rate claimed [ ]

Work done on documents	[ ] hours [ ] minutes
Time spent in meetings with the client	[ ] hours [ ] minutes
Time spent in meetings with others	[ ] hours [ ] minutes
Time spent preparing correspondence	[ ] hours [ ] minutes

Or

Number of letters written	[ ]
Total for solicitor's charges	£[ ]

Expenditure

Instructing expert	£[ ]
Travel expenses	£[ ]
Court fees paid	£[ ]
Counsel's fees	£[ ]
Total expenditure excluding VAT	£[ ]
Total of solicitor's charges and expenditure	£[ ]
Add VAT	£[ ]
Total claimed	£[ ]

[*I certify that the fees claimed do not exceed the charge made to the client in this matter*]

....

Signed

....

Dated

Appendix 11

Mediation Settlement Agreement, Form N182

HM Courts & Tribunals Service

Mediation Settlement Agreement

Case No:

Claimant:

Defendant:

Date:

Mediator:

In a voluntary telephone mediation today, you agreed terms as set out in the mediation settlement agreement overleaf. This agreement is in full and final settlement of all parties' claims in this case, including in relation to costs.

The terms of the agreement have been read back to each party and you have each agreed to those terms.

If you believe that there is any inaccuracy in the terms of the settlement agreement set out below, you must reply to the court within five days of the date of the settlement agreement.

You should keep a copy of the agreement. A copy of this agreement will be placed on the court file.

If there is a breach of the agreement by the other party and you wish to take further action, you should complete an N244 General Form of Application. This form can be found at http://hmctsformfinder.justice.gov.uk/HMCTS/FormFinder.do. You must state clearly on the form which of the two options below you wish to be considered:

1) That the court enters judgment in your favour for the unpaid balance of the outstanding sum of the settlement agreement. You will have to send the court a copy of your settlement agreement and on the accompanying N244 General Form of Application:
   a) Specify the amount you say is still owing to you
   b) Give full details of the breach of the settlement agreement you say has been committed by the other party.

2) That your claim be restored for hearing for the full amount claimed.

Please note that if the settlement agreement contains non-monetary provisions (for example, agreement to provide a service to a specified quality before a specified date), it is only possible to apply for your claim to be restored for hearing for the full amount claimed.

Send your completed application to the court at

Please quote your case number and **include the payment of £45.00** (cheques should be made payable to HMCTS). If you wish to pay by credit or debit card please include a contact phone number and a member of our team will contact you to arrange payment.

Your application and court file will be referred to a District Judge and you will be notified of the judge's decision in due course.

N182 Mediation Settlement Agreement (04.14)   © Crown copyright 2014

Mediation Settlement Agreement

Name and address of court	

Claim no. [ ]

Name of claimant	

Name of defendant	

On   the parties agreed that:

Terms:-

  1. The parties have agreed the following:

  The --option-- agrees to pay to the --option-- the sum of   (the settlement sum) in full and final
settlement of the claim to be paid

  By

  or

  by instalment amounts of   per month
for a period of months commencing on the
with a final payment of   due on

  2. The court will stay the case (i.e. the court will take no further steps in relation to the case) and the claim, defence and any counterclaim will be struck out without further order of the court (meaning that the case will no longer be treated as active) if the court has not heard from either party by   .

  3. The parties will keep the information contained in this agreement confidential and not use it for any other purposes. Other than a final written agreement, any information – whether written in a document prepared for mediation or written or spoken during the mediation – can only be used for the purpose of mediation and cannot be referred to in any court action unless the parties agree. The parties agree that they will not call the mediator to give evidence in any court action.

Page 2 of 3

4. In the event of any default by either party, the other party shall be entitled to apply to the court:

    a. for judgment, without any further court hearing, for the unpaid balance of the settlement sum; or

    b. for the claim to be restored for hearing for the full amount claimed.

5. This agreement is in full and final settlement of both parties' claims, including any claim for costs, court fees, expenses or interest.

> The terms of this agreement as set out above have been read out to both parties, and both parties have given their verbal agreement to all of the terms set out above.
>
> Mediator:
>
> Date:

Index

References are to page numbers

ABTA (Association of British
    Travel Agents) — 14
Address for service — 26, 29–31, 82
Adjournment, request for — 81
Admission of claim — 103
Advice organisations — 14, 15, 16, 99, 108, 161
Advocacy — 182–3
    appeals — 217
Advocacy skills — 200
    closing speech — 203
    cross examination — 202
    examination in chief — 201–2
    legal points — 204
    opening speech — 200–1
    practical tips — 204
    re-examination — 203
    taking notes — 204
Agents, claims against — 28–9
Allocation — 55
    case management categories — 56
    changing or challenging
        allocated track — 68
    claims involving disputed
        allegations of
        dishonesty — 59
    claims of no financial value — 60
    claims which do not qualify
        on financial grounds — 60
    directions questionnaire *see*
        directions questionnaire
    disposal without hearing — 66

housing claims — 56, 58–9
IPEC *see* Intellectual Property
    Enterprise Court
orders of the court's own
    initiative — 66–7
personal injury claims — 32, 56, 59
powers of the court — 57–8
qualification for the small
    claims track — xvii, 5, 36, 56–7, 58
striking out claims — 66, 73–4
views of the parties — 60
voluntary referral — 68
Allocation hearings — 67
Alternative Dispute Resolution — 130
    see also mediation
Amended claim/defence — 103
Appeals — 5, 123, 209, 211
    against case management
        decisions — 215
    appeal rules — 211–12
    costs — 170
    flowchart — 218
    grounds for appeal — 212–13
    hearing — 217
    paperwork for — 215–16
    permission to appeal — 206, 213–14
    respondent's cross appeal — 216
    review and not re-hearing — 214
    second appeals — 217
    summary table — 210
    terminology — 211

Appeals *(continued)*

time limits	211
Applications	77–9
adjournment, request for	81
consent applications	79
costs	79
orders without a hearing	80
telephone hearings	79–80
without notice	80
Applications for directions	159–60

Applications to set aside

judgment	123, 218–19
credit repair applications	222
judgment in default	220–2
procedure	219–20
Arbitration	5, 7, 12, 14, 130, 139

Association of British Travel

Agents (ABTA)	14
Attachment of earnings	228–9

Banking Ombudsman Scheme	14
Bankruptcy	29, 226–7
Bland denial	49
Burden of proof	197

Businesses

claiming against	
individuals	14, 107–8
representation in court	183

Case management

appeals against case	
management decisions	215
civil restraint orders	74
powers of the court	72–3, 103–4
orders made on the court's	
initiative	77
relief from sanctions	74–7
sanctions	74
striking out	66, 73–4, 103–4
Charging order on land	229–30
Circuit judges	210
Citizens Advice Bureaux	16, 108
Civil practice books	8

Civil Procedure Rules

applications, provisions for	
making *see* applications	
case management powers *see*	
case management	
European Small Claims	
Procedure	96–7
overriding objective	71–2
rules excluded on the small	
claims track	92–6

service of claim form and

other documents	82
address for service	26, 29–31, 82
alternative methods	85–6
deemed day of service	83–5
delay: 4-month rule	86
method of service	83–5
slip rule	90–1
statement of truth	34–6, 81–2
summary judgment	88–90
time for compliance with	
judgment or order	91
time limits: calculation	91–2
transfers of cases between	
courts	86–8
Civil restraint orders	74
Claim form	17–19, 20, 21, 23, 39
service *see* service of	
documents	

Claimants

address	25–6
name	24–5
Claims of no financial value	60
Commercial debts: late payment	34, 112
Community Legal Services fund	15

Companies

claiming against	
individuals	14, 107–8
representation in court	183
Company insolvency	227
Consent applications	79
Contempt of court	195–6
Contract disputes	122

Contractual interest 33
Costs
   ability to pay 11
   application for summary
      judgment 90
   applications in small claims
      cases 79
   evaluating the case 10–11
   following allocation, re-
      allocation and non-
      allocation 178–9
   frequently asked questions 176–7
   judgment 205–6
   legal representatives 37
   no costs rule *see* no costs rule
Costs in the case 176
Costs reserved 176
Counter service 6, 21
Counterclaims 50–1, 102, 114
   road traffic cases 103, 117
County Court Money Claims
   Centre (CCMCC) 20, 38, 44
Court orders 207
Courts Charter 39
Court fees *see* fees
Credit repair applications 222
Cross examination 200, 202

Debt advice 14, 108
Debtor's assets 224–5
Deemed day of service 83–5
Defective goods 119
Defence: drafting rules 101–2
Defending the claim 49
   bland denial 49
Defence by way of set off or
   counterclaim 50
   see also counterclaims
   full defence 50
   states paid defence 49
Defendants
   address 29–31
   identity 26–9
   name 25, 29

response to claim *see*
   responding to claims
Delay: 4-month rule 86
Directions questionnaire 61
   court's power to dispense with 67
   failure to return or complete 65
   received by court 65–6
   requirement to co-operate 62
   section A – settlement/
      mediation 63, 131
   section B – contact details 63
   section C – track 64
   section D
      expert evidence 64
      hearing 65
      hearing venue 64
      witnesses 64
   signature 65
   time limit for returning 62
Directors, claims against 28
Disclosure rules 93–4
Discretionary judgment 45
Dishonesty 59
Disposal hearings 53
Disposal without hearing 66
Dispute of jurisdiction 48
Disputed items 156, 162
District judges 7–8, 210
Documents
   court file 187
   definition 149
   introduction of new
      documents at final
      hearing 187–8
   photographs and sketch plans 156–7
      costs of 170–1
   service of 82
   standard directions 149–51
   used as evidence 198
Drafting rules 99
   letters before action 100
   precedents *see* precedents
   statement of case and defence 100
      admission 103

Drafting rules *(continued)*
  admission *(continued)*
    amendments 103
    defence to counterclaim 102–3
    detailing the claim 101
    detailing the defence 101–2
    reply to defence 102

Email 6
Enforcement 223
  attachment of earnings 228–9
  bankruptcy 226–7
  charging order on land 229–30
  company insolvency 227
  costs 170
  finding out about a debtor's
    assets 224–5
  injunctions 60
  interest on judgment debts 230
  order to obtain information 225
  overview of steps after
    judgment 230–1
  register of judgments, orders
    and fines 226
  third party debt order 228
  timescale 230
  warrant of control 227–8
European Small Claims Procedure 96–7
Evidence 9–10, 94–5
  burden and standard of
    proof 9, 196–7
  documents 198
  expert evidence *see* expert
    evidence
  limiting cross examination 200
  prohibited evidence 200
  rules of evidence 197–8
  settlement discussions not to
    be mentioned before
    hearing or judgment 199
  taken on oath 200
  without evidence 198–9
Examination in chief 201–2
Expert evidence 10, 64, 95,
    153–6, 162

  procedure at hearings 199
  single joint experts 154
Expert fees 168

Fairness 191–2
Fast track 56
Fees 12, 62, 163
  expert fees 168
  issuing a claim 37
  remission 16, 37
  unpaid professional fees 113–14
Firms, claims against 27
Forms
  EX160 16
  N1 17–19, 20, 21,
    23, 39, 109, 110
  N20 153
  N149A 61
  N153 67
  N164 123, 214,
    215, 216, 218
  N180 61
  N182 136
  N208 23
  N225 44
  N225A 46
  N226 47
  N244 78
Free advice 14, 15, 16, 108
Full defence 50

Garage repairs: negligence 111, 124
Glossary xxi–xxvi

Hearing date 65
Hearing venue 64
  last-minute change 149
  transfer by court order 145, 149
Hearings 96
  advocacy skills 200
    closing speech 203
    cross examination 202
    examination in chief 201–2
    legal points 204
    opening speech 200–1

practical tips 204
re-examination 203
taking notes 204
appeals 217
court room etiquette
addressing the court and
judge 187
documents 187
friends and observers 189–90
interpreters 188
introduction of new
documents at final
hearing 187–8
mobile phones and
computers 187
special needs and personal
safety 191
Welsh language 188
witnesses 189
dealing with cases justly 181–2
ensuring that parties are on an
equal footing 182
evidence *see* evidence
frequently asked questions 207
judgment *see* judgment
layout of the court 186
non-attendance 162–3, 196
preparation for 143–4
application for directions 159–60
case settled before hearing 157
checklist 160–3
decide whether to attend
hearing 162
documents needed 149–51, 161
evaluate and consider
settlement 160–1
expert evidence 153–6, 162
lists of disputed items 156, 162
note date and time 160
payment of hearing fee 163
photographs and sketch
plans 156–7
preliminary hearing 158–9
special directions 158
standard directions 144–5, 146–8

time estimate 157–8
visiting the court before the
hearing date 163
witness statements
(non-experts) 151–2, 161
witness summons 152
private hearings 184, 185
procedure 191, 192
consequences of non-
attendance without
notice 196
contempt of court 195–6
fair hearing method 191–2
informality 195
notice of non-attendance 196
order of hearing 193–5
preliminaries 192
usual sequence in civil
trials 193
recordings 185–6
rights of audience (advocacy) 182–3
trial in public 184–5
Holiday cases 53, 105–6, 112–13
Housing claims 56, 58–9, 110–11
Human rights element 32–3

Indemnity basis costs 175
Informality 195
Information
order to obtain 225
requests for 93
Injunctions 60, 170
Insolvency 226–7
Inspection of documents 93–4
Intellectual Property Enterprise
Court (IPEC) 6, 8, 57, 61, 97–8
Interest calculation 33–4, 112,
113, 116, 125
judgment debts 230
Interim remedies 95
Interpreters 188
Invoices, unpaid 105, 107, 112
Issuing claims
address for service 26, 29–31
brief details of the claim 31

Issuing claims *(continued)*
  by post 20–1
  calculating interest 33–4
  checklist 22
  claimant's address 25–6
  court fees payable 37
  diary note 39
  form N1 17–19, 20, 21, 23, 39
  formal issue by the court 38–9
  human rights element 32–3
  identifying the defendant 26–9
  legal representative's costs 37
  naming the claimant 24–5
  naming the defendant 25, 29
  online xviii, 21
  over the counter 6, 21
  particulars of the claim 32
  preferred court 37–8, 44
  procedure between response and allocation 40
  specified claims 23, 24
  statement of truth 34–6
  unspecified claims 23, 24
  value of the claim xvii, 5, 36, 56, 58
  see also statement of case

Judges 7–8
Judgment 204–5
  costs and witness expenses 205–6
  court order 207
  overview of steps after judgment 230–1
  permission to appeal 206, 213–14
  reasoned decision 205
  setting aside *see* applications to set aside judgment
  time to pay 206
Judgment on admission 43–4
Judgments for unspecified sums 52
  allocation to the small claims track 53
  deciding the value without a hearing 52–3
  disposal hearings 53
Judgments in default 51–2
  applications to set aside 220–2
Jurisdiction, dispute of 48

Landlord and tenant *see* housing claims
Late payment: commercial debts 32, 112
Lay representatives 170, 183, 189
Leading questions 202
Legal advice 14, 15, 16, 99, 108, 161
Legal aid 15–16
Legal fees *see* fees
Legal representatives 182–3
  costs 37
Letter of claim 12
Letters before action 12, 14, 100
  precedents 104
    businesses claiming against landlords 107–8
    complaint to a holiday company 105–6
    defendant's response 108–9
    simple debt claim 105
Limited companies
  claims against 27
  directors 27–8
Liquidators 28, 29
Litigants in person 5, 15, 99, 161
  appeals 217
  costs 175–6
  voluntary referral to small claims track 68
Loss of earnings 169

McKenzie friends 183, 189–90, 217
Means testing 16
Mediation xvii, 6, 12, 14, 20, 129–30
  civil mediation providers
    outside the court system 138
    customer feedback 137, 138, 139
    definition 130

directions questionnaire 63, 131
face-to-face mediations 135–6
frequently asked questions 137–8
hints for successful
    mediation 134, 136
mediation appointment 134–6
outcome 136
preparation for 135
procedural table 130
procedure between selection
    for mediation and
    mediation 132–4
role of the mediator 134–5
selection criteria
    category of case 131
    judge's decision 132
    willingness to negotiate 131
telephone mediations 134, 135
time limits 134, 135
Medical reports 154
Money Claim Online
    (MCOL) 21, 33, 38, 104
Multi track 56

National Mediation Helpline 6
No costs rule xvii, 5,
    15, 79, 166
costs terminology 176
court's discretion on costs 174–5
definition of costs 165
electing to use the small
    claims track by
    agreement 167
frequently asked questions 176–7
offers to settle 167
overall discretion 167
Part 36 offers 172–3
practice direction on pre-
    action conduct 167
qualifying the costs 167
routine awards for costs
    costs of appeal 170
    costs of enforcement 170
    court fees 167–8
    expert fees 168

fixed commencement costs 168
injunction cases 170
lay representatives 170
low value personal injury
    claims 171
photographs and sketch
    plans 170–1
witness expenses 169
standard basis costs and
    indemnity basis costs 175
summary assessment 175–6
unreasonable behaviour 171–3
No order for costs 176

Offers to settle 47, 96, 161, 167
Part 36 offers and the no costs
    rule 172–3
settlement discussions not to
    be mentioned before
    hearing or judgment 199
Ombudsman schemes 12, 14
Online service xviii, 21
Order for sale 229–30

Part 8 procedure 23, 52
Part 20 claims 57
Part 36 offers 172–3
Partnerships, claims against 28
Pay on Time website 34
Perjury 222
Personal injury claims 32, 56,
    59, 98, 118
costs 171
medical reports 154
Photographs 156–7
costs of 170–1
Pre-action conduct 11
businesses claiming against
    individuals 14, 107–8
consequences of non-
    compliance 15
letters before action *see* letters
    before action 14
practice direction 11, 12,
    13–14, 167

Pre-action protocol 5
Precedents
    application to set aside 123
    brief description of type of
        claim 110
    grounds for appeal 123
    letter to court manager 109
    letters before action 104
        businesses claiming against
            individuals 107–8
        complaint to a holiday
            company 105–6
        defendant's response 108–9
        simple debt claim 105
    statement of case including
        defences and
        counterclaims
        claim against garage for
            negligent repairs 111, 124
        claim by landlord for
            unpaid rent and service
            charges 110
        claim for unpaid invoice
            under Late Payment Act 112
        defective goods 119
        defence to claim against
            garage for negligent
            repairs 111
        defence to claim by
            landlord for unpaid
            rent and service
            charges 111
        holiday claim 112–13
        personal injury claim 118
        road traffic case 115–17
        unpaid professional fees 113–14
        unpaid school fees 120
    witness statements
        contract dispute 122
        road traffic case 121
Preferred court 37–8, 44
Principals, claims against 28–9
Privacy 184, 185
Professional fees, unpaid 113–14
Public counters 6, 21

Publicity 184–5

Recordings 185–6
Reference materials 8
Register of judgments, orders and
    fines 226
Rent *see* housing claims
Requests for information 93
Requests for time to pay 45
Responding to claims
    acknowledging the claim 48
    admitting the claim 43
        discretionary judgment 45
        judgment of the court's own
            initiative 45
        judgment on admission 43–4
        request for time to pay 45
        summary table 46–7
    defence to counterclaim 51
    defending the claim 49
        bland denial 49
        defence by way of set off or
            counterclaim 50
        see also counterclaims
        full defence 50
        states paid defence 49
    dispute of jurisdiction 48
    failure to respond in time:
        judgment in default 51–2
    judgments for unspecified
        sums 52
    allocation to the small claims
        track 53
    deciding the value without a
        hearing 52–3
    disposal hearings 53
    reply to defence 54
    response pack 41–2
    third party proceedings 51
    time for response 42–3
Rights of audience 182–3
Road traffic cases 103, 115–17
    effective advocacy 204
    photographs and sketch plans 156–7
    witness statements 121

School fees, unpaid 120
Scott schedules 156
Service of documents 82
    address for service 26, 29–31, 82
    alternative methods 85–6
    deemed day of service 83–5
    delay: 4-month rule 86
    method of service 83–5
Setting judgment aside *see*
        application to set aside
        judgment
Settlements 12, 63, 136,
        160–1, 185
    see also offers to settle
Shops, claims against 27
Single joint experts 154
Sketch plans 156–7
    costs of 170–1
Slip rule 90–1
Small claims track
    advantages xvii
    appeals *see* appeals
    avoiding court proceedings 11–12
    directions questionnaire *see*
            directions questionnaire
    efficiency 5
    election to use 6, 68
    enforcement of judgments
            see enforcement
    evaluating the case 9
        applying the law 10
        cost of proceeding 10–11
        evidence 9–10
    flowchart xix–xx
    history and overview 5–6
    judges 7–8, 210
    mediation *see* mediation
    pre-action conduct *see* pre-
            action conduct
    procedural table xxvii–xxviii
    procedure
        allocation stage *see*
            allocation
        hearings *see* hearings

    issuing a claim *see* issuing
            claims
    response to claim *see*
            responding to claims
    qualifying financial
            limit xvii, 5,
                36, 56, 58
        terminology 6–7
        voluntary referral 68
Special directions 158
Specified claims 23, 24
Standard basis costs 175
Standard directions 144–5, 146–8
Standard of proof 9, 196–7
Statement of case 100
    admission 103
    amendments 103
    defence to counterclaim 102–3
    detailing the claim 101
    detailing the defence 102–2
    precedents
        claim against garage for
            negligent repairs 111, 124
        claim by landlord for
            unpaid rent and service
            charges 110
        claim for unpaid invoice
            under Late Payment Act 112
        defective goods 119
        defence to claim against
            garage for negligent
            repairs 111
        defence to claim by
            landlord for unpaid
            rent and service charges 111
        holiday claim 112–13
        personal injury claim 118
        road traffic case 115–17
        unpaid professional fees 113–14
        unpaid school fees 120
    reply to defence 102
Statement of truth 34–6, 81–2
States paid defence 49
Statutory interest 33, 112, 113, 116, 125

Striking out   66, 73–4, 103–4
Summary assessment of costs   175
Summary judgment   88–90

Telephone hearings   79–80
Telephone mediations   134, 135
Third party debt orders   228
Third party proceedings   51
Time limits: calculation   91–2
Tomlin orders   130
Transfers of cases between courts   86–8
Travelling expenses   169
Trust Online   226

Unreasonable behaviour   171
Unspecified claims   23, 24

Value of the claim   xvii, 5,
                            36, 56, 58

Voluntary referral   68

Wasted costs   176
Welsh language   69, 188
Winding up   227
'Without prejudice'   161
Witness evidence   198–9
Witness expenses   169
  judgment   205–6
Witness statements   104, 151–2
  contract dispute   122
  road traffic case   121
Witness summons   152
Witnesses   64
  cross examination   200, 202
  examination in chief   201–2
  procedure at hearings   189
  re-examination   203
Woolf, Rt Hon Lord   5